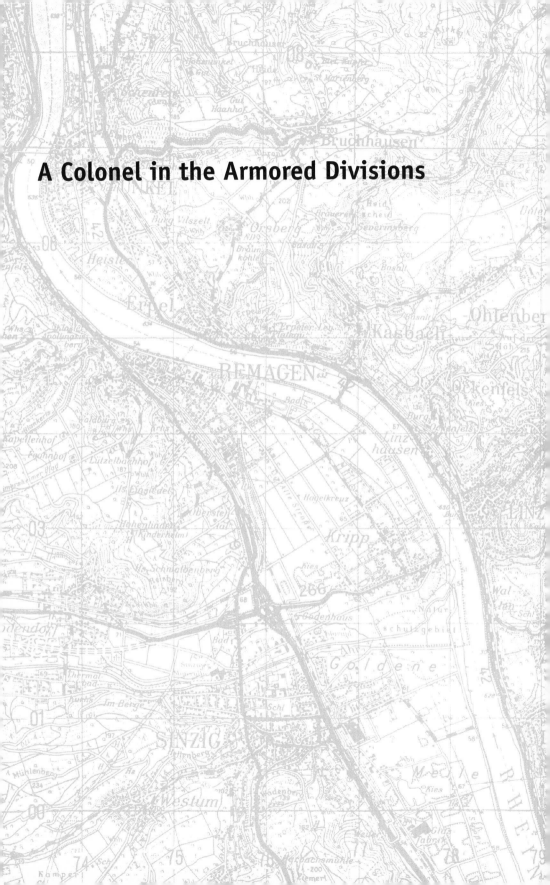

A Colonel in the Armored Divisions

A Colonel in the Armored Divisions
A Memoir, 1941–1945

William S. Triplet
Edited by Robert H. Ferrell

University of Missouri Press
Columbia and London

Library of Congress Cataloging-in-Publication Data

Triplet, William S. 1900–
    A colonel in the armored divisions : a memoir, 1941–1945 /
William S. Triplet ; edited by Robert H. Ferrell.
        p.   cm.
    Includes bibliograhical references and index.
    ISBN 0-8262-1312-X (alk. paper)
    1. Triplet, William S., 1900–   2. World War, 1939–1945—Personal
narratives, American.   3. United States. Army—Officers—Biography.
4. World War, 1939–1945—Tank warfare.   I. Ferrell, Robert H.
D811.T75 A3 2001
940.54'8173'092—dc21   00-050781

⊗™ This paper meets the requirements of the
American National Standard for Permanence of Paper
for Printed Library Materials, Z39.48, 1984.

Text designer: Vickie Kersey DuBois
Jacket designer: Susan Ferber
Typesetter: BOOKCOMP, Inc.
Printer and binder: Thomson-Shore, Inc.
Typefaces: Officina Sans, Veljovic

The Press gratefully acknowledges the contribution made by the Hulston
Family Foundation toward the production of this book.

Contents

Preface

Readers of the present book will recall Colonel Triplet's *A Youth in the Meuse-Argonne: A Memoir of World War I, 1917–1918* (University of Missouri Press, 2000), and it is pleasant indeed to introduce his equally fascinating account of World War II. This doughty soldier from Sedalia, Missouri, one of the many professional military men who despite discouragements remained in the army between the two great wars of the twentieth century, proved ready to assist in the country's defense when the time at last came, and helped make it possible for the American nation to survive and flourish in subsequent years when one dictatorship after another threatened the peace of peoples everywhere.

As mentioned in the introduction to the World War I memoir, Triplet enlisted in the Sedalia company of the Missouri National Guard in 1917 and was made a sergeant because he was tall for his age (seventeen) and possessed a hog-calling voice. After the company was taken into federal service, brought into an infantry regiment of the Thirty-fifth (Missouri-Kansas) Division, and sent overseas, he proved himself an extraordinary soldier and during participation in the actions of 1918 took part in the battle of the Meuse-Argonne. The latter was the largest and most costly battle in all of American military history, one million men taking part, with deaths numbering twenty-six thousand.

Having obtained more than a taste of military life, Triplet chose to become a professional military man, a Regular, and entered West Point in 1920, graduating with the class of 1924. Thereafter his assignments were the usual sort, to regiments in the Southwest and in Panama or as an officer in charge of Reserve Officers' Training Corps units (he was at Purdue University in Indiana) or in charge of men sent to a tank school. In 1940 he received assignment to the infantry board at Fort Benning, Georgia, a good assignment because the small group of senior officers and their assistants, to which latter group Triplet was assigned, looked over and tested new weapons for the enlarging army. Moreover, beginning in February 1941 it was headed by an officer with a future, Brigadier General Omar N. Bradley. Triplet remained with the board until after Pearl Harbor, when he requested and with difficulty managed an assignment with troops.

The present brief drawing of Triplet's background for participation in the second great military action of his country in the century just past is not the place to detail his experiences, save to remark that the business of obtaining a truly satisfying assignment required more time than the colonel (he became a full colonel in December 1942 and carried that rank through the war) anticipated. He first served with the Thirteenth Armored Division, a badly led group—the division's commander was incompetent—that came to a bad end, wasting one billion dollars, as Triplet morosely recorded years later. His second assignment, the training of army troops with amphibious tanks and troop carriers on the West Coast, in anticipation of capturing Japanese-held islands in the Far Pacific, was much more appealing work but paled in attraction after a while, and led the colonel to request, virtually insist upon, reassignment with troops either in the Pacific or Europe. A third, once he arrived in Paris in December 1944, with the Second Armored Division, known as the "Hell on Wheels" Division, resulted in discovery that the Second Armored was not exactly hell on wheels, that the men and officers were lackadaisical and gave his tactical and strategic advice little attention. Sent to the Seventh Armored, he "lucked out," received a four-thousand-man unit known as Combat Command A, and soon was moving from triumph to triumph as he led his big group, CCA, into Germany. His command ended up on the Baltic, with a mission of preventing German troops from transferring to the defense of Berlin against the oncoming Russians. In the last days of the European war Triplet's CCA captured a German destroyer. The ship appeared in front of a port controlled by the colonel's group and began working its way up the channel, feeling its course because of the danger of mines. One of Triplet's commanders sent a platoon of tanks to confront the destroyer, in what if it would have happened might have been a unique action, a ship versus M4 guns, and the destroyer captain promptly lowered his swastika and came on in for surrender.

The preface to *A Youth in the Meuse-Argonne* has sketched Triplet's duties thereafter, until retirement in 1954, which encompassed varying assignments in the Far East and in the continental United States. The colonel sought to take part in the war against Japan but arrived in the Philippines in October 1945, too late for that conflict. He remained a while in the islands and in Okinawa, returned for stateside duty, and went back during the Korean War when he advised a South Korean division. He retired in a ceremony at West Point in 1954, thirty years after his commissioning.

What is interesting about the next long period in his long life—born in the year 1899, he died in 1994—is that he spent forty years in retirement in West Germany, Florida, and last in Leesburg, Virginia, not far from Washington, and during those years he worked to produce, apparently for his grandchildren, a massive memoir, hundreds of space-and-a-half typescript pages done on what appears to have been an old manual typewriter. The memoir was very interesting and highly informative. It was an altogether untypical action on the part of a professional soldier. Yes, many officers of the Regular Army produce memoirs, but no, most of the memoirs are not interesting, and those produced by senior officers usually are helped along by writers and perhaps are insufficiently interesting for that reason—the accounts are glib, or half-and-half (with the putative author interfering with the writer). In Triplet's case the resulting memoir was entirely his production. Moreover, although produced by an experienced writer—the colonel had published articles in the *Infantry Journal* and in 1943 the *Journal* brought out a paperback book of his describing infantry tactics—his account quite apparently was not something he planned to publish. One suspects he simply enjoyed writing it, remembering what he had done in the wars. Shortly before he died he sent copies to the U.S. Army Military History Institute at Carlisle, Pennsylvania, the army's archives, a part of the Army War College at Carlisle Barracks.

The present editor, seeking information on the battle of the Meuse-Argonne for a book on the subject, found the portion of the memoir dealing with World War I in the Thirty-fifth Division files at the institute, which led to discovery of the World War II part in the papers of the Seventh Armored. The literary quality was its first attraction, followed by a sense that the military judgments were of much interest and, taken with the writing, made the memoir of World War II equally worthy of publication with that of World War I. And so, in the following pages, readers may see what a real professional in the U.S. Army felt was worth recording about America's participation in the second war against Germany as well as the army's preparation, or lack thereof, for that war.

Acknowledgments

Again it is a pleasure to acknowledge the assistance of the staff of the U.S. Army Military History Institute, which is part of the Army War College at Carlisle Barracks, Pennsylvania: the director, Lieutenant Colonel Edwin M. Perry; assistant director, Richard J. Sommers; head of the search room, David A. Keogh; and Pamela Cheney and James Baughman.

The family of Colonel Triplet contributed a great deal—the late Catherine T. Fitzgerald and her husband, Colonel Byron Fitzgerald, and Catherine's sister, Elizabeth T. Hennig. Their help has included, respectively, a disk copy of the memoir, digitalization of the memoir's pasted-in photographs, and guidance through the family's history including memories of the closeness and enjoyment of each other's company. Catherine and husband and Elizabeth have been joys to work with.

Similarly, the staff of the University of Missouri Press, in particular the director and editor-in-chief, Beverly Jarrett; the managing editor, Jane Lago; and manuscript editor John Brenner. I can only repeat what appeared in volume one, that the director's enthusiasm was infectious, the managing editor's care invariably helpful, and the editor never failing in catching errors.

Betty Bradbury made many changes in the disk, John M. Hollingsworth was the cartographer, John K. Hulston again was interested (he fought in World War II), John Lukacs the historian, also a veteran, remembers. Brigadier General James Lawton Collins, Jr., read the manuscript and pointed out the range of the 105-mm. gun, among many other things. Russell F. Weigley of Temple University was equally helpful, as one would expect of the distinguished author of *Eisenhower's Lieutenants.* As always, a thank-you to Lila and Carolyn.

A Note on the Editing

In writing the second volume of his memoirs, Colonel Triplet appears to have had some sort of detailed diary, as was clearly the case with his memoir of the war of 1917–1918. But all one can say is that what survived, what forms the basis for the present book, is a massive typescript, 708 pages, much of it space-and-one-half, put together by the colonel, typed by the colonel, with no evidence of its source or sources. Triplet's wife, Fiona, whom he married during June Week in 1924, has passed on and cannot testify. Of their three daughters, the oldest, Lee, died in 1998 and left no explanation of her father's writings. The youngest, Catherine, died this year, 2000, and did not know the source or sources of the memoir of World War II apart from her father's prodigious memory. Elizabeth, who survives, does not know either.

For the most part the typescript narrative runs along in fair order. The colonel wrote in vignettes of several pages, and a considerable part of the editing has consisted of gathering and ordering them in chapters. Within the chapters as they at first came together the logic sometimes wandered, in which case I cut vignettes by sentences or paragraphs and in quite a few cases eliminated them. Some would have been of little interest to readers. Side issues of interest, memories of years later, appear in quotation marks in the notes.

Smaller details of the editing included reducing capitals, exclamation marks, dashes, and commas, changing "which" to "that" if a comma did not precede, adding or removing hyphens, and placing percentages in arabic numerals. I took the liberty to write out acronyms such as AIB (armored infantry battalion) on first use, thereafter the acronym. All numbered units including divisions have the numbers written out, contrary to U.S. Army style, which is to write out numbers of older units.

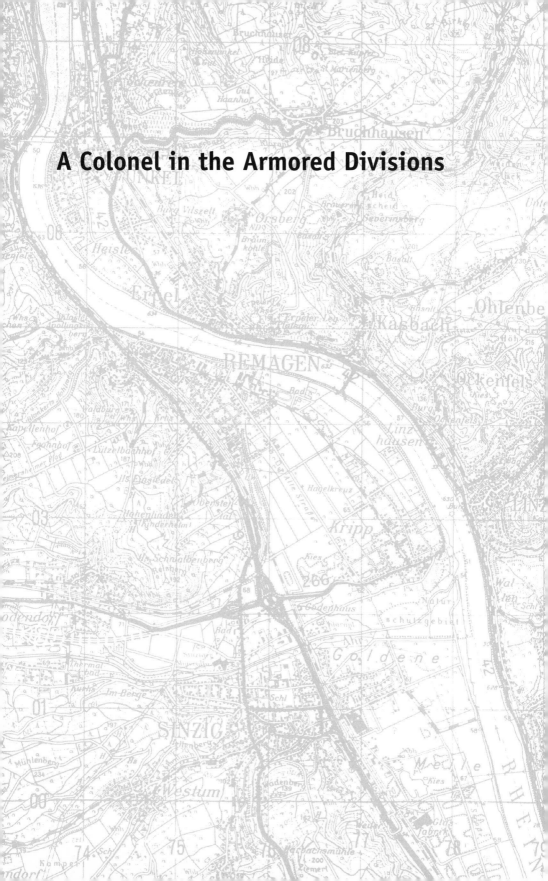

A Colonel in the Armored Divisions

One

The Infantry Board

I reported for duty to the president of the Infantry Board, Colonel Taylor, on December 4, 1940. Colonel Taylor always reminded me slightly of George Washington—features, reserve, and leadership. He gave me a general briefing on the mission of the board. The board proper was made up of experienced field officers who were known as the thinking section. As an appendage the test section was composed of company-grade officers (the nonthinking section) under Light Colonel "Count" Melasky. I was assigned to the nonthinking section to test vehicles and weapons as well as any other prototypes that were submitted to the board. I reported to Count Melasky, a well-built, heavy-set middleweight, sandy haired, ruddy complexion, relaxed manner, and most courteous to his crew of junior officers. I was assigned to a metal desk in the basement of the headquarters of the Infantry School—the thinkers had individual rooms on the floor above. I was anxious to get to work but was advised by my classmate, Captain Chazal, who acted as supply officer and a sort of executive to the count, to take it easy, look over the shoulders of the other test officers, and learn the ropes.

The two years I spent in the test section of the board were the most interesting, entertaining, and probably useful that I have spent in the army. New ideas were welcomed by the chief, innovations praised, improvements on prototype equipment were encouraged. There were seldom deadlines or schedules to meet. Every officer worked on his projects in his own time and in case some hard thinking was required a day or two of doodling or feet on the desk was not questioned. The one requirement was absolute neutrality and honesty in test reports and recommendations: "Is it acceptable for field use by the infantry?"

The Molotov Cocktail, Fougasse, and Road Builder

The gasoline-filled-bottle bomb allegedly used by the Russians against tanks with great success was and still is the most over- and falsely praised weapon ever advertised by the press. Our reporters alleged that when a gallant Russki patriot lit the cloth fuse in the neck of the bottle and flung it to break on the German armor, the tank crew would hysterically fight their way out of the turret to avoid being roasted alive when the armor turned red and glowed with the heat. Then the engine would catch fire, the fuel tank would explode, and the ammunition fire would reduce the tank to a large glob of melted metal.[1]

1

I was ordered to check these rumors out and invent a better incendiary bomb for the use of our infantrymen.

The first test was to check the alleged rise in temperature. I filled some two hundred bottles with gasoline and plugged the necks with cloth fuses. Clark and I went to the antitank range where the carcass of an obsolete M5 medium was used as the target. Thermometers placed in the fighting, driver, and engine compartments would register the heat increase of the melting armor.[2]

We flung bottles to burst over the turret, the driver's apron, the air intakes, and when the flames had died checked the thermometers. No change or just a degree or two of increase. The outside of the armor was a little warmer, detectable by the palm of the hand. Dozens of bottles of precious gasoline were sacrificed in volleys. Same result.

OK, let's back off and do a little thinking.

1. Steel is a fair conductor. Heat applied in one area will eventually warm up the whole mass slightly to imperceptibly. The warming effect of a quart of gasoline on thirty-five to forty tons of steel is less than that of ten minutes in the sunshine of a Georgia summer.[3]
2. If a gasoline bomb burst on the air inlet the flames and smoke would be sucked in by the fan and would for about one and a half to two minutes interfere with the cooling of the engine—an ineffectual length of time. Unless there was a serious leak in the fuel tanks, they would not be affected.
3. If a quantity of gasoline bombs were burst on the air intake louvers the smoke might interfere with the carburetion of the fuel by depriving the engine of oxygen and the tank might be stalled until the gasoline burned out and the driver restarted the engine.

So there was no need to test the gasoline bombs on a live tank after all, and the project was dropped.

The one constructive idea that I contributed on this test was the development of a better bomb.

I requisitioned a jar of phosphorus, which came in the form of small cylinders about a half to one and one-half inches immersed in water. Remove one of the cylinders and in a few seconds the water would evaporate and the phosphorus would burst into flames. If one used gasoline as the liquid, the flame was almost instantaneous.

A problem: how does one pop phosphorus into a bottle and then fill the bottle with gasoline? Very carefully, and with risk of having the thing blow up and singe your eyebrows.

OK, we'll pour enough water in the bottle, enough to keep the phosphorus damp, first. Then pop the phosphorus cylinder into the water. Last, pour in the gasoline and cap the bottle firmly.

It worked. That is, it worked if the phosphorus capsule stayed with the bulk of the fuel when the bottle broke. But most of the time the capsule bounced clear and the gas simply evaporated harmlessly. Back to the drawing board.

Aha! Place the phosphorus capsule with the inhibiting bit of water in a pestle and grind it into small chunks, practically a powder. Pour the soup of water and phosphorus powder into the bottle, add the gasoline, and cap the bottle.

It worked magnificently. And not a damned soul was interested.

The fougasse had been used since the invention of gunpowder in the fifteenth to seventeenth centuries as a poor man's cannon to cover a weak point in fortifications. A slanting hole was dug with the opening facing the expected target. A keg or kegs of powder placed in the bottom of the hole was the propelling charge. A load of stones was shoveled in on top of the powder. A fuse fired at the appropriate moment would strike the attacking force with a half ton of flying stones.

From time to time when a test officer had a particularly important or interesting test to make he would invite the members of the test as well as the thinking section of the board to witness the show. It was much more convincing than reading the dry factual report. Captain Sydenham issued such an invitation to witness the effect of a gasoline fougasse on a target vehicle such as a truck, armored personnel carrier, or tank. The booted and spurred seniors arrived on the test site and milled around while Sydenham explained his idea.[4]

Sydenham showed the tunnel three feet in diameter and five feet deep that was scooped out of the clay bank beside the road. He explained the loading—fifteen pounds of TNT, electrically detonated at the bottom of the hole, and a fifty-five-gallon drum of gasoline. A truck would tow a target along the road, he would push the plunger at the appropriate moment, the TNT would shatter the drum and blow the liquid gasoline over the target, the explosion would fire the gasoline, and the target would be eliminated. Sounded very logical. His first test with water (due to the cost of gasoline) had been most successful. The board gathered in a semicircle thirty feet from the fougasse, watching with interest.

Here came a one-and-a-half-ton truck towing a sled with a paper-covered frame the size of a three-quarter-tonner 150 feet behind it.

Sydenham pushed the plunger.

There was a dull subterranean thump and the genie was out of the bottle. An immense black, red-slotted cloud shot out of the hole toward the target on the road, changed direction, and went straight up thirty feet and spread like the angel of death mushroom. The cloud stayed black but it was burning, pulsing with flickering lights and flames. Looked as though it was going to settle on us.

I was amazed at the physical fitness displayed by the senior members of the board. Booted and spurred, hampered by ten to fifteen years' seniority, some of them still outran me in our dash for the safety of clear sky.

The paper target was unscathed. Burning, vaporized gasoline does not fall, it rises, and as air gets into the cloud it burns further. The elders of the board departed with scathing remarks about safety, pretesting, brainstorms, and wasted time.

Sydenham went into a morbid depression for two days, doing nothing but sketching and reading. Then he was absent from his desk for a week. Finally he passed the word that the board was invited to witness the test of fougasse II. Only one courageous member of the thinking section showed up and took his post well in rear of the younger set, who were hoping for another such adrenaline-stirring result as before.

The same hole was used for the fougasse and the same truck dragged the carcass of a wrecked three-quarter-ton reconnaissance car. At the critical moment the same dull whoop sounded, but a dark, burning flood of liquid gushed out of the bank, sloshed over the target, and gutted it to its steel skeleton.

Sydenham had used fifty gallons of old crankcase oil and four gallons of gasoline this time, and all that rose was the smoke.

Due to the greater ease of installing land mines the fougasse was recommended only for the use of guerrillas.

But the idea of napalm was born and adopted by the air force in a later war.

"Mr. Le Tourneau, this is Major Triplet. Triplet, Mr. Le Tourneau. He wants to talk to you about a road-building machine that sounds interesting." Colonel Melasky promptly departed to consider problems more interesting to the infantry than roads, which were, after all, an engineer's responsibility.

I came out of my trance to find that I was shaking hands with a dynamic, forceful, energetic, and enthusiastic civilian, medium-sized, unremarkable figure, nondescript features, mousy brown hair, and penetrating eyes, dark brown. It was shortly apparent that he had a powerful imagination and was well qualified as a salesman or con man.

He presented a card, "Le Tourneau. Earth moving machines," followed by more data on the address in Florida, phone numbers, and branch factories.[5]

"We build bulldozers, backhoes, graders, dump trucks, rollers, power shovels, and earth movers," he began. "I want to build a road-making machine for the army, a machine that can make a road right across any kind of country at five miles an hour, fighting if necessary, so that all the army has to do is follow along behind it. Here's the idea—," and he unfolded sketches of an "artist's concept" that he pulled from his bulging briefcase. Colossal. Herculean. Unbelievable. Damnedest idea I ever saw or dreamed of.

The thing reminded me of the old Mark VIII tanks in a way, except that this one was scaled at 160 feet long, 40 feet high, and 40 feet wide counting the 9-foot width of track on each side. The body was only 20 feet in width. On the front a prow like the extended cowcatcher of a locomotive was equipped with pointed, sharp-edged prongs like the blades of a mowing machine. A sloping front apron was topped by a hemispherical turret from which protruded a sixteen-inch gun like a phallic symbol. About a hundred feet of body extended behind the turret and the machine was propelled by those monstrous tracks with track plates 4 by 9 feet equipped with grousers 2 feet in height.[6]

In a see-through sketch more machinery was shown inside and under the body, a set of grader blades set like arrows pointing rearward, a sheepfoot roller, a mechanical centipede with ponderous flat feet operated on the ends of knee-jointed legs, another gigantic roller with a conventionally smooth surface. In the artist's concept the prow was plowing up and tossing aside four to six feet of earth, boulders, trees, and brush. The grader blades were cutting soil, gravel, and rock back into the shallow trench formed by the prow. The sheepfoot roller was driving boulders and tree trunks into the foundation with three-foot feet two feet in diameter. The tamper drove all projecting material down to a flat level and the final roller was spraying a coat of bonding oil and rolling the roadbed smooth. Mr. Le Tourneau explained the concept:

"This machine in front carries the plow. The plow can be adjusted in height from the carrying position six feet high in the tap-root cutting depth of six feet. It can cut the rocks and roots through a virgin oak forest at five miles an hour, throws the trees and soil to each side like the bow of a ship throws a bow wave. Up here behind this sloping front apron is the control bridge for steering, depth of cut, engine control, and gun direction. This turret carries the sixteen-inch gun; that's why the army won't have to do any fighting as long as they follow on the road we build. Back here we have the engine room with diesels adding up to sixty thousand horsepower. Fuel tanks for fifty thousand gallons. We don't have to economize on weight—in earth-moving the weight of the machine is our friend. Look at those tracks and grousers. With eight to sixteen inches of armor around her this machine can go anywhere. With this much weight and power she can cut through solid limestone like a knife through Limburger cheese."

I was beginning to understand why Melasky had introduced Mr. Le Tourneau and then thought of something important elsewhere. The genius continued:

"Next the planer pulls the dirt back into the roadbed and cuts the camber and drainage ditches, mounds the loose material for the sheepfoot roller. Controller in here lifts the blade on either side if it hits anything too big for the roadbed. This fifty-ton sheepfoot hammers the debris into a hard mass way down. The stamper is driven by three track sprockets and the stampers operate with the speed of the machine so there is no complication by the use of a separate power source. Finally this roller—notice how it's shaped to give the right drainage slope to the surface—is teamed up with the sprayer here so we roll in a thin layer of oil. And you have five miles of macadamized road for your army every hour.

"Well, what do you think of it?" he asked, bright-eyed as ever.

"Hmmm, interesting, impressive, stupendous. Takes a little getting used to. It's about coffee time. Let's go over to the bar while I think it over."

I tried to turn the conversation to jeeps, horses, coon hunts, Halley's comet, anything else, but he was obsessed by big machines and like Archimedes was just looking for a place to anchor his lever so he could move the world.

After coffee we went back to my desk and he unfolded his sketches but this time I beat him to the punch:

"You have a magnificent idea here, Mr. Le Tourneau, but I have a few minor suggestions that might make it more acceptable to the army. It seems to me, Mr. Le Tourneau, that while the size and weight of your machine are an advantage in doing its job you might have a little difficulty in getting it to the place where the work is to be done. The war is going on in Africa, Europe, and the Orient, and the only way we can get to it is by plane and ship. There's no ship in the world that can carry your machine and if there was a ship big enough no skipper would accept a deckload of sixty thousand tons. The only way it could be transported by water would be to drive it into a drydock and build a ship around it."[7]

"That's a wonderful idea!" said Le Tourneau, scribbling in his notebook. "Build the hull around the machine and use the power plant to drive the propellers. Magnificent!"

"Another slight problem occurs to me—how are we going to get the machine to the port or drydock? Such a weight on grousers like that would completely destroy any road it moved on. The height and width to say nothing of the weight makes transport by railroad impossible. Move across country under its own power? I doubt if any of our present bridges would stand up under it and so far as I see in this sketch it can't swim.[8] Now to vulnerability, as our tankers have learned no armor has ever been made yet that cannot be broken or penetrated. Your proposed sixteen-inch belt of steel around the most important parts of the machine can be smashed, and remember that over twenty years ago the Germans were using the 42-cm. (sixteen-inch) howitzer to smash the forts and the deepest dugouts at Verdun. A sixteen-inch shell from a railroad gun could knock the turret off or give such a shock to the structure that the machine would be crippled and pounded into scrap.[9] And your tracks, massive as they are, could be wrecked by a field gun.

"But you're talking to the wrong people when you advocate size and weight. In the infantry we prefer to keep our targets small, low, and well dispersed. And put lots of these little targets into the fight.

"Oh yes, every machine that we've had any experience with does break down occasionally. Let's say you have thirty thousand two-ton machines instead of one sixty-thousand-ton machine on a job and you have a mechanical failure. You still have 29,999 working on the job.

"So I suggest that you scale down your idea to the point where any machine you build is transportable by rail and ship and that each machine has a separate function. That way when one gets hit or breaks down you have a lot more to continue the work.

"Another reason is you're talking to the wrong people—in the infantry we don't build roads, we just use the roads the engineers build or maintain for us. I'll give you the address of a man in the engineers you ought to start with, Captain Everett, on the staff of the chief of engineers.

"Thank you for dropping in, Mr. Le Tourneau, sure was interesting."

So Mr. Le Tourneau, his enthusiasm only slightly dimmed, took off to sell his machines to the engineers during the war, and continues to build the biggest and best earth-moving machines in the world.

Mummy Bag, Helmet, Jeep

During the long night marches of the spring of 1918 when the Thirty-fifth Division was the mobile reserve of the British Fifth Army, I had frequently dreamed of an improvement in the sleeping gear of the front-line troops.[10] The tentage and blankets were the same size and weight for the 130-pound runt of the company as the 220-pound, six-feet-four giant.

We never used tents on or near the front and were always quartered in barns or bivouacked in forests.

Why couldn't we form the tent material and blankets into a form-fitting cocoon around the individual, trim away the excess material, and sew up the edges? Make these bedding rolls in four sizes, small, medium, large, and outsize. Then the big man would be carrying twelve pounds of bedding, the runt would be packing seven pounds, and both would be sleeping a lot more snugly on a cold night. This idea, while basically worth a trial, remained a dormant dream for twenty-four years.

During a lull in the frenzy of testing weird ideas the dream returned and now I was in a position to do something about it. I went to the quartermaster salvage dump and drew a tattered Sibley tent and five salvaged olive-drab blankets.[11] Took this debris to the post saddler's shop where with the saddler's guidance and help I cut and stitched the sleeping bag of my dreams with four blanket liners. The saddler furnished the hooks, eyes, and thongs for the closure.

Never have I had an idea approved, developed, and adopted so fast. And in so many forms.

The board sent it to the quartermaster general as a requirement. In three weeks I received ten prototypes for test. They had interesting variations. Some bright lad in the quartermaster research and development had put a lot of thought into the development. They had made the following additions to some of the prototypes: heavy brass zippers, tabs inside and outside, from throat to toe; rubberized waterproof canvas; heavy, abrasive-proof canvas on back and sides; snap fasteners for liners; feather-filled quilt liners for the winter bag; durable cotton liners for tropical use; a dome three feet in diameter covered with mosquito netting supported by umbrella-rib-like rods that collapsed to a twenty-inch length when packed.

The weather at Fort Benning was warm to cool at the time so the tests could not be completed by us. I sent the tropic bag to the hot test center in Arizona and the winter bag to the mountain troops in Colorado.

I then borrowed a squad of riflemen from the Twenty-ninth Infantry and trucked them to a distant part of the reservation with eight days' rations. Gave them the easiest mission a soldier ever had—sleep. Each man was to sleep one night in each bag and report to the corporal the next morning how he had slept. The corporal had the job of making notes and taking down any ideas the men had for improvements.

A couple of interesting discoveries were made. The tropic bag was too cold for the lower end of Death Valley. After sunset the air cooled rapidly and by morning it was cold. They wanted two blanket liners. The mountain troops recommended a buttoned or laced closure. The moisture from the body froze and clogged the zippers so that a man had to have assistance or wait till sunup to get out of the bag.

By the fall of 1942 the quartermaster was making tropic liners, summer liners, winter liners, mountain liners, and Arctic liners for the basic mummy bag.

The proliferation of sleeping bags, blanket, cotton quilt, down-filled quilt, feather-filled quilt, wool-filled quilt liners, and the zipper, lacing, button, and toggle type closures suggested by the users and offered by a most cooperative quartermaster required more testing.

But what testing was required? The preferences stated were made by the ultimate users, the troops in the field, and under field conditions. It would be downright stupid and arrogant for the board to tell the troops on the front or in the snowdrifts what they really needed. So I weaseled on that test.

Again I visited the commissary, the laundry, and took my test bags and ten five-gallon milk cans full of water at 150 degrees to the butcher, stowed each can in a sleeping bag, and lined them up in the walk-in refrigerator under the eye of my friendly butcher.

Twenty-four hours later I read the thermometers suspended in the cans. The results were to be expected—the tropic bag can had frozen solid, since it had only the cotton quilted insulation. The Arctic bag with its waterfowl down liner had kept the water in its can well protected—temperature still showed a reading of 127. The other cans registered temperatures between those limits that could have been predicted.

So for this test I merely reported the temperatures registered in the comparative test and recommended that the requests of the troops in the field be granted. It was obvious that toggles and loops recommended by Alaskans could be more easily managed by men with frozen fingers than could buttons and buttonholes or lacings.

I don't know how many of these sleeping bags, originally meant for the sole use of the front-line, foxhole footslogger, ever got to the front. But a hell of a lot of field officers slept real comfy in them.

Some of them got to the front in the Pacific, I'm sure. I read a serious complaint by some GI who told a sad story. His best buddy was sliced to ribbons during a Japanese suicide attack because he couldn't find the zipper tab or the zipper jammed. Slaughtered like a pig in a poke. Well, anybody who would zip his bag to the chin when he was that close to the Japs.

And there was the sad story of the lad in Alaska who couldn't sleep in the snowdrifts while on maneuvers because his feet got so hot.

* * *

The board received a requirement for the development of a better helmet for the infantry. Since it was to be a development from scratch, the imaginative genius Major Sydenham got the job.

During World War I the United States had been stamping out the silly shallow washbasin-type helmets for the British. When the United States came belatedly into the fray we just accelerated the stamping and used them for our own troops. Now that we were in a war again we started to begin to commence to initiate action to get our frontline troops better head protection. Better protection for the temples and neck was required.

I came in next Monday morning and saw that Sydenham's desk was a veritable museum of helmetry—German, French, Italian, current American, and a weird composite that looked like the parade helmet of the British horse guards or the Garde Republicaine. Looked familiar. It was my brainchild of 1935. Sydenham had his feet on the desk—looked like he was asleep.

In 1934, I was maintenance officer of F Company, Sixty-seventh Infantry (medium tanks), and responsible for maintaining thirteen mechanical abortions offered by our moronic ordnance corps research and development geniuses. I also tested and turned in disapproving reports on new types offered.

F Company was attached to the First Battalion, Sixty-seventh Infantry (light tanks), commanded by Lieutenant Colonel Stutesman. Colonel Stutesman was always having new ideas that he passed on to me to work on. One morning in 1935 he caught me at the coffee break in the Sixty-seventh mess hall. "Triplet—the tankers need a better helmet. See what you can do about it. We need to have splinter protection, lead splash protection, chin straps, and chin flaps to include earphones for these newfangled radios. Get going on this project."

He was right. We sure did need a better type of helmet. The square, padded leather things the tankers used in 1918 to soften the bumps on the cranium were absurd anachronisms. With no chin or neck straps the only thing holding them on was gravity and in rough going tank crews immediately lost their helmets and suffered from bumps, bruises, and concussions when they were flung against the armor. "Yes sir," I replied enthusiastically. "That football helmet that I use is better than anything the government puts out. And it costs only $5.25 as opposed to the $14 for the leather boxes we copied from the British. We could save $8.75 a helmet if we went to football helmets and they have chin straps as well as neck and ear protection."

"That's right. Now all you have to do is add the splinter proofing, lead-splash eye protection, and earphones," agreed my heartless commander.

OK, after a lot of doodling I chiseled an old French helmet from the friendly sergeant in charge of the museum and removed the crest and rim. Went to the blacksmith shop and hammered sheet iron until I had the right curves, and asked the interested horseshoer to braze the neck flap onto the skull piece. The rest was easy. A pair of shatterproof goggles were set in a strip of sheet iron that was riveted at the temples of the skull piece, so the goggles could be raised or lowered. Large iron ear flaps lined with the padded earphones on each side and riveted in place, and the chin strip from a standard steel helmet added.

Colonel Stutesman looked over this crude model and speculated about adding a gas mask but finally sent the model and my sketches to the ordnance research and development section, requesting that they furnish a finished prototype for test.

Their wizards did a wonderful job and returned a helmet that would do credit to the horse guards in beauty and filled all of the colonel's requirements in detail. The padding gave protection against the bumps, the steel was the same gauge as the standard washbasin helmet, the temples and neck were protected, the goggles gave clear vision through the antique observation slits we were still using, and the earphones plugged into the experimental radio kept us in touch with the outside world. Blindness would no longer be the cause of casualties among tank commanders and drivers.

Colonel Stutesman made a heroic effort to have the helmet standardized, produced, and issued to all tank units. The request was disapproved at the highest level due to the cost. So the prototype went into the tank section of the Fort Benning museum where it remained until I recognized it among the other helmets on Sydenham's desk.

"What the hell is that?" I asked, indicating my brainchild.

"Borrowed it from the museum—a screwy idea of some idiot trying to make a tanker's helmet."

Since I was the idiot he was talking about I had an unreasonable rise in blood pressure, ire, choler, and a primitive yearning to smack Sydenham into the middle of next week. But too many witnesses, and the insult was certainly unintentional. So—"Well, Syd, you shouldn't have to spend much time on this requirement. Just recommend that they turn out yeah-million copies of the German helmet. It's the best in the world and proven in two wars. One thing, delete those silly knobs on each side for the hinging of face pieces. Even the Germans don't use face pieces except for snipers, and we never would."

"Yes, I'm thinking of that, but there's the matter of recognition. Our men would always be wondering, 'Is that guy under that helmet a Kraut or one of ours?'"

"Paint 'em a different color."

"Yeah, but what about a dim light or at night?"

"Yes, that's so," I agreed, and there my involvement with the new helmet ended.

Sydenham was lost to the world for about two weeks. Sometimes he just sat and stared at the collection of armored headgear on his desk. Sometimes he doodled and sketched. He was frequently absent from his desk and some days just didn't show up.

Then one morning he appeared wearing a helmet the like of which no one had ever seen before. It faintly resembled the German model in that it protected the neck and temples but was more rounded. He went into the chief's office and remained closeted with Melasky for half an hour. When he emerged he was evidently back in this world, bright-eyed and bushy-tailed. Chazal and I went to see the new headpiece. Chazal picked it up. "Why—this thing is plastic!" exclaimed Chazal. "It's not a helmet."

"That's right," agreed the genius. "That's the helmet liner. It will replace the campaign hat, the garrison cap, and the overseas cap. We're going to wear the helmet over it when the shooting starts. Then for garrison duty we take off the helmet and wear the liner."

It was a revolutionary idea, the plastic hat with the adjustable webbing and straps riveted to the shell, then a snug-fitting steel copy jammed on it for wear in the field. But it worked beautifully. The ordnance people responded nobly and in an amazingly short time sent us twenty helmets and liners for testing.

One of the liners became my constant headgear while testing vehicles. And since the war the Third World armies have been almost entirely equipped with surplus helmets and liners dreamed up by Sydenham.

The hard hat idea has also been adopted by labor and industry the world over, and in most states any motorcyclist who doesn't wear a helmet liner gets thrown into the slammer.

There was another world-ranging development made by the Infantry Board personnel during the 1940–1942 period. The Willys miniature trucks were sort of square-cut, looked a bit more rugged and capable than the Bantam, and were two hundred pounds heavier.[12] This should have resulted in an immediate disapproval, but I had committed the greatest crime of a test officer—I had fallen in love with the small recon car concept.

The major obvious differences were the Willys was shod with 4.5-inch tires as opposed to the Bantam's 3.5, and had a slightly more powerful engine. In appearance the Bantam was softly rounded while the Willys' hood was flat and all corners were square. The Willys also had the newfangled hydraulic brakes instead of the more reliable brakes actuated by cables and muscle power.

Mr. Martin, who accompanied the Willys fleet, was an unimpressive little washed-out brunet, very retiring and most knowledgeable and capable. He was cooperative in the extreme and was of outstanding assistance in selling the jeep (general purpose vehicle) to the infantry, the army, and the navy, to say nothing of the rest of the world.

I started testing the Willys just as soon as I could get a pair of them away from Sergeant Snyder and the mechanics. But the automotive tests were interspersed with tests and development of other interesting equipment that I carried out while Snyder and Mr. Martin were repairing the results of my last failure (or when my own frame had to be bent back into shape).

My principal job while on the Infantry Board (test section) was the testing of the quarter-ton GP vehicle, and getting it approved for production was the hardest work of that period. The principal trouble was that in the previous year the gray-haired thinkers of the board who were quite competent in dealing with matters concerning Custer's massacre, San Juan Hill, or World War I, had stated that the three-quarter-ton GP truck, as a truck, a command car, or as a reconnaissance car was the ultimate vehicle of all time. How could they now admit that there was a midget vehicle that could outperform their darling? These Indian fighters were very difficult and it damned near required miracles to get a majority vote of approval. The thinking section of the board was resistant to change. They called any suggestion for improvement "rocking the boat." Typical encounters in the club coffee bar ran something like this when one of the thinkers joined me for coffee: "Triplet, when are you going to conclude your test of that ridiculous motorized roller skate?"

"I'm working on it. I still think it'll make a good recon car."

"But we've already got a recon car. Just last year we swore the three-quarter-ton GP was the idea. We can't change our minds so soon, make us look like we didn't know our own minds."

"Well, the quarter-ton is proving that it can outrun, out-climb, and out-wade the three-quarter-ton job, and I see no reason to throw it out on account of you people making a mistake last year."

"The three-quarter can carry fifteen hundred pounds or six men satisfactorily. Why do we want to complicate the supply system with a midget that has a load capacity of six hundred pounds or four men?"

"Because the three-quarter-ton job has a silhouette like the Woolworth Building and would never live within sight of the enemy lines. You called it a satisfactory reconnaissance car because there was nothing better in sight. Now there is. Even the Germans have a better recon job, their

Kubelwagen. It has a four-man body, bucket seats, and a low silhouette, and the quarter-ton with its four-wheel drive and multi-gear system is way superior to the Kubelwagen."

"Well, when you turn in your report there's no member of the board will approve it. Complicates the system."

Naturally the board had fought the adoption of the Christie tank, which had been bought by the Russians and turned into the T-34, the best tank in the world.

I didn't perform any miracles, but Mr. Martin and his friends at the Willys factory did. They met every request that I made for modification except one, and the improvement they made instead was the right decision.

I started with the routine tests, weight (too heavy), speed (OK, I held down on the throttle till the speedometer hit sixty-eight and chickened out), braking ability (satisfactory), steering (OK considering the short wheel base that made sixty-five the top safe speed), steering radius (too large to make a U-turn on a two-lane road).

My first request to Mr. Martin concerned the steering radius. "Mr. Martin, for a reconnaissance vehicle we need something that can make a 180-degree turn with a fifteen-foot radius. How about a four-wheel steer?"

"I'll call up about it right away, captain."

Three weeks after I'd suggested a four-wheel steering machine we had it. She could turn around in a woodland one-track lane, so she answered my requirement for a fast getaway perfectly. But she had her bad points too. On the speed test I chickened out at forty-eight miles an hour. Short-coupled and with all wheels steering, she was always trying to go somewhere else, and fifty miles an hour would have been suicidal.

I drove her up against a curb in front of the school one morning, a perfect parking, with both tires not more than an inch from the curb. When I tried to leave I found that it was impossible. My front tires would turn slightly away from the curb and the rear tire would turn into it. It took a lot of muscle volunteered by amused bystanders to get my front wheel out to where I could leave my perfect parking position.

Since the four-wheel steer had the agility and turning radius desirable in a hit-and-run operation I took her to the ordnance shop and had the rear axle of a 2.5-ton welded to the reinforced frame with a ball-bearing mounted swivel on which I mounted our pitiful 37-mm. antitank gun. The tank destroyer M1.

Sergeant Simmons was a damned good gunner and was able to get excellent groups in the accuracy tests. He theorized that the shell was out of the gun before the recoil started, but as a bachelor of science whose best marks had been achieved in physics I'm sure the excellent shooting was due to the regularity of gun recoil and his shooting eye. But the four-wheel-steer jeep sure did recoil. The gun would crack and recoil. Then the jeep would leap up, sideways and backwards. So Simmons was right in part. The antics of the jeep did not affect the shot; the target was probably hit before the vehicle remembered to jump.

So the four-wheel-steer jeep became known as Leaping Lena, the idea of the front and rear steering was dropped, and Lena was only shown thereafter as a curio or for comedy effect.

Lucky Thirteenth: I

Escape

While in the test section of the Infantry Board at Fort Benning, I had broken up a score of prototype jeeps and taught the survivors to jump ditches, swim, climb trees, pull trailers, and carry weaponry far beyond their original design. With the acceptance of the modified vehicle by the army (navy and marine corps) I began to write letters to the personnel section of the War Department requesting assignment to a combat unit. These requests were forwarded with disapproving endorsements by the president of the board stating that I was indispensable in my present duty.

With the fall of Corregidor, I realized that the war was passing me by and that if I didn't get into it pretty soon I would retire for age as a major and the United States would probably lose. They hadn't done so well so far without me.

During a lull in the test section's activity I spent three days composing, perfecting, and polishing a letter to the War Department stating the many tests of equipment I had made, the several items that I had developed, and the few that I had invented. I pointed out that there was nothing in the foreseeable automotive or weapon future that could not be done as well by my well-qualified assistants, Captain Myer and Lieutenant Crosman. I modestly proclaimed that I was one of the very few officers of my grade in the continental United States who had had combat experience and such experience was presently needed on the front. The last paragraph of this opus was very specific, verging on the sarcastic: "Therefore I request that I be relieved from my present post as test officer, Infantry Board, and be assigned to command duty with the infantry, parachute infantry, glider infantry, mountain infantry, ski infantry, motorized infantry, or even to the armored force in armored infantry or tanks." That last phrase did it. Two weeks later I received my orders to report to armored force headquarters at Fort Knox for orientation and assignment.

General Wogan, the commander of the skeleton cadre of the Thirteenth Armored Division, was in the lounge of the officers' club attended by his staff of alert, positive, bright-eyed young artillery and cavalry officers. All were booted and spurred, clicking, clacking, and clanging with every movement.

Wogan was a swart, smallish man, alert, positive, bright-eyed, booted and spurred. The *Register* listed him as West Point class of 1915, field and horse artillery, so his selection of a horsey staff for mechanized warfare was understandable.[1] He was coolly courteous but seemed to have more important matters on his mind than the qualifications and assignment of his unit commanders. "Ah yes—infantry. But I already have two infantry colonels. Had no experience with armor I suppose."

"Yes sir. Tank School, 1929–30, company commander Second Tank Regiment, 1930–32, maintenance and test officer F Company, Sixty-seventh Infantry (tanks) with thirteen experimental types plus the platoon of Christies, 1934–36, and tested the Bren gun carrier for the Infantry Board this spring."[2]

"Hmmm, I think I'll put you in charge of the division trains."

The trains! Dear God! I'd pried myself from a safe, cozy, but fairly useful job only to be shunted into the noncombatant transportation, supply, repair shops, and hospital business. I put it into words. "But general, I came out here for a combat assignment and—"

"It's a matter of experience, colonel. I've got a senior cavalry colonel and a horse artillery colonel that I've asked for to command the tank regiments and the infantry colonels are already assigned."

"If we're talking about experience, general, I don't know these other officers but I'll guarantee that I've had more time with more types of tanks than both of your cavalry and artillery colonels and more time in contact with the enemy in the last war than all four of these colonels put together."[3]

I could have made this statement to include Wogan and his staff but that wouldn't have been tactful. When the War Department had started taking the horses away from the cavalry in 1935, General Chaffee had formed the experimental mechanized cavalry brigade with trucks and a platoon of three Christie tanks.[4] That took care of the cavalryman if he had served in the brigade. And as for combat experience, since World War veterans were given the opportunity to retire with three-quarters pay in 1935, combat veterans were very scarce and no cavalryman had seen combat. But my outburst was in vain.

"No—I had a letter from General Devers when he returned from Africa. He said that from the British experience the trains should be commanded by the youngest and most vigorous officers available. And from what he said the protection of the trains is a combat type job. So you'll be assigned as trains commander."[5]

I briefly considered requesting that he throw me back into the pool, but no, I might be ordered to a staff job or made the post gardener at Fort Knox. Better the devil I knew than the unknown around the corner. And I remembered the poly-negatived advice of my alley-rat friend of long ago, "Ya don't never wanta start nothin' ya ain't sure ya can't lose."[6]

So I said, "Very well, sir," and took my leave for the bar, defeated at all points. OK, if that's the way it's got to be, I'd be the youngest and vigorest goddamn trains commander in the goddamn armored force.

The two-week instruction put on by the Command and General Staff School was a "gentleman's course."[7] Homework in the way of reading was advised but not required, the battle films were interesting, and the lectures were entertaining and sometimes instructive.

I learned little beyond the confirmation of my opinion that we (and the British) were still far behind the Germans in all aspects of armored warfare and weaponry. Our antitank guns were 37-mm., to be changed (and we hoped) to 50-mm. The corresponding German guns were the 50-mm., 75-mm., and 88-mm. They were sloping their heavy armor; our tanks had too many vertical surfaces and thinner armor. Our new M4 medium tanks used a short-barreled 75-mm. The German tanks of corresponding size had long-barreled, higher-velocity 75-mm. guns with muzzle brakes (blast deflectors) that reduced recoil and directed the smoke to each side—the German gunner could fire a second aimed shot while our gunner was waiting for the haze to clear. Their diesel fuel tanks when penetrated sometimes caught fire and burned slowly—our gasoline tanks usually whoofed up and burned rapidly.

As a British lecturer described tank combat, "It is quite difficult when we are outgunned. The Jerry tank waddles up to fifteen hundred yards and stops. The gunner dismounts and dusts off the lens of his telescopic sight, then climbs back in and begins to dot off our chaps one by one. And we have to move in to half that range before our shot will take effect on him."[8]

Latta and Edwards

Captain Latta, who was cadred to the trains as the intelligence officer, was a self-starter with brains, initiative, and enthusiasm. The G-2 (intelligence) is the last staff position I would fill and I would not need him in that capacity for many months. But I did desperately need a headquarters company commander, antitank platoon leader, and a column commander. Latta filled all of these spots with distinction. He made quite a reputation with his antitank platoon.

The platoon was armed with four 37-mm. jeep-towed guns, later six guns—pitifully light armament for use against modern German tanks. So I gave him several ideas about their use as follows.

"The turret and frontal armor of the German tanks is thick and sloped, impossible for 37-mm. shot to penetrate, might as well throw pebbles at it. The side armor is thinner and more vertical, you have a chance of getting through the side. The rear armor is even thinner. And any time you get a shot through the armor you have a good chance of hitting the engine, a fuel tank, or ammunition. So try to hit them in the side or rear. Hitting the front or turret would be like slapping Jack Dempsey.

"So don't site your guns for frontal fire. Hide them behind hills, buildings, or in woods where the enemy tanks are apt to pass. Place them within three hundred yards of the flank of probable tank movement as on each side of a defile between steep hills or heavy woods.

"For your gunner three hundred yards is point-blank range. He can make a first-round hit on a vital spot, the shot will penetrate at full velocity, and the tank will probably explode, burn, or be abandoned.

"If the tank does not burn and the crew does not bail out, hit it again and again, fast, until it does. One tank exploded has more effect than five tanks merely scarred. So drill your crews in rapid fire.

"Guns should be dug in until the barrel barely clears the ground when covering the target area. Take the excavated soil away and hide it. If you use it as a parapet it will attract attention and will not protect your crew from a shell strike. Gun positions must be camouflaged until they are undetectable at three hundred yards."

Latta took the above advice seriously. A few days after our talk he came into my office. "Colonel, I have something out here that I'd like to show you."

"Fine, Latta. Bring it in."

"I can't, sir. It's a hole in the ground."

So we went out to see it. On the plain behind headquarters a 37-mm. gun was dug into a shallow pit, muzzle two inches above ground level, and niches for the crew and ammunition. The crew demonstrated their invention, a gigantic parasol of canvas on a light wooden frame. The canvas had been painted with light earth tones and sprinkled with sand and dirt while it was wet. Cords sewn through the canvas and knotted provided the tie strings holding a few clumps of the native buffalo grass.[9] The crewmen slid the slightly domed cover over themselves and the pit and from a distance of one hundred yards only a small sandy knoll was visible.

"Well, Latta, you sure took that ball and ran with it. I'd like to have you keep this a top secret a couple of days."

On the next training day I assembled the trains officers in the school room and gave them a short talk on concealment and camouflage in defense, then asked them to follow me. I led them out in a straggling column, passing Latta's covered and camouflaged crew until we were one hundred yards beyond the gun. "Gentlemen, there is an antitank gun in position within two hundred yards of you. The gunner has you in his sight. The muzzle is looking right at you. Can you spot it?"

They were interested, turning this way and that, searching the plain from underfoot to the horizon, noting and discarding clumps of brush, smears of fresh earth that the gun crew had scattered at a distance, and a wind-blown, rumpled sheet of tar paper that had gotten away from the carpenters. But no one saw the insignificant little grass-grown rise in the ground that they'd just walked past.

I waved a hand as the agreed signal for the crew to throw off the camouflage cover and stand up. Instead the gunner (also a man of considerable initiative) fired a heavily loaded blank round. Startled the hell out of everybody. Including me.

The muzzle blast of the shot had thrown up such a horrendous cloud of dust, sand, and pebbles that the rapid aimed fire I had prescribed was obviously impossible. I had never fired a 37-mm. before in such a dry and dusty climate or terrain and was quite discouraged about mounting the gun near ground level. But two days later the platoon sergeant proudly demonstrated his invention, the muzzle blast muffler M3. Under the muzzle and in front of the gun he had pegged an oval of painted, sand-sprinkled, and camouflaged canvas six by ten feet in size. He fired another heavily loaded round and, behold, no dust. His crew then pulled up the pegs, folded the muzzle blast muffler, and showed how it could be used as padding to make the rear seat of the towing jeep more comfortable.

"Nice going, sergeant. You call it the M3? We'll standardize it."

Captain Latta had worked his gun crews through all aspects of normal training until they were expert at putting their guns into position, digging in, rapid fire with dummy rounds, and accurate with shot or shell at stationary targets. It was time to do something more realistic and entertaining.

I found Major Edwards at headquarters. He was a dark Welsh type, brown hair, medium dark complexion, neat middleweight build, soldierly carriage and alert. He was cautiously reserved at first—seemed to feel that anything he said might be used against him. Understandably so, being rated as unsatisfactory by his regimental commander is inclined to put an officer on the defense. But he listened with interest as I talked about the organization and missions of the division trains and asked intelligent questions about the several vague areas.

"I'd like to have you take a trial run as executive officer," I concluded. "You'd be responsible for all administrative matters, you'd supervise a good deal of the training, and in some situations you'd probably act as column commander. Will you take the job?"

"Yes sir." A decisive type, and one of the ten best men I've known in thirty-eight years of soldiering.[10]

"Edwards, let's give the antitankers some moving target firing next week, say Wednesday or Friday. You've seen the Benning moving target demonstration, haven't you, something like that?"

Edwards went into high gear, selecting and arranging for the firing area, and finally presented me with next week's training schedule. I evidently hadn't made my instructions clear. "What's this item for Friday, Edwards? Subcaliber firing on moving target? They're way past subcaliber firing now and if we have the tow rope long enough we can use solid shot with no danger to the truck driver. No, we want to shoot at a full three-hundred-yard range, panel target on a sled one hundred yards behind the tow truck, no more of this one-thousand-inch stuff."

"No sir, the firing will be at three hundred down to two hundred yards. Captain Latta has tested all of the subcaliber shells ordnance has on hand and has selected twenty shells, that's five per gun, that will shoot true. And I've borrowed a light tank for the target. The colonel in the Forty-fifth wasn't too enthusiastic about it but I pointed out that it would be valuable experience for his crew."[11]

"You mean we're going to shoot at a moving tank with the crew inside?"

"Yes sir, more realistic."

"I'll say. But come to think of it the M5 certainly should take all the small-arms fire we can throw at it. How does the crew feel about it?"

"They're gung-ho about the idea. As you just said, it'll be more realistic."

After mulling it over I concluded that it was a good idea. The tankers had turned in their old-model riveted tanks with the observation slits to be melted down as junk, and the new M5 light tanks were the welded armor, lead-splash-proof type with periscopes.[12] They were proof against .30 caliber armor-piercing bullets, to say nothing of the ordinary ball or tracer rounds. And if Latta had been able to find twenty subcaliber rounds that shot true—

The subcaliber cartridges looked and felt like the normal 37-mm. armor-piercing shell. They were bored longitudinally to receive a .30 caliber chamber and barrel as long as the shell. Loaded with the .30 caliber rifle cartridge they gave the gun crews realistic practice in firing at landscape targets on the one-thousand-inch (twenty-yard) range. An ordnance officer had told me that due to the short barrel the muzzle venting was reduced to two thousand feet per second from the normal twenty-seven hundred but was reliable at short ranges. The principal trouble with the subcaliber barrels was they were not usually perfectly aligned when they were soldered into the shells. Load the shell one way and the bullet would strike three inches to the right, load it the next time and it would be three inches high left on the one-thousand-inch target. At one thousand yards it would be three yards off target, a complete miss.

But we were going to be shooting at three hundred yards so the strike would be within three feet. And if Latta had selected shells that shot in the same place no matter what way they were loaded, yes it might work.

We were out in the firing area bright and early on Friday. Latta's gun crews were digging in on the forward slope of a low hill, facing a steep hill in the distance that would serve as a backstop. Between the two hills a wide sandy road, or rather an unditched, unimproved trail, ran from a clump of woods a quarter mile on the left front, curving toward us to within two hundred and fifty yards on our direct front. The curve continued to the right front until the trail disappeared around the shoulder of the next hill on our right. Edwards briefed the tank commander, a chunky, cheerful, red-headed Sergeant Billings.

"Now, sergeant, your starting point will be the edge of those woods over there on the left. See that red flag by the side of the trail? That's where we open fire, when you pass the flag. You keep generally on the line of the trail, across our front, and around the curve to our right. We cease firing as you pass the next red flag. You keep on until you're under cover behind the next hill. Then turn around and get set for the next run. Same thing back.

"When you're making a run I'd like for you to do anything you can to throw our gunners off, no straight and level stuff. Change speeds, zigzag, stop, back up as you like, just stay within fifty yards of the trail."

"Sounds like fun," grinned Billings. "When do we get to shoot back?"

"Not this time. Be sure you've got the turret and hatches buttoned up, and all you'll get out of it is a few burred-up scars on your paint, and the ordnance promised they'd give you a brand-new paint job if we hit you."

"OK, sir, and Captain Latta will give us the word to go on every run?"

"Right, he's on your frequency, and let us know any time you have trouble. Anything else you need to know?"

"No sir." And Billings took off at a trot down the slope to his tank that was idling on the trail. He climbed into the turret hatch, slammed down the lid, and the tank moved out with a puff of black smoke from the exhaust.

The whole show was a great success. The sergeant maneuvered his tank well, changing speeds and swerving to throw the gunners off their lead and aim. At first he was quite successful, with no more than four hits ricocheting off his armor. But by the fourth run the gunners had gotten into the swing of it, lay a little ahead, and fired when he started to move into the crosshair of the sight. The tracers were bouncing off the side plates with monotonous regularity.

We took a break at the end of the first hour to allow Billings and his crew to climb out of their sweat box, cool off, and have a smoke. General Wogan and Colonel Frost jeeped up as we were about to resume firing. Wogan's reaction was identical to my own. "Came out to see your subcaliber—"

The tank clanked into view at the edge of the woods and the gunners swung toward the red flag.

"You're shooting at a tank with the crew inside?"

"Yes sir, just scars the paint up a bit and the ordnance people are going to do a repaint job."

"Hmmm."

The M5 clanked and rattled, zigzagging around the course, and the tracers clanked and rattled on the armor, ricocheting like screaming, flaming tennis balls.

"I'd like to make the next run in the tank, Triplet."

"Yes sir. Captain Latta, clear your guns and tell Sergeant Billings to come up to the midpoint and pick up the general and Colonel Frost. Have him dismount a couple of his crew here."

Latta must have improved on the order. Instead of halting on the road below us the tank waddled up the slope to the firing line, all hatches open. Sergeant Billings, the gunner, and the bow gunner dismounted. Billings saluted the general. "Sergeant Billings, Forty-fifth Tank Regiment, sir. She's all yours, general," with a courteous wave at the open turret.

"Oh no you don't," objected the general. "You handle the tank. I'll be the gunner. Frost, take bow gunner."

Billings and the VIPs mounted and clanked away to the starting point in the woods.

"What's it like in there?" I asked the displaced crew members.

"Like backin' up rivets in a boiler factory," said the gunner.

"More like a maniac tryin' to get in with a sledgehammer," corrected the bow gunner.

Once more the tank weaved, halted, zigged, ran, and zagged through the course; the fiery-tailed bullets cracked, clanged, and bounced off the armor. More radio conversation arranged an armistice and the tank returned to the firing line. Our overheated guests dismounted and walked around the tank, counting bullet splashes and fingering the scarred paint. They didn't look happy.

The gun crews were ejecting the expanded cartridge cases and inserting fresh cartridges into their subcaliber shells, while the leaders placed the reloaded shells carefully in position on the ground behind the gun for ready handling during rapid fire. Wogan walked along the line of guns, grimly observing the activity. I hoped that he would give them some commendatory remarks about their shooting. No, he returned without comment, rejoining Frost at the jeep.

"I don't like to see ammunition in the dirt," he remarked sourly.

"Yes sir," said Latta and took off to see that his crews handled their ammunition according to the book.

Our visitors mounted their jeep, returned my salute morosely, and drove away.

"What kind of burr has he got under his tail this morning?" I wondered aloud.

"I'm not sure but I could make a pretty good guess," said Edwards, jerking his thumb toward the tank crew who were still counting bullet tracks on their paint.

Come to think of it, so could I.

Instruction

My reportedly mutinous, order-exceeding, hard-to-hold executive had turned out to be a star-spangled jewel. Over a morning-break cup of coffee with him I conversationally mentioned that during the next month I wanted to put the trains through their marksmanship courses. "It will have to be done in two or more echelons so that their primary work can go on," I added.

Three days later I went to division to confer with the concerned staff on training time and allotment of ranges. The understandably puzzled operations officer opened up his range schedule where we were slated for range firing during the second and third weeks.

"Oh yes, it's all set up, no conflict. You're the first to apply. Major Edwards arranged it yesterday."

So I tried to pass it off as though I was just checking and took my somewhat embarrassed leave. On getting back to the office I dropped in on Edwards and found him struggling with the detailed program. Did I yell at him for jerking the rug from under me? I did not. Having him as executive was like having a fairy godmother on call. "Nice going, Edwards. I'd like to see your program when you've got it firmed up."

"I've run into a little trouble. I was planning on two echelons as you directed but we'll have to make it three. They'll have to have two-thirds of their strength to keep the shops, supply, and medical installations going. I've cleared it with G-4 and asked operations for a third week on the ranges, so that's all set. Now I've got to rework the schedule, should have it finished by noon tomorrow."[13]

He used the specialist method of instruction as demonstrated at the Infantry School. Selecting fifty experienced cadre men, he gave each man one part and patter that he recited like a phonograph record for each successive class. One NCO instructed in sight settings, another in aiming, a third in positions, and so on, to include the dry firing. The students were organized in fifty-man classes that rotated every hour to the next instructor. Machine-gun Kelly of the Infantry School couldn't have done it any better.[14]

The ordnance and quartermaster battalions were instructed in the carbine and the truck-mounted machine guns. Since we might be sent to the Pacific where the Japanese do not operate according to the rules of "civilized" warfare, the medical battalion was also armed with the carbine for all ranks to include captains. All officers of field grade were to qualify with pistols.

While on the Infantry Board, I had tested and influenced the board to approve the .30 caliber carbine only to replace the .45 pistol, which is a romantic but almost useless weapon in a shooting war. I had never expected to see the carbine with its low-velocity light bullet and three-hundred-yard effective range replace the rifle that could reach out three times that far. But the army had gotten overly enthusiastic about the little guns and I was disgusted to find that the trains were totally equipped with them.

A handful of determined riflemen in position a quarter to half a mile away could totally block our supply columns bringing up fuel and ammunition until infantry was brought up to clear them out— my two carbineers per truck sure couldn't do it. And visualizing what bullets, especially tracers, would do to a load of gasoline cans or artillery ammunition was nightmarish. But OK, we had carbines. We'd learn to use them.

I had very little to do during the marksmanship period. Every good outfit has to have the cast-iron son-of-a-bitch on its tail and Edwards filled that role to perfection. So all I had to do was stroll about looking benevolent and handing out advice or encouraging words here and there. Few changes in the program or methods were necessary.

One change that I did make was in the instruction of left-handed, left-eyed men. We had an astonishing number in that category, since they were supposedly going to a noncombatant unit, not quite fit for front-line combat service. Several men were functionally blind in the right eye. They could never have been used as riflemen with the bolt-action rifle, but with the semiautomatic we had only to teach them the left-handed positions and how to load.

I also insisted on the two-round burst with the machine guns. Our men had been badly influenced by the example of their tomato-catsup-daubed movie heroes firing hundred-round bursts while waving their guns from side to side with 100 percent deadly effect. That is wasteful and ineffective. I had to demonstrate that a rapid series of two-round bursts with constant correction of aim between bursts will get more pounds of meat per bullet, whether the gun is tripod- or swivel-mounted. It is especially more effective if the truck is moving.

I was satisfied with the results of the range firing, barely satisfied, but we'd done the best we could. It was not until the end of the range season when all units had finished their firing that I realized what my noncombatant heroes had done. The average carbine score of the ordnance battalion was the highest in the division, the quartermaster battalion stood third, the medical battalion averaged with the median of the infantry battalions, and the machine gunnery compared favorably with that of the tank regiments. Not bad.

The American soldier is notoriously reluctant to protect himself by shelter trenches of any sort—they require digging. Having read about the Revolution and Indian wars, he will take cover behind rocks (which add stone chips to the destructive effect) or trees (which have the defensive value of pasteboard against military bullets) but he will not willingly use pick or shovel until the enemy is in sight. That is too late.

I conducted the officers school on field fortification, since as a retread from the World War I knew more about entrenchments than any of my staff or anyone in the division. My instruction, verbal, mimeographed, and demonstrated, can be summarized as follows:

"In modern warfare Mother Earth is your best friend. Stay close to her and in time of danger crawl back into the pouch like a scared baby kangaroo—dig. Dig your cover before you need it and you'll live longer. The wise soldier sleeps in his slit trench.

"We will use the slit trench for passive protection against bombing, strafing, or artillery when ground attack by infantry or tanks is not probable. The slit trench is dug as long as the man, as wide as his shoulders, and deep enough to protect him from a projectile falling at twenty degrees. Place and stamp down the excavated soil in a crescent at each end of the trench, piling it high enough that a splinter coming over either end at twenty degrees will not strike him. Make the crescents at the ends thirty inches thick to stop small arms fire. Camouflage thinly with native vegetation.

"Although an enemy ground attack is not expected site the slit trenches of each group for all-round defense with the long axes pointing outward like the spokes of a wagon wheel.

"For defense against ground attack we will use the rifle pit. Each man digs a circular pit wide enough so he can kneel or squat in it and deep enough for his head to be eight inches below ground level when he crouches as low as possible.

"Place your group for all-round defense so that every man can shoot in any direction.

"Each man spreads his shelter half or blanket, tosses the excavated soil on it, carries it one hundred yards or more to the probable rear, and dumps it to form a dummy entrenchment. Raw dirt will attract the enemy fire and it is best to have the bullets strike behind you.

"For rifle pits we do not use parapets. Use camouflage of natural vegetation—thinly.

"Make and carry spider-hole covers for your rifle pits, one per man. Cut a circle of beat-up salvage canvas three feet in diameter, stiffen it with two or more sticks tacked across each other. Tie several pair of cords into the fabric for use in tying on clumps of grass or a small bush. Laid flat over the pits they will shield your men from observation. Propped up on one side they protect from sun or rain. Flipped aside, your men can fire in any direction.

"If you have time, camouflage the dummy positions heavily.

"Under threat of possible enemy attack in bivouac, machine guns will be dismounted from vehicles and emplaced in machine gun pits.

"Site the gun for all-round fire.

"Mark out a circle on the ground four feet in diameter. Dig a slit trench around this circle deep enough for the man to crouch with his head eight inches below the surface.

"Cut down the top of the center mound until when the gun is mounted on it the muzzle will be just above the ground surface.

"Again, carry the excavated soil away to build a dummy emplacement behind you.

"Camouflage your emplacement thinly—the dummy emplacement heavily.

"When in a dangerous area for a long period you will build the luxurious duplex apartment fighting-living quarters like this.

"Starting with a rifle pit or machine gun emplacement dig a deep slit trench from it at right angles to probable attack. Make it two-man wide and four feet deep. Cut the sides down a foot and a foot wider. Cut six-foot logs, planks, or branches, and roof over the trench. Spread shelter half over the logs. Cover shelter half with excavated soil to ground level. Dispose of surplus soil. Camouflage lightly. Furnish interior with sleeping bags and decorate with pinups as desired.

"Notes: these entrenchments will protect your man from bomb or shell splinters and from being crushed if a tank runs over his hole. Do not dig deeper than specified. A close bomb or shell burst may move the side of your hole and crush or bury you.

"Special note for machine gunners: The soil may not stand up under the vibration of firing your guns. Therefore you will make T-boards with cross cleats on the under sides and with notches cut to fit the spades of your tripods. Always carry them on your vehicles."

After my talk, blackboard sketches, and a mimeograph distribution the class inspected the slit trench, rifle pit, spiderhole cover, machine-gun pit, T-guard, and the duplex that Captain Latta and his young men had made, and I gave the class the word, "Go thou and do likewise."

But in vain. When urged by their officers the men would dig in shallowly with a few feeble swipes of pick or shovel, just enough to keep them out of the stockade for direct disobedience. The ordnance battalion was especially difficult; no shelter that was defensible against a child with a BB gun was dug by ordnance personnel.

Until one day I went out to inspect an ordnance company in bivouac and was amazed to see them dug in, not professionally or neatly but thoroughly.

When I complimented the captain on his unusual success he beamed and proudly explained. "Put the company in the woods, trucks parked outa sight, and told 'em to dig in. The trenches they dug wouldn'ta hide a rabbit. Took the lieutenants out there on the flat and we started shooting carbines through the treetops, then a little lower, and a little lower. After half an hour of that we went back and this is what we found. Nobody hurt but by God they're all dug in, and just look at those blisters."

I have always been careful never to reprimand an officer for initiative, constructive action, or an original idea—those officers who are aggressive and able to think and act on their own must be encouraged. But in this case I almost strangled holding back caustic comments or worse. Finally made it. "Seemed to be very effective, and I'd include your idea in our training program, except, you know, these carbine bullets are so light that they're easily deflected in any direction by hitting a tree limb. Even a rifle bullet can be turned by a tree or a branch. I'm glad to hear that you didn't kill or cripple any of your men. But we won't do any more shooting over the men except with a concrete-base-mounted machine gun on the infiltration course."

Three.

Lucky Thirteenth: II

The Antitank Show

After the range season was completed for all weapons, I scheduled an antitank demonstration for the education of all trains personnel. I wanted to show the smashing power of the 37-mm. gun, the .50 caliber machine gun, and the new hollow-charge antitank grenade; the use of intense .30 caliber machine-gun fire against observation slits or periscopes; the blinding effect of phosphorus smoke grenades; and the effect of the explosive satchel charge when placed under cover of smoke.

I was outlining this program to Major Edwards during our morning coffee break in the mess. "I want to convince the last truck driver, roustabout, and mechanic that if every man uses everything he's got we can stand up to an armored attack and win."

"Right," said Edwards. "And how about some Molotov cocktails?"

"No, I don't think so. They've been given a lot of romantic publicity by bar-bound war correspondents and Hollywood actors but I don't think they've blistered a buttoned-up crewman or stopped a tank yet. Scared them maybe, but the phosphorus grenades are more effective."

"OK, we'll use phosphorus," agreed Edwards.

"Let's try to set it up for first Thursday of next month for all trains personnel except skeleton medical crews on duty. I'll invite the infantry and tankers to send observers if they like, so let's make it good."

He did. The dress rehearsal was impressive, well nigh unbelievable.

"Are you sure that tank attack will work?" I asked.

"This is the third run like this. The drivers aim 'em right, put 'em in low gear with full throttle, jump out, and they follow their same tracks every time. The hairy part is the driver climbing out of his hatch and over the turret to jump off the tail, but they're getting good at it."

At 0900 on D (demonstration) Day the audience was assembled behind the staked and roped-off safety lines. It appeared that in addition to the trains battalions, most of the officers of the infantry and tank regiments and a scattering of engineers were present.

A few yards in front of the audience the four guns of the antitank platoon and six tripod-mounted machine guns were dug into position, unrealistically close together, but due to safety requirements and angles of fire we were pressed for room. On the flanks and forward of the line of guns a few men were putting the final touches on their spider-hole rifle pits and camouflaged covers.

29

Three hundred yards down-range and slightly to the left were two hulks of an early breed of tanks, one facing the guns, the other presenting a flank view. A long ridge six hundred yards distant and three or four hundred feet higher would serve as a backstop for the firing.

Since it was Edwards's show, I had required that he run it. He mounted the jeep rostrum.

"Gentlemen, the demonstration this morning is intended to show the members of the division trains that tanks are not invulnerable, that they can be stopped.

"How can a tank attack be stopped?

"In order to be successful tanks must be accompanied by infantry. If we shoot away their infantry support the tanks will turn back. We would like to show this aspect of antitank warfare but the infantry units all declined to take part in the realistic show which we proposed." (Appreciative snickers from infantrymen present.)

"Tanks can also be stopped by mines which we will normally have to protect our installations in the field. Unfortunately due to supply requirements no mines are available for training at present.

"Tanks can be seriously hurt by artillery fire but a current shortage of ammunition for training does not permit its use for this demonstration.

"So we have nothing but our own gunfire, grenades, and explosive charges, an admittedly weak defense but the best we have to offer.

"Now, gentlemen, please observe the ridge on the skyline in front of you." Latta spoke briefly into his walkie-talkie.

Where the hell was General Wogan? The VIP bench that I'd had set up for him, the brigadiers and staff, was still empty. Hitchcock should have them here by this time.

A faint rumble was heard from the ridge in the distance, tank engines being "jazzed" by their anxious drivers to prevent stalling. The gun crews came to the alert like bird dogs awaiting the shot and the word "fetch." The men on the forward flanks disappeared into their rifle pits and pulled their camouflaging covers into place.

A line of the obsolete Mae West twin-turreted light tanks appeared over the crest of the ridge, two, three, five tanks, covering a front of three hundred yards. They waddled ahead and down the gradual slope at a sedate four or five miles an hour, bobbed across the slight swale, and continued up the rising plain toward me.

I hoped the drivers had all gotten clear without getting stepped on.

The tension was building up. Two months ago the tankers in the audience had been training in these very tanks. Now that they'd been rescued from the ordnance junkyard and tuned up for a last run before going back to the melting pots, they were really impressive as they bobbed and weaved over the slight irregularities of the terrain. They were getting close. As the first of their irregular line passed the bush that marked the three-hundred-yard range—

"Commence firing." Captain Latta gave the word without emphasis.

Four tracers darted out and disappeared into four frontal plates. One tank stopped as though it had run into a wall and black smoke began to seep from the turrets. Another started burning but staggered gamely on for another hundred yards. The gun crews were getting their rounds off fast and within a minute four of the tanks were stopped and were burning furiously. That idea of stowing partially filled gasoline cans and crankcase-oil-soaked rags in hull and turret sure made a realistic show.

"My God, that's Beatrice," I heard someone wail. Couldn't blame him, it hurt me in a way to see still working machinery pounded to death like that.

One of the Mae Wests had not stopped. Latta had promised to skin any gunner that fired on Number 5 on the right of the line. Engine roaring at full throttle, Fiona clanked on toward the line of guns.[1] When she reached the fifty-yard mark, spider-hole covers were flipped off and half a dozen phosphorus grenades were thrown. The tank was concealed by the blinding white smoke that succeeded the bursts. Two carbineers who were farthest forward and behind the tank on each flank dashed out of their cover. One of them found the long wire that Fiona was trailing behind her and yanked it hard. With the switch pulled "off" the engine died and Fiona stopped with her front apron plate just visible through the cloud.

A man carrying a heavy canvas sack ran forward from his flanking hole, tossed his package on the apron under cover of the thinning smoke, and fled for cover. A few seconds later the audience was stunned and deafened by the horrendous blast of the satchel charge (shouldn't have done that—too much and too close). Fiona whoofed up and joined her sisters in emitting flames and a cloud of black oil smoke.

The firing of two of the new hollow-charge antitank grenades against the flank of the burning hulk was an anticlimax. With half of their smaller explosive force penetrating the armor and sounding inside the hull, they were not impressive to men who had just been blasted by the satchel charge at point-blank range. (We should have fired them before we'd smoked her.)

Major Edwards stood up in his jeep, raised his arm, "Gentlemen!" and resumed his spiel.

"The natural tendency of light-armed men facing an armored attack is to run or hunt cover and stay down.

"There is one more alternative, to stay and fight.

"We will now show you the possibility of success if we stand our ground and fight with our light weapons. David versus Goliath.

"We intend to concentrate the fire of three .30 caliber and three .50 caliber machine guns with a few carbines, first on the tank hulk facing you, then on the hulk with its flank exposed.

"Both of these hulks have their observation slits backed by the bullet-proof glass with which you may be familiar, instead of the modern periscopes. We will try to smash, sear, or lead-splash this glass so that it would be useless for observation and have to be replaced. Granted that the enemy will carry spare periscopes, we should then keep up a heavy fire to smash the replacement glass.

"Carbines will fire normal ball ammunition for lead splash. The .30 caliber guns will fire one tracer, two armor-piercing, and two ball-round series. The .50s will fire one tracer and four AP series.

"One belt of 250 rounds will be fired by each gun at each target."

Edwards turned to the waiting gunners.

"At the first target—commence firing."

The guns chattered in fast short bursts, the tracers darted and ricocheted. A total of three hundred fiery balls representing fifteen hundred rounds smothered the turret for a long minute, five tracers or twenty-five bullets per second were searching for the vulnerable glass. The belts ran out, the silence was deafening. The gunners fed new belts into their guns and cranked the first round into the chamber, then traversed to lay on the second tank hulk.

"At the second target—commence firing."

The tracers arced down-range and glanced from the armor—the larger .50 caliber balls from the side of the hull while the .30s searched the turret for the observation slits. Again the guns ran dry.

"Gentlemen, this concludes our demonstration. We trust that it will show you of the trains that you are not defenseless, that tanks are not invulnerable, and that your best chance of surviving an armored attack is to stand your ground and hit them hard and fast with every weapon at your disposal. Please move forward and inspect the targets."

The barrier ropes were dropped and the crowd surged forward toward the burned-out wrecks. The demonstration had gone off without a hitch. I'd never seen a better show at Benning, where convincing demonstrations were the rule. I drifted along with the mob in a mild state of euphoria, exchanging light chatter and mordant humor with exuberant trains people, cheery infantry officers, and morosely thoughtful tankers as they hand-spanned the eighteen-inch gaps in front of Fiona's driver's hatch; poked their fingers in 37-mm., .50 caliber, and grenade holes;

examined the scarred, shattered, or lead-smeared glass; or felt the armor to learn just how hot a gasoline fire may be.

After completing the rounds I turned back, almost colliding with Major Hitchcock and his VIPs—General Wogan, the brigadiers, the former horse artillery and cavalry tankers, and Colonel Wysor of the infantry. Wysor was obviously in a good frame of mind and B. General Evans was his usual bland, neutral self, but the others looked as though they'd washed down a dose of liquid quinine with vinegar.

"Good morning, general," I babbled. "Sorry you missed it. Major Edwards put on a really good show. Had a place reserved for you up front."

"I saw the whole thing, colonel. I'm certainly sorry you invited the tank officers." He left without further comment, trailed by his entourage. Hitchcock remained.

"Sorry I couldn't move them up, colonel. They wanted to stay back in that truck, said they'd get a better view."

"Small matter, Hitchcock."

The general was right. I wish that nobody but the trains had seen the show.

Relieved

The speed marches were killers, especially for the trains personnel. It was asinine (pardon me, General McNair) for army ground forces to require my clerks, mechanics, cargo handlers, stretcher bearers, and surgeons to measure up to the marching standards of infantry.[2]

They had the muscles, lungs, and hearts to make the marches, but not the feet. After all, a man who stands behind a counter, twists nuts on bolts, removes appendices, or taps a typewriter four days a week just doesn't develop the calluses of a rifleman by two days of fieldwork a week.

But we had it to do. So well in advance before we started the conditional marches I conducted an officers' school on "blisters."

"Next month we will meet the AGF requirement for speed marches of your units, in combat packs and carrying your personal weapons. The first march will be eight miles in two hours, the second test will be twenty-five miles in eight hours.

"Your men are physically able to meet these requirements, but they will have trouble. Blisters. Raw, infected, and ulcerated blisters will cripple your men for a week or two after each march unless they take care of their feet.

"Blisters are caused by the heat of friction on soft skin. You and your men will take these precautions: Starting now, don't wear socks during normal duty—grow calluses. Stop using soap on your feet. Don't wash your feet—just rub them with a dry towel. Trim the toenails very short, straight across. On field marches wear two pairs of socks, cotton under wool. Pull your socks taut at every halt. Wear shoes that you've shaped to your feet by soaking and wearing till dry. Use foot powder on your feet, on both pairs of socks, and inside your shoes. It's the dry lubricant that reduces friction and heat."

All of this was good advice, and we didn't have the epidemic of crippling blisters that I had expected. But there were two notable exceptions.

Lieutenants Rosenblatt and Sopranzi were a highly educated pair of young doctors who naturally knew a lot more than I did about dermatology. They were familiar with the miraculous curative qualities of balsam of Peru, the chocolate-colored, resiny concoction that they so frequently smeared on lacerations, burns, and blisters. Theorizing that such an effective cure should also be a preventative, they coated their feet liberally with the gooey stuff, then pulled on their socks and shoes for the twenty-five-by-eight march.

They finished with their units and in no unusual state of fatigue or misery. They removed their shoes without difficulty. But after trying in vain to pull off their socks they were evacuated to the hospital. There, after administering a mild oral anesthetic to my unhappy heroes, one of their colleagues carefully peeled off the socks with the complete skin of the feet firmly glued therein.

The horrified surgeon shipped them to Letterman General Hospital for intensive specialized treatment, and we never saw them again.[3]

Moral: an educated person is not necessarily intelligent.

In August of 1943, one year after the "Lucky Thirteenth" had started training, the big day arrived. A horde of agate-eyed, coldhearted, emotionless, humorless hatchet men, a team made up of armored force and army ground forces led by a suave and heartless brigadier general, descended upon the division to determine our combat readiness. They stayed, examined, looked, peered, pried, and tested throughout a harrowing week.

Just what they did during that week I can't say from my own experience or observation—I just heard the plaints of my peers and the battalion executives about unreasonable insistence on accurate records, unguessed shortages of equipment, unsatisfactory maintenance, wild gunnery, poor march discipline, minor tactics, etc., ad nauseam. The division staff and regimental commanders seemed in a state of deep depression but apprehensive of worse to come. While everyone else was moving rapidly about like a stirred ant heap, headquarters and headquarters company of the division trains stayed close to office and barracks, hopefully waiting for and fearing a visitation by the test team.[4] But though the dumps, warehouses, shops, motor parks, dispensaries, and barracks of the trains were thoroughly combed over, we were ignored. We were not even listed on the schedule of inspections, and a query to Colonel Frost brought the inconclusive answer, "They may get around to you." Then I alternated between feeling outraged at being left out and damned glad we were.

During this week I observed, was told, or got the impression that a drastic change took place in the women of the area around Camp Beale. Previously hostile or indifferent wives became more like the girls the boys had married. Several lassies who had been playing hard to get with majors settled for hastily arranged weddings with lieutenants. One ambitious young lady (who was not apprehended until after V-J Day) married four of the men, carefully choosing her husbands from different battalions of the armored infantry and saying "I do" only after making certain that the allotment of pay and government life insurance was made out to her. Others not so shrewd thoroughly seduced their young men in the hope of marriage. Naturally the rumor was that in a few days the division would be pronounced combat-ready and shipped to England or to fight, bleed, and die in the mountains of Italy.

At the end of the week the inspectors took flight like a cloud of full-fed locusts, and like the locusts leaving complete devastation behind them. At a meeting of all field-grade officers in the division theater the verdict was announced.[5] General Wogan's exhortation condensed to the unhappy essentials may be expressed as follows: The Thirteenth Armored Division after a year of training is credited with six months toward combat readiness. This 50 percent rating is directly due to incompetence or lack of diligence on the part of field officers of the division. Beginning now, training for combat will be the primary objective of all ranks. Field officers are and will be held personally responsible for the efficiency and combat readiness of their units. Heads will roll.

Many of the long-term wives resumed their previous poisonous personalities. The recent brides began to nag their husbands about previously unnoticed or unmentioned faults. The sirens who had seduced their boyfriends in vain accelerated their activities in order to get pregnant and show cause for immediate marriage within the six-month period of grace. The female financial wizard found time to marry two tank gunners, one from each regiment. Then pleading illness in the family she retired to her home in San Francisco to await the mailman bearing the allotment checks, or better yet telegrams of condolence from the secretary of war followed by government insurance and settlements.

Stimulated by Wogan's stirring speech, commanders drove their units through the training program with vigor until a man who was crawling through a wire entanglement under machine-gun fire stood up at the wrong time, and a tank commander was shot through the head by one of his supporting riflemen during a combat firing exercise.

Once again, extreme caution reigned, and any field training that was more vigorous than a Boy Scout summer camp schedule was not encouraged.

Situation normal.

Shortly after the disastrous combat readiness inspection and the general's stirring speech I received a call at 0900 from the chief of staff, Jack Frost.

"Colonel Triplet."

"Triplet, the general would like to see you in his office right away."

Seven minutes later I entered Wogan's office. It was quite an unusual tableau. Instead of the long expanse of empty carpet one normally trod in approaching the distant desk, only an aisle between three rows of folding chairs remained. The general had evidently been having well-attended conferences in addition to his general assembly in the theater. The front row of chairs was completely occupied by an array of the rank and file, the inspector general and one of his junior hatchetmen, two of the equestrians, G-3 and G-4.[6] The ordnance and quartermaster staff officers and the surgeon were the rank. The file were my three executives of the trains battalions.

Wogan, seated behind his desk, was reading a training manual with his back to the windows in the right side of the room. The staff were conferring in hushed whispers like choir boys in church. The general swiveled around as I clumped down the aisle and clicked to a halt.

"Colonel Triplet, reporting as directed, sir."

"Good. We were just discussing the state of training and the allocation of training time, colonel, and I thought you should be here."

"Yes sir."

I looked for a seat. The front row was fully occupied, four to a side. As the ranking field officer present and the one who was most concerned, I certainly wasn't going to take a back seat, so I pulled an end chair from the second row, took it to the wall on the right front of Wogan's desk, and positioned myself where I could see what was going on. It was an odd performance, and even with memory clouded with age and prejudiced with rage I can clearly remember some of the lines of the show. General Wogan opened the conference.

"The technical training of the support battalions was found to be unsatisfactory during the recent inspection. This may be due to inadequate training programs, poor instructional methods, or lack of training time. What do you have to say on this, Colonel Smythe?"

The G-3 uncrossed his boots, stood up, and read from his notes on the legal pad he'd been studying. "It is my opinion that the fault lies in the time and emphasis spent on tactical training by the trains commander. The technical training schedules and instructional methods were followed exactly as prescribed by armored force headquarters, so time must be the prime consideration.

"I have made a compilation of the time used for tactical training. I find that the division trains have been occupied in this training during the past year as follows: Officers' school (nights) 100, physical training 250, tactical training (day) 700, tactical training (night) 48, marksmanship and combat firing 128, total 1,226.

"I believe that if the support battalions had been given more time, say six hundred hours, to devote to more useful subjects, their technical readiness would have been found to be satisfactory."

So that was the way it was. I looked along the line on my right front. Smythe was now earnestly proposing that tactical training be eliminated for the coming six months so they could catch up on their technical homework. G-4 appeared blandly neutral. The inspector general was the very picture of a dedicated IRS auditor who has just discovered where the undeclared loot was hidden. The surgeon was thoroughly enjoying the show. The weedy young ordnance type was walling his eyes nervously and twitching like a cornered rabbit. The quartermaster glumly studied the spit shine of his shoes. And the trio of battalion executives gave the impression of the night watch before the funeral, which it was. I was the corpse lying in state.

I had friends in the group but they had evidently been so well worked over before my arrival that while I had their sympathy, I did not have their support. Smythe had finally run dry. The inspector general could contain himself no longer.

"As I have seen it, the basic trouble with the training of these battalions is that they'd rather go out in the field with Colonel Triplet and play soldier than attend to their primary duties."

The viciously contemptuous manner in which he said "play soldier" gave me a rush of blood to the head. I yearned to squelch this brawny little CPA type, but it wasn't my turn yet. The surgeon cut in with his poisonous contribution.

"There has been so much concentration on weapons that the only way the medical battalion could help the wounded in pain would be to shoot them." Major Busch, the battalion executive, twitched and reddened. Spencer's nervousness and Aldenhoven's unhappiness obviously, increased when the inspector pointed out that the ordnance mechanics could dig perfect rifle pits but couldn't time an engine.

So it went. The general listened and doodled without comment while the G-3, the IG, and the surgeon laid the entire blame for the technical failure of the support battalions on me. I had taught them motor marches, cross country navigation, field fortifications, marksmanship, and combat firing as though they were in the infantry. I had required the quartermaster clerks to dig. I had taught the medics to shoot. That clearly was the reason for their 50 percent efficiency rating. This trio alternated without prompting by Wogan; as soon as one man came to a period the next broke in with a further accusation. The rest of the witnesses (or jurors) remained morosely silent.

In spite of my flaming rage I kept my jaws clamped, waiting for the general to call on me for my views. Instead he gave judgment and pronounced the sentence. He swung his swivel chair toward me. "You see how it is, colonel?" he asked. "We believe that the tactical training of the trains is presently quite sufficient and your time with the battalions should be reduced. We will try giving you one day a week and see how that works out. Say Wednesdays—and all physical training will be under control of the battalion commanders. That should give you enough time for refresher courses. Well, colonel?"

I couldn't talk, just nodded.

"Very well, gentlemen. Colonel Triplet will have the responsibility of working with your battalions on Wednesday of each week. That is all. Thank you."

I moved out (appropriately) at the tail of the column as they left the office. In the hallway I stopped. Counting ten did no good. I turned and marched back in to Wogan's desk in a blue flaming rage. He was again turned with his back to the light, reading the manual, and removed the specs. I didn't stop for the usual formalities.

"General Wogan, I request immediate relief as trains commander and a transfer to a soldiering outfit as soon as the armored force can find a spot for me. I'll have my letter to the commanding general, armored force, up here for your endorsement by noon."

He was evidently amazed by my request and attitude.

"Why, why? What do you mean?"

"Sir, this was the goddamnedest business I've ever heard of."

I had to get control of my voice and words, didn't want to get my buttons pulled off for insubordination. So I continued, choosing my words carefully and speaking slowly.

"I thought that I was called to take part in a conference. Instead I was put on trial by your staff before officers whom I command in training.

That action completely negated my position as trains commander. I was not even given a chance to offer a defense and the accusations that I was responsible for the inefficiency of your staff members were so absurd that I could easily have saved the situation. But it's too late now.

"I'll point out to you that a year ago I was given two days per week for the tactical training of these battalions and at present they can drive safer, dig deeper, and shoot straighter than any other outfit in the division. I've made soldiers out of the mechanics, clerks, and doctors I started with. Now that I've been publicly humiliated before the men I'm supposed to command in the field, I have no alternative, I'm quitting."

Wogan leaned back in his chair amazed, puzzled, thoughtful. I think he was seeing me for the first time.

"You honestly believe I let you down," he mused aloud.

"You certainly did, sir."

He evidently hadn't the slightest grasp of troop leading or the fragility of command. But he was thinking.

"Well, I'm not going to relieve you of command, it wouldn't look good on your record. And you just hold off a few days on that letter to the armored force. We are going to have a few changes in personnel very shortly. Would you take command of a tank regiment?"

"A tank regiment? Yes sir, that's what I've been hoping for."

"Good, we'll see how it works out."

"In that case I'll hold off on the letter and keep my present quarters until it works out, but I'm still through with the trains. I recommend Colonel Edwards as a good man and I'll turn the job over to him."

"Oh yes, Colonel Edwards. He put on your antitank demonstration. Yes, he'll do very well. All right, colonel, I'm sorry that you feel that I let you down. Stay with it."

"Yes sir."

I stayed with it, or rather I stayed there. I notified Edwards of the results of the conference and gave him the total command in effect. I never issued another order nor talked shop with another member of the trains, didn't want to undercut Edwards. Gave myself a three-day pass and a long weekend to visit Fiona, the youngsters, and the goats in Grass Valley.[7] And while in camp I sulked in my tent like Achilles—no, Ajax at the siege of Troy—except I had several paperback whodunits to sulk with. And no more "come over and have a nightcap" at the evening mess.

Sure saved on whiskey.

Forty-fifth Tanks

Heads did roll.

Some ten days after I'd quit the trains—

"The chief of staff is on the phone, sir."

"Triplet here."

"Hi, Trip. The general wants you to take command of the Forty-fifth Tanks, VOCG (verbal order commanding general). I'll have the orders out and copies to you by 1700, but he wants you to go over and start getting acquainted this morning."

"OK, Edwards has everything in hand here, so I'll get over there right away and get a briefing from Leighton."

"I'm afraid you can't, he left yesterday."

"The hell, where's he off to so fast, and why? To win the war by himself?"

"I can't say." (Can't? top secret? forbidden to? don't know? won't?)

"OK, I'm off."

From the condition of the regiment as outlined on the combat readiness skin list Colonel Leighton was probably reassigned as a recruiting officer in Arkansas or as post gardener in Fort Knox. The most serious deficiencies appeared to be tank gunnery, marksmanship with individual weapons, and tank maintenance.

Throughout the first week I did nothing but study the skin list of the inspecting team, walk through the barracks, training areas, and parks, observe, and say nothing. My most serious faults are instant decision and immediate action; this time I was going to study, weigh, and measure every situation as deliberately as a federal court judge.

No—one positive action that I did take immediately that first morning was to call in the adjutant. "Lieutenant Mueller, I'd like to meet all the officers and their ladies as soon as it may be practical, and believe that we might best arrange that at a party of some sort. What is the current social schedule?"

"Nothing is on at present, sir. But I suggest that we lay on a dinner dance at the mess on Saturday night. I'll get the announcement out today, RSVP by Friday noon, string quartet from the band. And the mess crew will have plenty of time to prepare menu, decorations, table settings, and so on."

Hmmm. He was evidently a damned good man, grabbing the ball and running with it like that.

"Very good, let's make it so. But remember the second lieutenants. Keep the cost down to, say, $1.50 per person."

"At $1.90 we won't be able to have wine, sir. I think that most of the officers and especially the lieutenants would rather pay $2.25 and have a real wingding party."

They did. It was a nice affair they put on, very Old Army. A receiving line with Fiona and Lee, our seventeen-year-old daughter, on my right, name cards at the tables, soft music in the background, and the wit and beauty of the Forty-fifth dining and dancing.

At one point, about the dessert and coffee, I stood and expressed my pleasure at meeting the officers and ladies of the regiment and proposed a toast. "Ladies and gentlemen, to the unfailing success of the Forty-fifth!"

As the diners rose and sipped I was startled, no horrified, to see my teenager sitting at a distant table with her escort rise and toss down her quarter-bottle-sized glass of 12 percent California vintage apparently in one gulp. Oh oh, as far as I knew it was her first bout with the Demon Rum. But to her everlasting credit she carried it better than several of her elders for the rest of a very fine evening.

Remedying the unhappy maintenance situation was simple. The next Monday, I had an assembly of all officers and gave them the word, which can be condensed as follows.

"Thirty-two percent of the tanks were currently on deadline. We will consider 10 percent or less on deadline to be acceptable, only for the prescribed engine checks. Maintenance and repairs are the responsibility of the crews and the chain of command supported by ordnance when necessary. When a tank is on deadline the crew will stay with it, lending their muscle to the mechanics in the higher-echelon shops. Since one tank is 20 percent of the platoon, the platoon leader when not in the field will supervise them. If a company has two tanks out of action or a battalion has eight on deadline, the company or battalion commander concerned will spend the major part of his time supervising the maintenance and repair work.

"The crews and officers mentioned above will remain in the regimental and shop areas as long as their tanks are out of action. Overtime work, nights, weekends, and holidays will be permitted and encouraged.

"Your tank crews and some of your officers will be very unhappy about being confined to their barracks and shops, and may complain through channels, but I have already informed the commanding general and the inspector general that this program is not cruel and unusual punishment. It is a means of ensuring that you and your crews take an active and informed interest in the care of your tanks. And I feel sure that within a month you will reach the 10 percent goal that I require and again enjoy the company of your ladies and the pleasure spots of Marysville, and you will know a hell of a lot more about your machines."

Actually the 10 percent goal was passed in two weeks.

Marksmanship qualification was even simpler. The adjutant told me of a major who was an ardent member of the National Rifle Association and I talked the problem over with him.

"The ranges will be no problem. The other regiments are going back to review basic training so you'll have a free hand for at least a month. There are 238 men who are unqualified. What do you need to qualify them?"

"That's about fifteen to twenty men per company, split three ways, pistol, submachine gun, and carbine. At first thought I think I should have one officer and three high-shooting NCOs per company. I'll plan the job in detail and let you know, sir."

"No, I'll be busy with the gunnery. Just ask the exec for what you want, you have priority. And the next I want to hear about it is that they're 100 percent qualified."

"Right, sir. I'll keep the bolo men shooting till they do make it, if the ammunition is available."[8]

"It is. And by the way, I'm putting out the word that no man leaves the post until he is qualified with his personal weapon."

"That will give them something to work for. And I'd like to give the instructing NCOs something if they put out well—"

"Certainly, passes, a short leave, see me at the end of the program. Well, major, it's all yours."

At the end of three weeks the major reported that he had four men left who were impossible and not worth the efforts of the four NCO coaches that he still had working with them. I told him to see the S-1 (personnel) about it and tell him to get rid of them.

I never did know where they went, only that they no longer marred the 100 percent qualification of the Forty-fifth. Maybe to the medics?

In studying the tank combat gunnery problem I found that Horse Artillery Leighton had taught the artillery method of gunnery, i.e., "range eight hundred, fire, over, range six hundred, fire, short, range seven hundred, fire, short, range seven hundred and fifty, fire," and they'd get a hit on the third or fourth shot. That is a good method when they're firing blind from two to three miles in rear of the firing lines, but would be fatal in dealing with enemy tanks or antitank guns. To stay alive a tank gunner had to make first-round hits, like a gunfighter in a barroom brawl.

Too many men were missing on the marksmanship program and a quarter of the tanks and crews were in the shops, so I did nothing but hold officers' schools on combat gunnery for the first three weeks. The major ideas that I taught are condensed below.

1. Guns will be bore-sighted at one thousand yards instead of on the one-thousandth-inch target. They will fire targeting shots at one thousand measured yards, adjusting the sight on the burst, until the burst is on the target. The gun will then be accurate at all lesser ranges.

2. Machine guns will also be targeted at one thousand yards. If the gun requires another sight setting (nine hundred or eleven hundred) the gun will be used as a range finder, firing single tracers at estimated ranges until a hit is made. The gunner will then use this range to get a first-round hit with the cannon. Note that a single tracer from a small-caliber weapon in a combat situation will probably be disregarded by a tank or gun commander. He will be looking for bigger game than a sniper.

3. When forced to fire the first shot with the cannon at an estimated range, aim low. An over is gone forever, probably unnoticed by the enemy. A low shot will wreck or burn the enemy tank, and a short will blind and frighten him and you will get your corrected shot off before he fires his first aimed round.

4. In firing at cardboard targets representing antitank guns on the combat range use this technique of firing short. Don't punch a neat hole in the target, destroy it by throwing a bushel of gravel, dirt, and shell fragments through it, instead of hitting it and having the shell burst fifty yards beyond.

5. Machine guns will be fired in two- to three-round bursts; the Hollywood method of long, swinging bursts is spectacular but ineffective and will not be used. When your tanks move down the combat range or into the enemy lines I want to hear your machine guns tattat-tattat-tattat and the dirt boiling in front of and immediately behind the target.

On my first morning on the combat range as I was accompanying the first platoon through their run a messenger from division jeeped up with the word that the general wanted to see me. That was in effect the last I saw of the Forty-fifth Tank Regiment.

General Wogan laid the situation clearly before me.

"The Thirteenth will be reorganized as a light division, in battalions rather than regiments. The combat command idea rather than brigades.[9] I'm three colonels over-strength for a light division. I've thought of giving you the trains command again but don't believe you'd want to take it. Is that correct?"

"That's right, general, I wouldn't care to go back to the trains."

"In the meantime General Simpson, Ninth Army, has asked for you to take over an armored group at Ford Ord, some sort of amphibious tank outfit. You'd prefer that to the trains?"

"Yes sir." What the hell were amphibious tanks? But I'd take it.

"Good. Frost is having orders for transfers cut now, so tell him you're off to the Ninth Army. Good luck."

So ended my service with the Lucky Thirteenth. The Thirteenth wasn't lucky. I was.

The next time I heard of the Thirteenth Armored was during a chat with an officer of the XVIII Airborne Corps. We were reminiscing about the Ruhr pocket.

"That's where the Thirteenth Armored stopped," he said.

"The Thirteenth Armored—I was in the Thirteenth in 1942–43. How'd they do?"

"Practically nothing. They went into the line and were shoving up this road to close the loop. Ran into a roadblock in a defile covered by a couple of platoons of real tough riflemen. Stopped cold. This general—Wogan—Wogan came boiling up, jumped out of his star-spangled jeep, and says, 'The Thirteenth Armored will never by stopped by a few infantrymen,' and *wham,* one of these Krauts put a bullet through his neck. That was the most profitable forty pfennigs that Hitler ever spent, that billion dollars' worth of men and machines stayed stopped."

"The hell you say—didn't they—"

"Nope, had to get some infantry outfit up there to leap-frog them."

On August 31, 1954, in company with several members of the class of 1924 and several senior generals I retired at West Point—the corps of cadets in review, a fly-over of a fighter wing, the banging of saluting guns, "ruffles and strumpets," a most impressive ceremony. After the review there was General Wogan in civvies, coming up with neck slightly crooked, to shake hands, smile, and congratulate me. (For what?) He lingered, obviously studying my ribbons (eight for combat and two for meritorious service), then turned away with a shake of the head. A puzzling performance. Still wondering about the ribbon reading, I looked him up in the *Register.* "Retired disabled 1946, DSM, SS, LM, PH." OK, he'd earned his Purple Heart and I suppose that any major general who moves up in small-arms range of the enemy deserves a Silver Star, but any major general who wastes a zillion dollars' worth of men, weapons, equipment, and training time does not deserve a Distinguished Service Medal or the Legion of Merit. He should have been court-martialed for treason and given a dishonorable discharge for the total elimination of one armored division from the strength of the army of the United States.

I think the timid, playboy, political sonofabitch should have been shot. But it evidently paid off to be a classmate of Eisenhower's.

Four

Eighteenth Armored Group (Amphibious)

The Presidio of Monterey, now the home of the Ninth Army, is built in tiers on the north slope of a large hill overlooking the town. The quarters of the officers and married NCOs form the lower level, the headquarters and barracks are the middle layer, and the stables are the line of buildings along the ridge. It was originally built by the Spanish, taken over by the Mexicans in the 1820s, and inherited by the U.S. Army in 1846. The post had been modified and expanded several times in the past three hundred years, but the original design had been maintained for good reason. It is common knowledge that high ground is healthful and the lower areas are cursed with *mala aria* and mosquitoes. So naturally the horses, so important to the Spanish, Mexican, and U.S. cavalry, were stabled at the highest level; the active part of the garrison was housed in the next most desirable area; and the comparatively unimportant wives and camp followers occupied the lower levels.

I found the Ninth Army well under the control of my classmates of the U.S. Military Academy, class of 1924. Tall, dark, and handsome Jim Moore was the chief of staff as a brigadier general, Colonel Red Mead, runty, ruddy, and feisty, was G-3 (operations), Colonel Dan Hundley, a solid citizen and a sandy, rugged-faced middleweight who had already commanded a regiment in the Solomon Islands campaign was G-1 (personnel).[1]

General Simpson was very tall and slender, with a shiny bald pate and a long dark cast of countenance. But when he turned on the charm with a welcoming smile I forgot my first impression, his resemblance to the current movie representations of Mephistopheles or Fu Manchu. We had never served together before so there was no chit-chat about old times. He outlined my mission. "You are to form and train the Eighteenth Armored Group (Amphibious) of six battalions, three of tanks and three of personnel carriers. Train your units for combat beach landings in cooperation with the navy. As soon as your group is combat-ready you will take them to the Pacific theater of operations."[2]

That was it, very simple.

"How much time do I have, sir?" I asked. "When are they needed?"

"MacArthur wants them last month," replied the general. "You'd better get going. Moore and Mead will fill you in on what they have to date."

They did. In a brief four-way conference I learned that the group would be stationed at Fort Ord, that the headquarters and headquarters company would arrive the next day, that two battalions would join at the end of the week, and that I would have my full complement by the end of the month.[3] The group would be formed of tank and tank destroyer battalions that had been trained for land warfare but were surplus to requirements in their primary roles. So my principal mission would be to familiarize them with their new machines and weapons and teach the tactics and techniques of amphibious warfare.

"What training or technical manuals are available?" I asked.

"There are no manuals of any type at present. The marines are starting to train five battalions at Camp Pendleton but all they have is the navy stuff on boat landings.[4] Training manuals will probably be written after a study of your experience."

"What about the equipment?"

"Some of it is on the way. You'll get the rest of it as fast as it comes off the assembly line at the Food Machinery Corporation."[5]

"OK, I've got a busy day ahead."

So armed with a notebook, pencil, and total ignorance, I began the formation of the Eighteenth Armored Group (Amph).

First Acquaintance

I checked in with Colonel Ramsey, the camp commander of Ord, a lean and lively lightweight with a bad limp, and with his executive, Lieutenant Colonel Wycoff, a plump middleweight with a roving glass eye that he sometimes replaced or covered with a patch. Both of these retreads from World War I were shining examples of the value of partially disabled but capable and dedicated officers when employed on duties within their capabilities. I could outrun Ramsey and see farther than Wycoff but I could never have managed as good a host camp for the many various combat units temporarily stationed with them.

Colonel Ramsey had already made preparations for the reception of group headquarters and the six battalions of tankers and tank destroyers, reserving a sufficient block of barracks, administrative buildings, and officers quarters in the south-central portion of the division-sized camp.[6] Transportation was laid on for the reception and for immediate issue. He was also able to give me my first firm knowledge of the strength of the tank and carrier units. The tank battalions would have 37 officers and 711 other ranks, the carrier battalions (officially tractor battalions) would have 24 officers and 480 enlisted men each.

The headquarters and headquarters company arrived led by Lieutenant Colonel Northridge, a veteran of the Guadalcanal campaign as a member of the Americal Division. He was a tall, slender, sandy-blond, schoolmasterish type, very deliberate in thought and action, and 99 percent right in both. I felt fortunate in having a number-one of this type to balance my own often erring impetuosity. He wore glasses and had an amusing conversational habit, sometimes disconcerting, of staring at the other party with the pupils of his eyes balanced on the upper steel rims of his spectacles. A damned good man and I put him in charge of practically everything during the period of experimentation in surfing.

Northridge had a good crew: Chisholm as company commander, Major Rathke and Captain Rolle in S-3, Major Howell as S-4 (supply), Dietrich as COMO (communications), Bost in S-2 (intelligence), Miller as athletic and recreation, and half a dozen more second lieutenants who were thrown into any position that needed reinforcement at the moment.

We entered a maelstrom of activity, jeeping over to the Presidio to contact our opposite numbers in Ninth Army, reconnaissance of land firing ranges, observation and testing of surf conditions, selection of sea and beach training areas, marking out vehicle parks in the sand dunes near the beaches, conferences with the local navy and coast guard commanders in Monterey, and inspection and trial of the first of the amphibious machines to arrive in Fort Ord.

I had my first view of these mechanical monstrosities as they sat on flat cars in the Ord railway siding. They were an imposing sight, vaguely reminding me of the Mark VIII M-1918 forty-ton tanks I'd lived with for a couple of years in the Second Tank Regiment.

The tank and carrier hulls were identical, twenty-six feet long, eight feet wide, and seven and one-half feet high. The Continental radial engine was mounted in the stern, taking in air through a vertical grill mounted at the rear of the cargo space and discharging through a horizontal grill forming the after deck. The machines were designed by the navy bureau of ships so they were painted a dusty gray-blue battleship gray similar to the French horizon blue, a hell of a lot better camouflage color than the army olive drab. In the forward compartment of both types the driver was in the left seat and the partner was the radio operator who manned a navy radio. The driver's glass port looked an inch thick.

The tank was decked over to include the mount for the turret, at the height of the driver's cab. The M5 light tank turret with its 37-mm. gun was superimposed on this deck, raising the overall height to ten feet. At the rear of the turret the deck dropped to the height of the hull proper and, partially protected by the turret mounting, two round open hatches with shielded swivel ring mounts for light machine guns provided protection for the tanks to the flanks and rear.

On the carrier the driver's cab added a foot to the overall height. Swivel mounts were installed for the .50 caliber and two .30 caliber machine guns. The hull would probably carry twenty-five or thirty men or three to four tons. The net weight was fifteen tons.

The engines were governed to a top speed of eighteen hundred rpm that gave us fifteen miles an hour land speed. In water the deep double-horseshoe grousers pushed the water to the rear and threw a heavy stream through chutes mounted on the stern at the rear of each track. Action equaling reaction—as the water shot to the rear the vehicle moved forward. "Full ahead" was a scant six miles an hour.

Steering was accomplished on water as on land by pulling one brake lever and stopping the track on that side. The other track then received all the power and the vehicle would turn sluggishly toward the braked side. Both tank and tractor had a great deal of inertia, and when the driver shifted to neutral they would drift on and on at six, five, four miles per hour in spite of his instinctive and useless hauling back on both brake levers, and *crruunnch* would ram the pier with a jolt that would fetch an audience from a block away to examine the damage. Since the grousers were designed to scoop water to the rear, the vehicles were even more sluggish in reverse. But by using reverse at full speed we found we would ram our objective at a more reasonable two or three miles an hour. These kindergarten driving lessons taught us to keep the engine at its full eighteen hundred rpm for all water work, to make decisions well in advance, and to act on them immediately and vigorously.

My first thought as a tank officer was that these craft wouldn't have a chance in combat. Their gun power was inadequate, their armor wouldn't turn anything larger than .30 caliber bullets or shell splinters, and their vulnerable target area was outrageous—even a scared enemy gunner couldn't miss. But they were built for seagoing operations and beach landings, so if they were smaller, and had two-inch armor and heavy guns, they wouldn't float—the M4 medium or M5 light tank sure couldn't swim.[7] So we'd give them a real good try.

My waking, dozing, and sleeping hours were taken up with mental arithmetic, theories of organization, training problems, and tactical uses of amphibians in combat. For instance, let's see, the tankers will remain organized as they were with the M4s and M5s. How many tanks will we need? Three for each battalion headquarters, four companies with three tanks per company headquarters, and three platoons of five tanks each. That's eighteen per company, seventy-two per battalion, plus the three for battalion headquarters is seventy-five per battalion. Three battalions is 225 plus three for group headquarters, a grand total of 228 tanks. (Turn on the light and make a note, requisition 228 tanks.)

For the carriers, no, they're called tractors. There'll be five per section with a sergeant in command. Three sections per platoon, a lieutenant commanding, that's sixteen tractors per platoon. Three platoons per company is forty-eight plus three for company headquarters is fifty-one.

Two line companies in the battalion makes 102 plus seventeen for the battalion headquarters service company totals 119 per battalion. Three battalions comes to 357. That's a lot of tractors. (Light and notebook, wait, I've forgotten the headquarters service companies for the group and the three tank battalions. They need seventeen tractors each, that'll be sixty-eight more. That makes a grand total of 425. Note: put in a requisition for 425 tractors and 228 tanks.)

Good Lord. That's a total of 653 of those monsters plus the administrative motor vehicles we'll have to have. Is the tank park we staked out on the dunes big enough? Have to check that again tomorrow. (Light and note, check park for size of battalion areas.)

And when I was exhausted by such serious calculations I was entertained by a series of lively dreams, trading my 37-mm. solid shot with a Japanese tank gunner who was using armor-piercing 50-mm. shell. The Jap always won, my gun would misfire, the barrel would droop like a strand of boiled macaroni, my tracers would fly wide or dart from here to there like butterflies, but his tracer would drive straight in like a flaming football and burst between my eyebrows. Another favorite—overtaken, broached, and capsized by a gigantic wave, trapped under the overturned tractor. And worst, timidly shrinking inside the comparatively safe armor of the tractor while Jap bullets pattered the plating and I didn't have what it takes to stick my head out.

After three or four hours of such adventures in color and with sound effects I certainly enjoyed hearing the rollicking notes of Reveille.

Sinkings, Towings, Painting

Mishaps were frequent throughout our training period since we were in the position of a ship's pilot approaching an uncharted coast on a foggy night. We had to learn from our mistakes. Sinkings in deep water were few—we lost only one tank and two tractors offshore and by employing a professional salvage firm we recovered the tank. All of our other machines were lost near the beach within recovery distance.

The sinking of a tank or tractor was a serious matter. Only one did I find mordantly amusing. We were practicing launching by platoons in calm water. A tractor platoon hammered down the beach in single column. On the flag signal of the platoon commander every tractor spun full right and plunged into the ripples. As they dashed out to full flotation depth the lieutenant's tractor started spouting water from the pump outlets on each side. Odd. There shouldn't be any water in the bilges. In spite of the three hundred gallons a minute being pumped the tractor was gradually sitting lower and lower in the water. Two hundred yards out the crew became aware that something was wrong and confusion reigned. The driver did a U-turn and the double-strength crew began bailing with the bucket and helmets. They almost made it. The drowned engine sputtered and quit just as the tracks touched bottom in four feet of water and the crew waded ashore in deep disgust.

"Why did you come back, lieutenant?" I asked the platoon leader.

"Forgot to put the drain plug back in," he confessed, blushing with embarrassment.

Other sinkings ranged from routine to downright horrifying. A water-flooded engine would conk out, the pump that was grafted to the drive shaft and normally emptied the bilges with dispatch would stop with it, and each successive wave would drive the derelict nearer the beach and the bottom. Since it had no superstructure a tractor would normally sink upright due to the weight of the tracks. A tank would capsize and rest with its turret or side on the sand.

The salvage team consisted of two tractors, each with two or more steel towing cables. When a vehicle was swamped, two or three hardy souls of the salvage crew would wade out and hook a cable to the wreck. The salvage tractors, cable-connected in tandem, would then drag the derelict ashore. A machine that was capsized or deadfalled would be approached from one side, the cable hauled over and attached to the track on the other side. A pull by the salvage tractors would then flip the wreck upright to release the sodden crew who had been breathing the air bubble trapped inside the hull and wondering what in hell was taking us so long.

The safety officer would radio the guard in the tank park and they would telephone ordnance shops for the wrecker and tank transporter. If there were serious injuries an ambulance would be requested from the hospital.[8]

It was a good system and I was pleased with our recovery operations until one late afternoon when Captain Wright appeared in the doorway of my office. "Is the coffee on, colonel?" So it was just a social call.

"Sure is, Wright. Come in and set."

I poured the thick black residue of the breakfast brew from the simmering pot and diluted mine to a pale tan with a dollop of milk.

"Well, how are the downtrodden working classes doing in the sweat-shops?" I queried. "All the wage slaves happily busy I trust."

"We're snowed under, colonel. That's why I'm here."

So it wasn't a social call after all. He went on.

"You're swamping so many of your machines that my crews just can't keep up with you. It's the corrosion that damages the engines and radios—"

"I agree, we're swamping too many. It's not only the engines and radios, what hurts me is when there's a crew mousetrapped in there. How many broken arms, necks, or backs are there under that hull? But we've got to push them hard to get them ready for the next port call to AFWESPAC."[9]

"Yes sir. I know that you've got to train your men in rough water and train them faster than you'd like. That means sinkings. But your salvage crews could help us a lot if—"

"What do you mean help you? I was there when they went after that capsized tractor this morning. I timed them. They went out in chin-deep water and had that thing flipped over on its feet and the crew out in six minutes. They reconnected the cable and had her towed high and dry in eleven minutes from the time she went over. They had the drain plug pulled and everything dried out and ready for your wrecker crew when they came in forty minutes later. I think that's helping you a lot."

"That's just the trouble, sir. They pull the wreck out of the water after they get the crew out. They let it dry out and corrosion sets in."

"But leaving her sit in the sea water sure doesn't do her any good," I objected.

"It really doesn't do much harm as long as she stays in the water. It's when you get the sodium chloride drying on metal in the presence of oxygen that iron rusts, aluminum and copper corrodes badly, and magnesium disintegrates. That's why I'd like to have your salvage crew let the wrecks stay right there where the splash of the waves will keep them wet till my boys get there. Then we can winch a wreck onto the transporter, rush her to the shop before she dries out, and hose her down with fresh water before corrosion sets in. Drain the crankcase and cylinders, give her a lube job, and she's ready to go again."

"I'll be damned, never thought of that," I confessed. "So I get the men out and leave the wreck for you to handle?"

"That's right, sir. Save us a lot of work in the long run."

"OK, after this we'll attach the tow cable and wait for you."

"Another thing, colonel, about the painting. A lot of rust is showing up on your hulls and we can't keep up with it. We've got too much serious repair work on hand to spend our time sanding and painting armor plate. You and I both know that it's eyewash but these corps and army inspectors carry on more about a rust spot on your turret than they do about a cracked cylinder head. Question is if I furnish the paint can your people put it on?"

"We sure will. These rust patches as big as my hat were beginning to bother me too. I'll have Howell see you tomorrow. More coffee?"

"No, thank you, sir. Good coffee, but—" He shuddered and departed.

After Captain Wright had given me his lecture on salvage, free oxygen, sodium chloride, and various metallic oxides, I whiled away a couple of hours of insomnia by thinking about painting. Next morning I caught Major Howell at the breakfast table. "Howell, I'd like to have you spend your day managing for paint, a lot of paint. Different colors. You can draw all the battleship gray you'll need from Captain Wright, and he'll be glad to turn over all the sandpaper and brushes you want. But see if you can con him out of some red, blue, yellow, green, white, and black. Then try Bigelow in utilities."

"Yes sir. Utilities has house paint in several colors. And maybe I can trade with some paint shop or hardware stores in town. How much do we need?"

"I want each tank battalion to have the turrets painted a distinctive color so we can recognize them with the naked eye a mile away. The tractor people will paint the drivers' cabs. Our own stuff stays gray. Any paint that's left over we'll use on the rusting hulls, sanding and painting in different colors like these modern artists, break up this solid gray, the camouflage idea."

Howell delivered the paint in quantity and I put out the word to the battalion commanders. Next Friday was designated as painting day and all other activities suspended. Saturday was set aside for paint inspection. I took Friday off to catch up on the accumulated paperwork and compose another boat-rocking letter to army ground forces.

Saturday dawned bright, clear, and sparkling. I left the mess, walked out to my waiting jeep, and did a double-take. The well-worn regulation olive-drab paint job was marred by five-inch block letters in dazzling white spelling the name "Great Mogul." I glanced with dour suspicion on T-5 Perkins but his lantern-jawed mug was blandly deadpan as usual, so I pretended I didn't notice the change.[10]

Arriving on the highway above the entrance to the tank park, we halted for a moment. Yes, the crews had done well and the idea would work out well. We could now distinguish between the 774th with their flaming red turrets and the green-topped 778th. The blue drivers' cabs of the 535th showed up well in contrast to the yellow cabs of the 539th. And the hulls! The hulls were speckled, spotted, striped, and splotched with a varied smattering of all the primary and secondary colors. Gave the general appearance of a lineup of crocodiles suffering from a virulent skin disease. It added up to a good job of camouflage painting for land warfare, a lot better than battleship gray or the dark olive drab of the land tanks, and a big improvement over the former splotches of rust red.

We drove on into the park for the rust inspection and I went into shock for the second time that morning. Sergeant Cole and his two-man crew were standing before the group command tractor, and Sergeant Schmidt had his five heroes lined up in front of the tank, all at rigid attention and all wearing the same bland, innocent "come to Jesus" expression of a soldier who is putting something over on his officer.

The bow of Cole's tractor was painted as a gigantic shark's head, a gray-green shading off to the basic gray about the gills. The wide open lips were lined with jagged white teeth the size of my hand surrounding the scarlet mouth and purple maw. An evilly slanted white, cat-pupiled eye stared from each side of the bow. It was a really artistic caricature that I haven't seen equaled until I was terrified by the film "Jaws" forty years later.

Schmidt's tank was even more of a jolt. On each side of the turret base in neatly blocked six-inch white enamel letters stood the name "Terry Bull." That was a low blow.

There was a story behind that name. As a poverty-stricken captain in the late 1930s, I had added to my inadequate income by writing prophetic stories of the war between the United States and Munga (acronym for Military Union of Germany and Asia) for the *Infantry Journal*. The heroes of these years were the Bull brothers, Terence (infantry) and Horatius (tanks), both rather rough diamonds and sergeants in their respective branches. The *Journal* paid five cents a word so the monologues in which Terry and Horry described their adventures and the latest thing in military hardware or tactics used lots of short words, very readable by the troops.

But this prosperity was not to last. Shortly after war was declared in 1941, I became a poorly paid major and the president of the Infantry Board called me in. "Triplet, you know those stories you're always writing for the *Infantry Journal*—from now on, if your ideas are any good they're top secret and you work on them for the board. If they aren't any good don't waste your time writing them."

"Yes sir." He'd never heard of freedom of the press.

That ended my outside income until I got a letter from the *Journal* stating that a selection of the Bull brothers' stories would be published in pocketbook form at the going rate of twenty-five cents a copy and that I would receive 20 percent in royalties. It was evidently sold in quantity—I could take Fiona out to dinner at the club every Saturday, and bought Lee that bracelet she was hoping for, on the proceeds. And Sergeant Schmidt must have been one of my customers.[11]

I'd intended to ignore Perkins's witticism and Cole's artistry but decided now that I couldn't deadpan all three of them. Turned back to where Perkins had parked "Great Mogul" on the right of "Shark."

"Perkins, I'm very much relieved. When I heard you were naming your limousine I was afraid you were going to call her "The Admiral.""

"Thought of that, sir." Perkins didn't change his sanctimonious expression but his tan did turn a dark brown. "But the boys talked me out of it—wouldn't be right for a tanker."

"Damned realistic paint job, Cole. Didn't know you were an artist."

"I'm not, sir," smirked Sergeant Cole. "Found a man in the 535th used to be a billboard painter."

"And where did you get the Terry Bull idea, Schmidt? Terence Bull was an infantry sergeant and ships and tanks are supposed to be named after girls."

"She is, sir, named for Terence Bull's sister Teresa." He must have lain awake all night planning that ambush, and I'd walked right into it.

"I'll be damned, didn't know he had a sister." Best I could do.

I turned away from these smug, smirking, likable wisenheimers and moved on to walk through the ranks of the artistically decorated battalions. Not a speck of rust.

Organizational Structure

From time to time the army would assign a surplus brigadier general to the III Corps. General Millikin would then assign him as commander of the mélange of troops stationed at or being processed for overseas shipment at Fort Ord.[12] Colonel Ramsey, the post commander, didn't need or want a troop commander to control the troops but the brigadier didn't interfere with his operations and the system kept the general out of the way. In fact we were seldom aware that we had a brigadier in charge. There was one notable exception.

The current general having expired from the cancer that had caused his assignment to this dead-end duty, Brigadier General David P. Hardy was announced as troop commander. He was vice president of production in some oil company when as a brigadier general in the reserve corps he was called to active duty. This sudden appearance of a one-star strategist with little or no practical experience was probably embarrassing to the War Department, which was rapidly expanding the army 8,000 percent. Reserve officers from second lieutenants to colonels were welcome, in inverse order of rank. They were the flesh and blood of the military skeleton, the Regular Army. But a general?

I can ESP a high-level conversation in the newly occupied Pentagon. "Here's David P. Hardy up for assignment. Where shall we put him? Can you use him in your—"

"No way! I know him. Maybe you can use him as assistant—"

"Uh-uh! He's been in the reserves long enough to make brigadier and what I need are Indians instead of so damn many chiefs. Find some spot for him where he can't do much harm."

"An idea, how about commander of troops at Fort Ord? It's a processing center for overseas shipment and I think there's some armored group permanently stationed there. We can assign Hardy to III Corps and suggest to Millikin that—"

"Good idea. Put out the orders."

And General Hardy took command of troops at Fort Ord.

It is only fair to admit that I did not like General Hardy. He was a large, squarish, horse-faced brunet. He was decisive and positive in his ideas, which he usually formed from a basis of total ignorance, and he had no desire to learn.

During our first meeting I found that he was not interested in our training program or the morale or welfare of the men. His concern was centered on costs—fuel and oil used, the price of machines and weapons, and the cost of repairs. He firmly declined my invitation to observe any of our activities.

During our discussion of maintenance I proudly described how our mechanics were coping with the problem of blowing sand during lubrication of the machines in our sand dune–sited tank park and how our wash rack had whipped the difficulty of sea water corrosion. His response to this bit of braggadocio was, "I don't want to hear any more of your goddamned belly-aching about training conditions."

But I suppose that's the way a vice president of production talks to the foreman of a drilling rig.

On the morning following our second aborted attempt to land on a strange coast I received a message from General Hardy requiring my immediate presence at his office. I was still stiff and sore in every muscle due to bracing for nine hours against the pitching and rolling of yesterday's misadventure. When I limped into the general's office I was not at my physical or psychological best. He touched a nerve with his opening.

"I've heard that you had some losses during the stupid trip yesterday."

I realized now that trying to land on another coast was stupid but didn't like anyone else saying so.

"Yes sir. We lost a tractor, a troop carrier."

"I hear that you've lost a hell of a lot more than that."

"Yes sir, two men drowned last month."

"How many vehicles have you lost so far?"

"Permanent losses to date are two men and one tractor. We've had a good many injuries and sinkings but the injured men are returned to duty and we've always salvaged the vehicles."

"How about the tractor you sank yesterday—are you working on it?"

"No sir. It went down in deep water west of Punta Piños. Salvage is impossible."

"Twenty-five thousand dollars tossed away! Did you save the weapons?"

"No sir. It was a bit rough and the crew—"

"That's another $3,000 you've lost in deep water. From now on you are not to go out farther than two hundred yards from shore. I will not have any more machines sunk where they can't be reached."

I was understandably horrified. The prospect of having to spend all of our water training time in white water was so awful that I protested.

"But general, that would be too dangerous. We can't maneuver in the breakers. We'd lose a lot of men if we try to do anything but launch straight out and land straight in. We can't turn—"

"Are you with me or against me, colonel? If you aren't with me you're against me. Now, in the future you are to do all of your training within two hundred yards from shore. Do you understand my order?"

There was no point in further discussion with this star-spangled embodiment of obstinate ignorance so I quibbled.

"Yes sir!"

Note that I did not answer, "I understand the order and will obey," nor did I shout the German "Zu Befehl!" (I'm off to carry out the order). My reply meant only that I understood. Quibbling.

On leaving his office I considered the problem very briefly. There was the safety of the men—I was putting too many of them in the hospital now. The value of the equipment I'd lose beyond reach. Most important, the mission and General MacArthur's reaction when I sent him amphib battalions that couldn't go more than two hundred yards from shore. I balanced these factors against my probable court-martial.

Our training program remained unchanged. I felt like I was walking a greased tightrope over Niagara Falls with General Hardy's razor-edged knife poised to cut the rope. And I was sure he would.

But my worry was for nothing. I doubt if the general ever raised his eyes from his bookkeeping and looked out the window at the swarm of LVTs launching, landing, navigating, and shooting in the safety of the smooth swells far offshore. Or perhaps he'd had second thoughts about the stupidity of his order, or maybe General Millikin had—[13]

For a brief period the amphibs had an organizational structure that compared in stupidity only with that of the Roman army when two consuls were in command on alternate days. General Millikin broke the news. "You're getting another group—the Thirteenth Armored Group for the amphibs. Colonel Charles S. Johnson, Infantry, commanding. Do you know him?"

"But we don't need another group, sir, we're getting along fine just as we are."

"You're getting one and since Colonel Johnson is senior to you he'll be in overall command. I don't like the change any more than you do but McNair seems to think that you have too heavy a training load for one group."

"Well, general, after building this outfit up from scratch I don't like to turn the command over to an imported Indian-fighting colonel and play second fiddle while he learns the business. Can you send me to the Pacific?"

"I don't want to send—here's an idea, you told me that you don't pay much attention to the land training, because your men already know how to drive and shoot. That's the answer. Colonel Johnson will be nominally in charge of both groups. He'll receive the new battalions and be responsible for their ground training. Then he'll transfer them to your group for sea training. And he'll endorse and forward the official correspondence of your group as the joint commander. That's the answer."

"If we split the training like that, general, I'd like to have you assign a brigadier for the joint command. Since Colonel Johnson has had no experience with the LVTs there's bound to be some disagreement between us regarding training methods. For example, I don't want to see any changes made in the gunnery methods I've prescribed. So I'd like to see a brigadier—"

"Impossible. I'll be in command of both groups. If there is any friction between you I'll settle it. I'll brief Colonel Johnson on his duties and I don't think you'll notice any real change in your operations."

Colonel Johnson and his Thirteenth Armored Group headquarters arrived as prophesied. After a briefing at III Corps he checked in at my headquarters for a cup of coffee and an orientation. He was a lightweight brunet with a lean-drawn, discontented, dark-complexioned countenance accented by a ruddy nose. He was obviously distressed by the transfer of the Thirteenth Armored Group to the amphibian business and as dissatisfied with the awkward situation as I was.

But Millikin was right. Probably due to his forceful briefing there was no real change in operations and no friction in our dual command role. Johnson moved his group headquarters into an office building and barracks immediately north of the amphib barracks area and took his people to the park and beaches for orientations on LVTs. He took charge of newly arriving battalions and supervised their land driving and gunnery. He endorsed our futile requisitions for spare parts and forwarded my boat-rocking letters to AGF with his approving signature as Thirteenth Armored Group commander, commanding.

It was an unfortunate relationship, but we made do. We were both very happy when his orders to the European theater arrived and he left to win the war for Eisenhower. For a short time I was the unhappy commander of two groups, but some unusually intelligent staff officer in AGF found something more useful for the Thirteenth to work on and they faded out of the picture. We reverted to our former overworked status quo. And loved it.

Five.

Waves

Practice

I took the first tank and tractor that were processed and issued by the camp ordnance detachment for my very own, and Captain Chisholm assigned very capable crews to handle them. I did most of the initial water driving myself to learn what I could about the capabilities and limitations of these aquatic—no, amphibian—monsters. After all, I did know more about water driving than my crewmen; I had sailed small boats in rough water and had tested the Ford amphibian jeep and the Chrysler amphibian half-ton truck in the Chattahoochee River in flood.

The surf near Monterey, sheltered by the Pacific Grove–Punta Piños peninsula, was usually a mere ripple, and became progressively stronger on the northern beaches that were exposed to the full force of the Pacific rollers. We therefore did our initial cruising near Fisherman's Wharf and ventured northward as we gained confidence in the ability of the machines to stand up to rough usage in the surf.[1]

We found that when we were out beyond the breaker line we could not accurately judge the height of the waves or the power of the surf. The white water of the breaking wave was on the landward side and the strongest surf on a sand beach would look like smooth rollers from the sea. A terrifying accident took place when an unpredictably large wave lifted the stern of a vehicle until it was near perpendicular as it surfboarded in until the leading edge of the prow struck the bottom and dug in. The hull then snapped forward and down like a fifteen-ton deadfall, trapping the crew inside.

The tanks had much more lateral stability than the tractors, caused by the inertia of twenty tons of tank as opposed to the fifteen-ton tractors. We had no trouble with the tank. The weight of the turret made it more stable against wave action and the full decking kept the hull from being overwhelmed by an overtaking wave, especially when the two scarf gunners partially plugged their hatches. It could drive into an eight-foot breaker that would fill and sink a tractor and emerge shaking off the water like a surface-running submarine.

The tank did, however, have one potential serious disadvantage—I foresaw that, due to the top-heavy weight of the turret and gun, if the tank were sunk in deep water it would capsize and sink turret first. That would create a most serious problem for the disoriented crewmen trying to get out. Damned serious.

Both machines were so slow that breakers overtaking from the rear would break over the rear deck where the horizontal louvers permitted the escape of the cooling air. Sometimes the blast of air kept the engine compartment clear of water. Often the foam would flood the compartment and short out the lower spark plugs. Most of the time the three-hundred-gallon-per-minute pump could cope with the water and the engine would sputter, slow, catch again, and pick up speed.

But once it just gasped and quit. Quite an experience. Sergeant Cole was driving, making an approach to the beach through a modest five- to six-foot surf. I was in the radio operator's spot on his right, staring at the blank wall of armor of the cab and apprehensively feeling what was going on through the seat of my pants. Several normal pitches as the stern rose to the overtaking wave, followed by a drop and slowing as the wave passed. Cole was hauling at his levers, keeping her tail to the surf in good shape. I could get only a slantendicular view of the beach we were approaching by leaning to the left for a sight through the driver's window, but it looked good. A terrified shout from Crewman Martin, "Here comes a big one!" It was. The stern started rising, and rising, and rising, until we were surfing down a seventy-degree slope and Cole had his right lever full back to offset our swing to the left. A kick in the tail and a muffled roar above the sound of the engine—no sound from the engine—Cole punching the starting button—water roaring into the compartment waist deep—not pitching now, just rolling, sluggishly.

"Let her go, Cole, get out!" More water. Cole and I stuck in the one-man door, popping out like two corks from a bottle just as she sank upright within forty feet of the normal high-water line.

We climbed out of her flooded carcass and waded ashore through the receding foam of the succeeding five to six footers that followed the rogue wave.

Lessons learned. You can't depend on the surf being regular, stand by for unpleasant surprises, always wear a life preserver tied on (we'd carried ours ashore in our hands), when the engine quits abandon ship. Get out one at a time, radio operator first (he can be out while the driver is untangling himself from his controls and turning around).

Colonel Henderson, USMC, commander of the amphibious group in training at Camp Pendleton, showed up at the Eighteenth Group headquarters one cool fall morning. I had asked for an adviser from the marine group to observe our infantile efforts and give us the benefit of his experience. Henderson had done us the courtesy of coming himself. He was a big, beefy, browned, round-faced six-footer, a very capable and confidence-inspiring type.

"Started last year with two battalions of the old sheet-iron Alligators made by the Roebling outfit," he told me. "Had to train them and get them out in a hurry. Now I'm putting two battalions of these new tanks and three battalions of carriers through the course. In addition to being armored, these LVTs are much better machines to work with and we've got a year to do it in."

"Good God! They're allowing me only a month for the first two battalions and they want six battalions on the way in two months. Why the difference?"

"Well, I guess it's just this interservice rivalry. MacArthur has pushed the army into the amphibian business and wants a lot of army LVTs and DUKWs out there right away to compete with the marines and navy.[2] We're not in such a rush because there're a lot of Alligator-operating marines in the Pacific already and all they need is the new type machines."

"What do you have in the way of training manuals?" I asked, hoping that the marines had developed something more useful than the pamphlet of directions that the Food Machinery Corporation furnished with the machines.

"There aren't any," admitted Henderson. "This Alligator and LVT idea was brand new and we've been so busy training the troops that nobody's had time to write any manuals. We just make it up as we go along."

"I'd like to get copies of everything that you've got in writing, your standing operating procedures, training schedules, safety precautions, anything in that line will give us a running start."

"We'll send you everything we've got, it won't be much."

We jeeped to Red Beach where the 776th Tanks were timidly dangling their tracks in a four-foot surf, then went north to Green Beach to see the more advanced 534th Tractors launching and landing by sections.

"What do you know about waves, colonel?" I inquired. "I've heard about the seventh wave being the biggest, but after counting a few hundred I think that's just a superstition."

"Down at Pendleton they say that it's the ninth but I've never counted them. I do notice that you have a different kind of surf here in the bay. You don't get any breakers until the rollers are close in to the beach. Down our way they start breaking as far as a quarter of a mile out on a rough day."

"The coast guard here says it has something to do with the slope of the beach—we have deep water pretty close in."

I was looking back toward the dunes to make sure that Captain Deutsch had his maintenance crew on the job and that the medics with their ambulance were waiting for customers at the end of the road.

"Great God!" exclaimed Henderson. "Look at that!"

I looked. We were standing high on the beach, fifty feet from the high-water line, ten feet above sea level, and we were looking up at the foam-tipped crest of a solid green wave, a terrifying picture. We had a full view of the interiors of the hulls of two tractors, one broached and overturning, the other standing upright on its broad bow directly in front of us with the crest beginning to curl well over the stern. A third tractor, still upright, was seen momentarily scuddling to the right squarely on top of the wave, then disappeared as the roller slid from under it.

The wave broke, the broached tractor vanished in the rolling white water, and the machine with its nose in the sand flipped forward and down with a crash like Lucifer slamming the gates of Hell. Henderson and I, starting toward the flipped tractor, were impeded by the knee-deep wash of foam.

The mammoth wave receded but was followed by a series of successively smaller monsters until they were running at a reasonable four to six feet. Five flooded hulks were visible in water three to five feet deep. Four had settled upright, the one that had flipped over remained capsized. The presently normal surf was dotted with a couple of dozen men in orange life preservers bobbing and paddling ashore, helped against the backwash by men wading out to reach them. I wasn't worried about them, but how many broken necks or backs did I have under that fifteen-ton deadfall? I had glimpsed a clump of five men falling, rolling, or hunching protectively just in rear of the cab as the hull had splashed.

Rescue work had started while the waves were still running high. A burly corporal had taken the two cables off his tractor, waded and paddled out to the capsized hulk, and was repeatedly submerging and coming up to blow, trying to find and engage the towing staple with the cat hook. Made it on the fourth dive and signaled his crew to "take it away." No result, not a quiver, until the next wave gave the wreck a slight lift and it slid a few feet shoreward. A horrible thought—

"Hold it, corporal! We don't know what shape those men are in. If they're hurt we don't want to grind that job in over them. Lead a cable over the wreck amidships and hook it around the track on the other side. Give it a sideward pull and we'll flip her over."

He was a very intelligent man and a damned good organizer. Got two more crews of the section coupling two cables together, carried the hook end out, and engaged it around the far track. The other end was taken by a tractor that had been backed into the surf as far as it could go without being water-borne. The slack was taken up slowly in low gear and the derelict raised and settled flat on its right side.

Colonel Henderson, I, the medics, and a dozen volunteer assistants charged into the hip-deep wash with stretchers and were met by half a dozen dripping, frozen, helmetless apparitions wading out of the hull, some rightfully scared, a couple laughing, and one man just downright indignant. "What the hell took you guys so long?" inquired the shuddering sergeant. "It was cold under there!"

Aside from a few strains, abrasions, contusions, and a dozen cases of exposure, the big wave had done little damage and given us some valuable experience.

"That thing must have been twenty-nine feet tall," I remarked as Henderson and I were jeeping back to the mess. "The tractor is twenty-six feet long and the water was breaking at least three feet over the stern."

"Let's round if off at thirty feet," corrected Henderson. "That was the goddamnedest wave I ever saw. I've heard about them, waves caused by an undersea earthquake like they have in Japan. The Japs call it a Tutsumi or Tsutsumi—they're scared of them."

"Can't blame them—so am I."

Gee. All the way from Japan?

Theory

As a result of our sinkings I became intensely interested in waves, their height, speed, and power. What was the relation between the height of a wave from trough to crest and its speed? How hard did a wave strike? We noted that we overtook small ripples of two to three feet, pushed through them, and left them behind. When they were the four-foot level we ran even, and catching a five-footer just right we could surf in and touch down as lightly as a fifteen-ton feather. At six feet they would sneak up behind, give us a smart smack on the rump, start us swinging broadside, and dump enough foam into the engine room to dampen the ignition. Most of the time we get by, but—

I went to see Captain Nielsen of the local naval office in Monterey. A startled chief petty officer in the office to which the surprised yeoman escorted me jerked his feet off the desk, slapped his comic book into a folder stamped "secret," obviously swallowed his cud of chewing gum or tobacco, and reared rigidly upright.

"Sir!" Captain Nielsen evidently did not have much business or many visitors but did run a tight ship.

"I'm Colonel Triplet, Armored Force," I announced. "I'd like to see Captain Nielsen."

"Aye aye, sir, just a moment sir." He turned and opened the door to the next room. "Captain, there's an army captain—ah, a colonel—here wants to see you."

"A colonel? Send him in."

Sounds of a creaking swivel chair, a pair of heavy shoes hitting the deck (I sure was getting nautical), and a desk drawer being jerked open. As I entered the well-nourished, ruddy, and gray-haired Captain Nielsen was shoving the latest copy of *Esquire* into the center drawer and closed it as he rose.

"Colonel Triplet of the Eighteenth Armored Group, Fort Ord, sir."

"Captain Nielsen, naval detachment." He seemed delighted to have company—had a handshake like a bear trap. "Eighteenth Armored Group—oh yes, I've heard about you people coming in. Do those idiots I've seen playing around in the breakers up there belong to you?"

"Yes, they're mine." No need to tell him that I was one of the idiots. "And since it's all new to us I came over to get the advice from the navy."

"Hmmm, how about a cup of coffee? Yes? Smithers! Coffee!"

And he hmmmed again and looked thoughtful until Smithers delivered two durable-looking mugs decorated with the navy seal. I sipped the black brew and got it down without wincing. It was vintage stuff, boiled day before yesterday and simmering ever since; tough people these navy types.

Nielsen swallowed a third of his mug, which brought him out of his reverie. "Don't know that we can help you much. Breakers, white water, very dangerous. I'm a battleship man myself. Stay as far away from it as we can."

"Well, you see we have these seagoing tracked machines that are supposed to operate on land and water; we have to come in with the breakers to land troops, and go out again through the surf for resupply. So far all I'm sure of is that going out is a lot safer than coming in. The tanks, the ones with turrets, can launch through eight-foot breakers and the open carriers can do six feet, but coming in through more than five feet gets pretty chancy."

"Hmmm—should think so. Navy landing craft won't come ashore in more than four-foot surf. Glad I'm in the navy."

"But possibly you can tell me what is the relation between the height of a wave and the speed it travels?"

"Never really thought about it. A ship overtakes the little ones and the big ones coming up astern catch up and smack her in the fantail. Never thought about it."

"Does the navy have any data or publication about wave speed, force, or regularity?"

"Not that I—let's see, we may have some material that you can use. Smithers!"

Smithers thumped in and assumed a sailorly position of attention.

"Smithers, look over our manuals and pull a copy of everything we have on beach landings, you know, marines, landing craft, boats away and all that, for the captain—for the colonel."

"Aye aye, sir!" He thumped out again.

"Another question. What is the force with which a wave strikes a boat? Is that a function of the height?"

"It might be. All I know is that the small waves don't hurt us and the big ones can warp frames, pop rivets, and open your welds. I suppose it's a matter of F equals MV^2."

"Undoubtedly, but when you don't know the mass and are not certain about the velocity it leaves you at sea, so to speak, in figuring the force, doesn't it?"

"Sure does. Say, why don't you go over and talk to Lieutenant Heinz at the coast guard station? Coast guard should know more about surf than we do. We try to stay out of it."

"Good idea, I'll do that. Lieutenant Heinz is it? Oh, by the way, we're going to be working with the tanks in six-to-eight-foot surf tomorrow and I'd be delighted if you'd join us. It might be entertaining for you and we'd be glad to get any pointers you could give us."

"I'd like to, but we're swamped with paperwork just now. Some other time perhaps."

So still ignorant, I departed with an armful of naval literature that told me more about small boat maintenance, anchors, knots, signal flags, and seamanship than I was really interested in knowing.

Lieutenant Heinz was an alert, lean young middleweight who was very cooperative but who could tell me little that I hadn't already found out or guessed. He did describe one outsized wave resulting from an undersea earthquake off Japan that was reported by a scared skipper to be a hundred feet high and traveling a hundred miles an hour. "But it did little or no damage to the ship, just lifted her a hundred feet like an express elevator and dropped her again just as fast. Blue water never hurts you, it's the white water on the crest that smashes you. And a big wave like that is running out from under its own crest, leaves a lot of foam on the reverse slope."

Then he cited some interesting facts and theories about Monterey Bay. "We never recover bodies in this area. The beaches are steep and slant right down to the Salinas Canyon that runs across the bay toward the northwest, five hundred fathoms deep. It was the Salinas River during the Ice Age a few million years ago. The steep slope makes for a shallow line of breakers near the shore and one hell of a strong undertow. So anyone who gets drowned rolls on down to the bottom of the canyon. If the fish don't get him on the way down he's still there."

"But doesn't decomposition bring them—"

"No, water's too cold. The Japanese Current runs down this coast, straight from Alaska and the Aleutians. It's fifty-two degrees on the surface even in the summer, that's good steak-hanging temperature, and at five hundred fathoms it's down in the high thirties or low forties. Preserves meat indefinitely. Interesting to think about what's down there."

I'll say it was. I was bobbing slowly down a steep slope through an ever darkening green landscape of waving seaweed with small fish flitting through the fronds. I was held now and then by a rock or weed but pushed clear by a slight current at my back. My semi-upright position was due to the small amount of dead air remaining in my flooded lungs, as opposed to the negative buoyancy (very nautical phrase) of my dangling combat boots. The water was getting dark, no, as I reached the bottom of the canyon there was a slight luminescence in which I could vaguely make out my surroundings, wrecks of ships, fragments of boats, and something, a humanlike figure, was swaying toward me, wearing a barnacle-studded breastplate and morion, heavily whiskered. He fixed me with the flickering green phosphorescent blobs under his beetling brows and waved a hand to his moss-covered morion.

"Salud, señor, Soy Sebastian de Portola y Montenmayor, a servicio suyo," he gurgled and bubbled in archaic but understandable Spanish. "Ahogado an anno Domino milseisoientoydos."

Drowned in 1602—no wonder his armor was corroded.

"Colonel Triplet, Eighteenth Armored Group," and I extended my hand, which he clasped with his cold, clammy claw and—

I snapped to life again. Heinz was going on with his lecture. " . . . times when you'll get a surf of twenty feet on a clear, perfectly calm day, undersea quake or the swells from a storm several hundred miles out."

"Twenty feet? That's a big wave!"

"That's a hell of a big wave when it breaks. How long are your craft?"

"Twenty-six feet."

"Hmmm, a twenty-footer'll pitchpole you, turn you over and over and even if you can hold your boat, hold your machine from broaching and rolling."

I'd heard enough bad news for the moment, and it was time to leave and digest what I'd heard. "I say, lieutenant, I'd like to take advantage of your experience in small-boat surf running. How about coming out with me in the tank tomorrow? Say 0900?"

"I'd like nothing better but we're awfully busy just now. Weather reports, submarine watch, distress calls from the fishing fleet, and paperwork. Some other time perhaps."

I tiptoed as I left through the outer office, didn't want to disturb the petty officer and his pair of yeomen who were napping, heads pillowed on their desks beside their neatly covered typewriters.

Waves, their behavior and effect, were fascinating. In the absence of solid information from presumably more knowledgeable and scientific sources I rigged anchored buoys at various depths and distances, took a post on the wharf just south of Blue Beach on a rough and breezy morning, and timed the waves of various heights as they passed the buoys in the distance.

Never was there a cruder attempt made in the course of a serious investigation. I should have used stakes or pilings placed at exact distances from each other, with the depth of water at high tide measured and marked accurately thereon. I should know the distance of my observation point from each stake and should have all these points accurately plotted on a large-scale chart. I needed a theodolite, a stop watch, and the trigonometry that I had forgotten in the last twenty years. Instead I used bobbing buoys approximately dropped at roughly measured depths at estimated distances from each other and the wharf. Accurate placement would have required a stable ship the size of the *Queen Mary*. I used my water-walking tank for the job.

On the wharf I unlimbered field glasses, guesstimated the heights of waves, and clocked their velocity in passing the buoys by counting in quick-time cadence, found you can't watch a wave and the second hand of a wrist watch at the same time. After a pageful of data came the calculations of wave speed by an exercise in simple arithmetic.

By the end of the day I knew a little more about waves and far more than Captain Nielsen or Lieutenant Heinz had been able to tell me. I'd learned these four facts or rather had developed four theories.

1. The speed of a wave in miles per hour was 1.5 times its height in feet, i.e., a six-foot wave moved nine miles an hour, an eight-footer made twelve.
2. According to the formula F equals MV^2, given plenty of water in the wave and the same area of the stern of my tank, a six-foot wave boots in the tail four times as hard as a three-foot ripple if we're waiting for it and a ten-footer means the equivalent of a rear-end collision at fifteen miles an hour. If we're moving at full speed as I intended we would, we ease the punch by six miles per—not bad if we can keep control. But heading into them, while safe from broaching or pitching, was something else again. The four-foot ripple hit us at twelve miles an hour and the six-footer was a head-on collision at fifteen. An eight-foot wave would strike at eighteen miles per hour and if we were so stupid or unfortunate as to dive into a ten-footer the tank commander had

better pull his head down or the twenty-one-mile-an-hour collision could break his back or neck.

3. The taller a wave the farther out it started breaking. The wave or rather the impulse of the wave seemed to be as deep as it was tall; at least half of the wave was under sea level. And as it approached the shore the undertow of the preceding wave was going out. So when the base of the wave struck the undertow it "tripped": the bottom of the wave slowed while the top kept moving until it started to fall forward, curl, and break into white water. It appeared that a six-foot wave would trip and break in nine feet of water, again the factor of 1.5 times the height.

4. My last theory was a real puzzler. Waves don't remain the same: the height, speed, and strength are always changing. The big wave moves faster, overtakes and absorbs its smaller cousins, becomes taller, swallows the next little fellow. But no, if that were true a ripple starting for Monterey from the middle of the Pacific would be big and powerful enough to wash right over the Sierra Nevada and fill Death Valley to the brim.

What keeps the size of waves within reasonable bounds? Gravity, of course, plus the friction of the wave impulse with the unmoving deeper water that constantly slows it down. Given a wave impulse caused by an undersea quake and no wind to drive it, a wave that starts out a hundred feet high at 150 miles an hour, pulled down by gravity and slowed by friction, would be a ten-foot, fifteen-mile-an-hour ripple when it came ashore in Monterey Bay. And a mere gale far out at sea would probably be unnoticed on Blue Beach.

Yes, wave study was fascinating. And if one is cursed by insomnia, trying to figure out why waves behave as they do is a sure cure. When I ended my two days of observation and calculating I still didn't know much about waves but I knew a lot more than the navy and the coast guard. Anyway I believed I did.

Six.

The LST

Two Ships

We saw only two navy ships at close range during our training years—one LST to give us practice in loading and launching our LVTs, and a destroyer that I presume was sent to furnish a military background while we were doing so.[1]

The destroyer came in first and dropped anchor two thousand yards off Red Beach. I've since learned that according to navy protocol I should have remained in my headquarters to receive Commander Lang when he made his official call. The next day I should have donned my best pink and green with polished brass, boarded the group launch, and returned the call via the starboard ladder. I would then have been received with four side boys, ultrasonic piping by a purple-cheeked bosun, fresh coffee, and cordial conversation.

But when Destroyer Number 216 (they weren't painting the names of ships then) dropped her hook I happened to be out on the bay in Terry Bull, checking on the water driving of a new tank battalion. Knowing nothing of naval customs, I decided to dash over and welcome the skipper to the bay.

"Wrobleski—left! See that destroyer? Put us alongside where they're lowering that ladder."

As we approached at six miles an hour someone shouted, "The Terry Bull coming alongside port ladder, sir," and a white-capped figure came to the rail at our end of the bridge to stare and wonder at our thrashing, foaming progress.

"Slow, Wrobleski, swing left, hard left—reverse! reverse!"

But LVTs were notoriously slow in responding to steering, and putting them in reverse had much the effect of braking an automobile on glare ice. We grazed the ladder and with both tracks thrashing backward were still plowing ahead with twenty tons of inertia at half speed when we made contact.

Clannggg! We glanced off the side. The ship rang like a Chinese gong and immediately boiled with the activity of a well-stirred ants' nest. All of the deck crew and a goodly number of the black gang were gawking over the rail as we swung around for another run. The captain was leaning over the rail to the over-balancing point and an ensign dashed down the ladders—everybody seemed to be quite concerned about our safety.

"It's all right, captain, we've got three-quarter-inch armor," I reassured him.

69

"I don't give a damn about you," he shouted. "I've only got three-eighths!"

Yes, now that I noticed, I could see some cause for his concern. An area of his armor a yard square seemed to be well shoved in, with a silvery horizontal streak three inches wide just above the water line where the corner of Terry Bull's bow had scraped it clean. Just a fender-bender. Nothing that a sledgehammer on the inside and a brushful of paint wouldn't cure.

We made the ladder on the second try. I was received by the officer of the deck with no side boys and no bosun's pipe and by Commander Lang with cool vintage coffee and cold courtesy.

But how could I have known that Buships was building destroyers with tinfoil hulls?

Then the long-awaited LST was seen at anchor in the cold gray dawn one morning, swinging at a safe distance from Destroyer 216. Odd-looking craft, something like a shoe box with a smaller box standing on its end on the stern. Certainly not beautiful, just practical.

I found Captain (Lieutenant, Senior Grade) Monck chatting with Northridge at headquarters. He was a medium-height, well-proportioned, deeply tanned brunet, and seemed altogether too young and soft a type to be the captain of a ship. Seemed to be a jolly, carefree, irresponsible character. I found his story most interesting. In common with all of his officers he was commissioned from ROTC, had trained on the Great Lakes, and had seen salt water for the first time three weeks before. He had taken command of LST 334 when she slid down the ways in Cairo. Not an Annapolis man. Must have been damned good.[2]

"Cairo?" I questioned. "Didn't know we were building ships in Egypt."

"Cairo, Illinois, sir," he explained with obvious patience.

"But that's up on the Ohio River—"

"At the junction of the Ohio and Mississippi, sir. We came by way of the Mississippi, the Gulf, Caribbean, and the Canal."

"Good God! A ship that size down the Mississippi? Must have been pretty hairy, all those bends and sandbars."

"Well, not too bad. The river pilots did all the official worrying on that part of the trip. All I did was chew my fingernails to the bone. But then I thought we draw only four feet of water forward and seven feet aft when we're fully loaded. Running with minimum ballast we'll float on a heavy dew. So when we touched down on a couple of unexpected sandbars I was able to tell the pilots, 'No sweat, that's what we're supposed to do. This just gives us practical training in how to pull off a beach.' So we'd out with the stern anchor, put the power to the winch, and slide off slick as a greased water moccasin. So now I've got an experienced crew."

Imagine that, building seagoing ships in the middle of the United States and floating them around all those bends and over the mud flats and sandbars that Mark Twain used to complain about.

Next day I went out in the launch, all gussied up in my class-A uniform, properly approaching the starboard ladder with two men manning boathooks and tenders. I was well braced for the ceremony and fanfare of navy custom that I'd been reading up on. When I had reached the level of the deck I would see two side boys on each side of the ladder, the officer of the deck facing me just beyond the side boys and waving a welcoming salute, and the boatswain apparently trying to blow through his closed fist. I must remember, do not salute the OD, face left and salute the flag at the stern, then return the OD's salute.[3]

OK, I did everything according to the book, but what? No white-gloved side boys, no piping boatswain, and no officer of the deck. Just Captain Monck dashing up with a pleased grin, waving a salute en route. And two more skinny adolescents stripped to the waist, sanding, pounding rust, painting, hauling, and greasing everything that didn't move.

"Glad to have you aboard, colonel."

"Glad to be aboard, captain." And that was it.

Monck led aft to the wardroom where we had the ceremonial mug of coffee and then showed me over the ship. Most interesting.

The after quarter of the ship resembled a five-story building, with the levels connected by interior and exterior stairways called ladders. The diesel engines and fuel tanks occupied the surgically clean, white-painted basement. The crew and troop quarters and mess were on the first floor. The officers' quarters and wardroom were up one flight, and the bridge was the penthouse with a bristle of AA guns on the roof. There was a lot of stuff and people squeezed most efficiently into very small spaces. Togetherness is the modern term. Glad I wasn't in the navy.

The deck was a wide-open space containing nothing but tie-down points for deck-loaded vehicles—preferably trucks. Tanks would put the weight too high. A powerful winch was the most important feature of the very small fantail aft of the superstructure.

The cargo space was a vast, empty, echoing cavern of dark, black nothing—the lights merely emphasized how dark the place really was. Then I noted the tie-down points and cables, pulleys, lines, chocks, and clamps festooned on the wall. At the rear of the cavern flush with the deck forward of the engine room was a king-sized platform, an open elevator for raising vehicles to the deck above when deck loads were carried.

The blunt bow consisted of two monstrous doors hinged at the sides and opening in the middle. They were backed by the upright ramp, which was to be lowered to permit loading or launching of tanks or trucks. The hull and tie-downs were designed to carry seven tanks, three abreast in the cargo space and the same number of vehicles in the deck load.

"Not much room for maneuver in here," I remarked, mentally measuring the thirty-foot beam.

"In the school they demonstrated loading light and medium tanks forward, turning them around and backing into position. But your LVTs— I don't know. How long are they?"

"Twenty-six feet."

"They can't make it. You'll have to back them in. No problem."

"OK, you know more about it than I do. We'll back them in. No problem." Little did I know.

What impressed me most about the ship were the loudspeakers. They seemed to be mounted everywhere and were in constant use at full volume. Somewhere in the bowels of the superstructure there was a tone-deaf, music-mad, hearing-impaired idiot with a phonograph and an inexhaustible stack of the latest and hottest jazz records from Tin Pan Alley. No, that's wrong. I said a tone-deaf idiot—they must have had three, one per watch. Probably a regular table of organization position, called phone operator, first class. The music was interrupted now and then by "Now hear this," followed by an official announcement, then the drums and trumpets would cut in again.

But it was evidently a happy ship. The crew of former Sea Scouts and high school dropouts was twitching, wriggling, sloshing paint, or pounding in time to the din—the officers and older petty officers seemed to ignore or not to hear the confusion.

Sure glad I was in the army.

The Concealed Maverick Sandbar

Monck eased his ship up to Blue Beach, the bow doors yawned wide, and the ramp was lowered to the sand for loading.

The first exercise was for the benefit of the medium tank battalion presently awaiting port call at Ord, so we of the amphibs were aboard simply as interested observers. As Lieutenant Monck had prophesied, no problem. The tanks waddled slowly up the slight slope of the ramp, swung right to graze the wall, turned, and backed into their slots where they were checked and cabled securely. Colonel Forsythe, a John Wayne type, intended to lead his men into battle, so his command jeep was loaded last, just clearing the ramp.

The ramp was raised, the bow doors slowly closed, slack was taken up on the stern anchor cable and, engines in reverse, LST 334 slid back into deep water just like a training film. Good show.

We took a turn a few miles out on the bay where the rollers became normal ocean swells. When we reached the open water the amphib observers noted an interesting phenomenon: standing on deck at the rear of the superstructure and sighting at the bow along a horizontal welding seam, we saw the bow rise and fall a foot or more. The ship flexed up and down as it slid over the swells. When we started a wide turn, striking the waves at an angle, the bow would rise and twist left on the next swell while the stern was dropping and twisting right on the last one. Then the twist would reverse as the bow dropped toward the trough. Monck should be warned. I caught a passing ensign.

"I say, lieutenant, this ship is crawling over the waves like a damned caterpillar. See how the bow swings? I think—"

"Yes sir, there's a lot of give in the hull. If there wasn't, that is, if she was rigid, she'd probably break her back in a high sea."

"I see. Then it's a choice between breaking her back if she's rigid and metal fatigue due to the bending?"

"That's right, sir."

It gave one to think. Still glad I'm in the army.

Five miles out our ship completed her turn and straightened out for Red Beach. She dropped her stern anchor and crept inshore until she groaned throughout her hull and came to a sliding halt fifty feet from the beach, aground in shallow water. The bow doors opened, the ramp dropped, and Colonel Forsythe's jeep dashed out—to drop off the end and disappear, almost.

While the crew was seated in the jeep their helmets were faintly visible just under the murky green surface. Standing, their heads were well above the danger line as they grabbed for the life rings flung by the ship's crew or the Mae Wests donated by amphib observers.

When the colonel and his men were fished back onto the ramp he seemed to be quite agitated. A short minute later he was dripping water all over the deck while he discussed the situation with a very embarrassed LST captain.

"—told me you'd put me ashore dry-shod! Christ on the mountain! That water's ten feet deep!"

"Very sorry, colonel. We're up on a sandbar and I thought the water was shallow enough. There seems to be a channel cut inside the bar. But I don't think it's over six or seven—"

"Well it's too goddamn deep for tanks and what I want to know is what you're going to do about it? Are you scared to put this crate up on the beach like you're supposed to?"

"Sir—I'll—"

"If you don't you're going to have us aboard here a long time, lieutenant. That's not a fleet of submarines I have down there."

Forsythe had fished out a soggy pack and a Zippo lighter. Now he flung the pack over the rail.

"Anybody got a dry cigarette—and a dry lighter?"

Monck, reddening with rage and embarrassment, turned and stomped up the ladder to the bridge. The ramp raised, the bow doors closed, the engines rumbled, and the ship slid easily off the underwater bar. We maneuvered out into the bay again and two miles distant turned and headed for Green Beach. It was different this time—we weren't slowing down. The loudspeaker blared. "Stand by to beach!"

No doubt the navy people aboard understood. For the benefit of the army he should have yelled, "Hold on to your hats!" Or an outright statement like "We're going to crash!"

The ship hit the beach at eight to ten knots, shoved her blunt bow up over the sand, and came to a screaming halt with her nose into the fringe of brush and a quarter of her length on dry land. My junior officers who were clustered in front of the superstructure started running briskly forward, trying to keep their legs under them when the ship struck; those standing at the bow leaned well over, clawing at the stanchions and steel rope of the rail. I was fortunate in having pessimistically secured a firm grip on the port rail.

The bow doors swung wide, brushing the bushes down, and the ramp dropped to flatten them. A roar from the loudspeakers—"D'you think you can make it now, Colonel Forsythe?"

Six hundred tons of M4 tanks rumbled up the ramp and through the scrub brush without dampening a grouser.

Monck shouldn't have lost his temper like that. It wasn't his fault that a concealed maverick sandbar had formed outside Red Beach. And Forsythe had been just too damned gung-ho in leaping before he looked. Most of all, after that trip down the Mississippi, I don't think Monck had to prove anything to anybody. But he did, and it cost him.

The engines roared, the winch chattered, and the rudder wagged from side to side. LST 334 just sat there in her sandy bow wave, didn't even quiver.

Next day a navy tugboat showed up from San Francisco and passed a line. Full power by 334, the tug beat the bay to foam, the tow cable snapped.

The ship sat there, steady as a monument, for the rest of the day, pumping out her minimum water ballast. Some of the crew manned fire hoses around the bow, vainly trying to wash away some of the sand that gripped her hull. "Like tryin' to empty the ocean with a goddamn teaspoon," was T-5 Perkins's dour comment. "Oughta put wheels on 'em," he added.

A bright young ensign walked from the ramp to where Perkins and I were perched on the dune admiring the king-sized salvage operation. "Sir, the captain would appreciate it if you would loan him six tanks until we get the ship off."

"Six tanks? Sure, but my tanks can't be of any help towing on a job that size."

"No sir. He doesn't want them to tow, he wants to stow them aft as ballast to get the stern down. We've pumped out our forward and midships water ballast and it helps, but not enough. Captain Monck thinks that six of your tanks stowed aft might give us the weight to lever the bow up."

"Sounds reasonable. But I suggest that my tanks are pretty light. The M4s are twice as heavy."

"I know, sir, and I suggested that to the captain, but he doesn't want to have anything more to do with Colonel Forsythe."

"Understandable. OK, tell Captain Monck they'll be here in half an hour." The lad turned out a pretty good salute for a naval officer and took off with the glad tidings.

I wrote a message. "Perkins, take this to the 772d on Black Beach. No answer is required."

Twenty minutes later B Company of the 772d was boiling down the beach to the ramp and the six leading tanks disappeared into the yawning maw of the LST. The crewmen walked out, mounted the backs of the other tanks, and B Company roared back to play in the surf on Black Beach.

Next day, Saturday, the tug made another attempt with a brand new cable. The cable held. So did the stranded ship. It looked like LST 334 was going to be a permanent fixture. It had occurred to me after leaving the beach, why couldn't the destroyer latch on and do some pulling? But she had pulled out during the night, ordered back to Mare Island.

Lieutenant Monck, resplendent in blue and gold, created quite a flurry among the ladies of the group at the Saturday night gathering but failed to take advantage of his opportunities. He couldn't seem to keep his mind on the business at hand, would just break off a promising line of sweet nothings with an admiring cupcake and stare glumly into space.

I could understand and sympathize. Here he'd brought his ship down the treacherous Mississippi, through a gale in the Gulf, across the Caribbean, and through the Panama Canal, without skinning the paint. And now in a moment of temporary insanity he'd converted yea-million dollars' worth of government property into an unwanted suburb of Monterey. He'd be lucky if the inevitable inquiry and probable court-martial didn't bust him to swabbie second class.

On Monday a second tug showed up, an ocean-going type, twice as big and eight times as powerful as the harbor tug that had been straining on the job. Both tugs took hold, all engines huffed and puffed, LST 334 slid into deep water as though that had been her intention all the time.

Hurrah!

I had heard from the 774th in the Pacific that reloading at sea was sometimes required after an engagement, since offshore reefs or coral heads frequently made it impossible for the LSTs to beach. And the 535th had reported that resupply missions usually required reloading at sea. They also stated that sea loading was much more difficult. Since we would be allowed the use of the ship only during the current week, sea loading was what we would do. If it was difficult we'd just about be able to put the group through the drill.

It was—more difficult, that is.

Loading the M4 medium tanks from the beach had been so easy. The ramp had been nearly level when it touched down on the sand. The rubber-soled tank treads took a firm grip on the steel cleats of the ramp and the tanks rumbled into their slots in the hold as surely as into a supermarket parking lot.

We found that loading at sea was very difficult. Difficult is a mild adjective to describe it. The ramp was lowered until the end was submerged. The ship held stern-on to the swells pitched gently but that slight pitch alternatively raised the ramp to the surface and lowered it three feet under water. Our LVTs had to back on, and moving in reverse in the water was our most difficult maneuver. Last, the action of the rounded portion of our horseshoe-shaped steel grousers on the steep, steel-cleated ramp made the climb nearly impossible. A slip by the grousers on one side would slam the stern over into the bow door and the discharge chute on that side would come unglued. So would a couple of grousers.

After much sweat, metallic clangs, unheard blasphemy, and minor damage, we had gotten three tanks aboard in an hour and a half. At that rate four hundred LVTs would take two hundred hours and we had, at the most, sixty hours to do it in.

"Colonel." A very capable-appearing sergeant leaning over the rail at my elbow was watching the fourth tank making its third try to grab a foothold on the bobbing ramp. Oh yes, I remembered him. He was guiding the second tank into position—tank commander.

"Yes?"

"I understand that when we unload in a shootin' war we'll be pretty well out on the water. Is that right, sir?"

"That's right, sergeant. We always unload at sea, form up at the rendezvous, and then go into the landing."

"Then we'll be out of range of any direct-fire guns, won't we?"

"Right. Nothing can hurt us except an accidental hit by heavy stuff or a possible strafing from the air."

"Then it don't make any difference if we unload backwards, does it, sir?"

"Not really."

"Well, seems to me it might be a lot easier to drive up that ramp forward and come out backward, because the—"

"By God, sergeant, why the hell didn't I think of that? Lieutenant Dietrich?! Get the word to Colonel Wilson, 'Load forward, launch backward!' "

Amazing. The LVTs charged accurately aboard the ramp at six miles an hour, the squared ends of the grousers took a firm grip on the steel cleats, the drivers could see where they were going, and the tanks and tractors came aboard in a steady stream.

Thank God for thinking sergeants.

The going-away party given by the group for Lieutenant Monck and his young officers was memorable. The navy was in fine flirtatious form and the ladies sparkled in appreciation. While Fiona was flirting with Monck and Lee was doing the cha-cha or cancan with the bright young ensign, I retired to the bar for a refreshment. A group of our married men were muttering morosely about "busting some blue-bellied bastard in the kisser" while the more romantic younger set were regretting the obsolescence of the code duello, all eyes glaring grimly at the carousing couples on the dance floor.

All hands seemed pleased when next midmorning the LST lifted her hook, blasted three farewell toots on her foghorn, and sailed over the northern horizon, out of their lives.

Seven.

Guns and Bays

A Bigger Gun

I was not satisfied with the 37-mm. gun as the main armament of the amphibious tank. When the gun was produced in 1935 it was a fair tank-antitank weapon, with a high velocity, flat trajectory, excellent accuracy, and punch enough to penetrate the light armor of those days. But it was already obsolete when it was issued.

As a platoon commander in F Company of the Sixty-seventh Infantry (Tanks) in 1935, I was directed to show a visiting Russian colonel the latest experimental models we were testing. He was astounded.

"Is this the heaviest gun you are using in tanks?" he asked, patting our brand-new 37-mm. on the shoulder piece.

"Yes, the Mark VIII with the six-pounder is obsolete now, but we find that this gun has the velocity to stop any tank that can be built. Armor them any heavier and they can't move."

"We are not so optimistic. We are putting a 75-mm. in our new series and are developing a semiautomatic 77-mm. that fires a three-round clip. We believe that tanks can be built with much heavier armor as the engines to move them become more powerful, and we want to be ready to meet them."

It was my turn to be astounded. It was generally known in those innocent days that Russians were too stupid to manage anything more complicated than a wheelbarrow. But after escorting Comrade Colonel Ivanovitch around for a couple of days I'd changed my mind. He was a smart mechanic and a good tank soldier. And my 37-mm. guns were no longer the best in the world.

And now in 1943 his prophecies had come to pass. Engines had improved, armor had thickened, and the Japanese were using 75-mm. guns in the tank-antitank role. So my boys would be playing David versus Goliath in every slugging match, accurately throwing their shot and shells that had the explosive power of a hand grenade, until a 75-mm. with eight times the power tore their turret off. But it was a difficult problem. The 75-mm. gun that I wanted or even the 50-mm. towed antitank gun if mounted in a turret would place a lot of weight topside and probably too far forward on the LVT. No, it just wouldn't do.

Then I remembered the brief appearance of the M8 motor carriage, one of the more stupid mistakes of our weaponry system, for which the ordnance corps, army ground forces, and the artillery board disclaim any knowledge or responsibility. The artillery wanted a motorized weapon so they could play their part in the newly formed armored force. There were hundreds of 75-mm. howitzers that had been turned in by the defunct horse artillery and were now stowed in cosmoline ready for use in the next Indian uprising. There were also plenty of armored half-tracks available. So our ordnance people took the howitzers out of storage, fitted them into Chrysler-produced turrets, bolted them on half-tracks, and proudly announced, "This is your armored force motorized artillery." They called it the M8.

The artillery line officers who had to use the guns were properly horrified and replied more or less as follows:

"The hell you say. We're not fighting Sitting Bull or Villa. We're in the big league now and those guys are using guns that you could throw a football down the muzzle. We want a full-tracked 105-mm. or better."

The armored artillery got the full-tracked 105 they wanted and the ordnance corps stored several hundred M8s away in whatever limbo they use to bury their major mistakes and hoped everybody would forget about them. But I remembered.

The 75-mm. howitzer might just be the answer. The gun was light and short. The shell was eight times as powerful as the 37-mm. and solid shot would have the mass required to bash in the two-inch armor of the heaviest Japanese tank. Used with full charge for direct fire, the velocity, trajectory, and striking power would be satisfactory and give us a fighting chance.

The tactical use of the 75 could be expanded as follows. During the approach to the hostile beach the leading waves of tanks could plaster the enemy shore, thickening the supporting fire of the destroyers, cruisers, and battleships. Accuracy would not be required; the only requirement would be to hit the island, and any gunner could do that in a normal sea. Once ashore the prime requirement would be fast and accurate shooting at point targets by the howitzer plus heavy machine-gun fire at anything that moved. Last, when the land-type tanks took over their normal role of infantry support the amphibian tanks would be available to give additional supporting artillery fire, using the howitzers for the high-angle fire for which they were designed.

A letter containing these cerebrations was dispatched to army ground forces with the recommendation that an M8 turret and howitzer be installed on an LVT (A-I) and turned over to me for a test of seaworthiness. Never was one of my ideas acted upon with more dispatch.

A hasty conference must have been called with members from army ground forces, the navy bureau of ships, the ordnance corps, the armored force, and probably the War Department. I can ESP the opening lines, probably by General AGF.

"Gentlemen, I have a letter from Typewriter Triplet, that insaniac who's training the tracked landing vehicle group out in Monterey. He wants to equip his tanks with the M8 turrets and 75-mm. howitzers instead of the M5 turrets and the 37-mm. guns. You all have copies of his weird proposal and I would appreciate your comments."

"Ridiculous," snorted Admiral Buships. "Even if the LVT could carry the additional ton and a half without swamping, it would capsize in any sea. And if it didn't capsize the recoil of the heavier gun would drive it under. And firing broadside—unthinkable."

"We certainly think it's worth a trial," stated Colonel War Department. "It will give us a chance to erase that yeah-million-dollar mistake made by ordnance."

"There was no mistake made by ordnance," shouted Brigadier Ordnance. "We made one pilot model exactly on artillery specifications and AGF wanted five hundred copies."

"We approved five hundred copies based on armored force recommendations," admitted General AGF defensively.

"The hell you did," rasped General Armored Force Artillery. "The first time we heard of the M8 was when a trainload of those short-coupled abortions rolled into Fort Sill—and rolled right back to Aberdeen."

"Gentlemen, as chairman of this conference (the navy made sure that their representative was chairman at any interservice conference if they had to pull an admiral from the firing line) I am not interested in the mistakes made by the several staffs and services or branches of the army. We will return to the subject. Colonel Tribble considers that the LVT (A-I) is undergunned and asks for the M8 turret and howitzer. We in the bureau of ships are sure that this modification would be unseaworthy and if Colonel Tribble tests it he will be drowned on the first launching."

"So—" remarked General AGF, meaning "So what?"

"Well, let's have him try one out," suggested Armored Force Artillery. "That way we'll either find out that this mechanical miscegenation is seaworthy or we'll be rid of a troublemaker. If it's dangerous—"

The dozing USMC captain awoke at the word "dangerous." "We ain't scared, we're marines."

The captain's contribution was ignored by all except the admiral who awarded him an irritated side glance. Brigadier Ordnance took up the discussion.

"Gentlemen, we have here an opportunity to put several hundred M8 turrets and obsolete howitzers to possibly useful work. We can then divert the M5 turrets to the British who seem to like the speed of the Stuart tanks, or we can use the 37-mm. in the M15 for antiaircraft work.[1] The M8 half-tracks will then be available to the armored infantry.

I make a motion that this solution to so many of our problems be adopted."

"Second the motion," was heard from four eager voices. When put to the vote there was one dissenting voice.

"I divorce myself and the bureau of ships from any part of this foolhardy project. We will continue to see that the manufacturer builds seaworthy tracked landing vehicles. What you put on them will be your own responsibility. Captain!"

The USMC captain who'd had a hard night awoke and followed the admiral as he stalked from the room.

As I said, I ESPd most of the above conference and verified my guesses by later conversation with various staff officers and with the admiral of the bureau of ships. Most convincing was the nonbureaucratic speed with which things began to happen.

I received a letter from AGF, which directed me to fasten three thousand pounds of iron around the turret of a tank, test it for seaworthiness, and report without delay.

Sergeant Wrobleski drove our tank into the ordnance shop and I presented the AGF letter to Captain Wright, who was initially horrified, then enthusiastically cooperative. I took a great deal of personal interest in his activities—assembling, weighing, and balancing worn track plates and the carcasses of discarded engines. I didn't want to go to sea with a built-in list, so the placing of the various weights had to be right. I also spent a good deal of time breathing down the neck of his welder who was tack-welding this iron to the turret. There was a fine line—I didn't want to destroy the turret, so the junk had to be removable, but I sure didn't want one of those eight-hundred-pound cylinder blocks to drop off under the shock of a heavy wave.

Three days after receiving AGF's directive, Wrobleski and I trundled the Terry Bull down to Blue Beach followed by two salvage tractors—our overweight tank would be too much for one towing tractor to recover.

"She sure drives solid," commented Wrobleski on arrival at the launching point. She sure did—rode more like a Grant or Sherman medium than the agile, bouncy Stuart she had formerly resembled. Well, that was what I was trying to do—get her out of the ineffectual light tank class.

"I'll run through it again, Wrobleski, just to be sure. Is your Mae West tied on?"

"Mae West OK, sir."

"Blow it up a quarter full and clamp the tube." I required all Mae Wests tied firmly and blown a quarter full by mouth, so that a man who was unable to pull the cords that activate the CO_2 would still float to the surface in spite of injury.

"Mae West blown up, sir."

"Guidelines on?"

"Snug on both arms, sir."

"Now listen, Wrobleski." I tried to put some healthy fear into his thick Polish skull. "I'll drive from the left scarf gunner's hatch. I have your guidelines slipknotted on my wrists. In case we go over or sink, this crate will hit the bottom upside down, sitting square on her turret. You just let yourself sink out of your seat and I'll start pulling on your lines. Don't try to dive out the turret, it'll be on the bottom and you'll get your lines fouled up on the gun. Don't panic."

"Panic, sir?" The poor devil didn't know the word.

"I mean don't get excited, just take it easy and let me pull you to this hatch. If I can't pull, you do. Got it?"

"Yes sir."

"OK. Keep your revs up to eighteen hundred and let's go."

We went into the calm water of Blue Beach in high gear like a floating flatiron. Felt like I'd breakfasted on cold stove lids, but she showed no tendency to list. Speed seemed the usual six miles an hour in spite of the additional load. Of course. She sat deeper in the water but the track was also taking more hold with more grousers digging in, and the full-open throttle would remain at eighteen hundred revs with any load. I twitched the right line for a shallow turn. OK, no perceptible list. A closer turn, a full hard turn, and she swayed ahead ten degrees outward, returning to level as we straightened out. Everything normal. No, there was one noticeable change. When I twitched the lines for stop, reverse, the tracks thrashed the water to foam but Terry Bull seemed to drift ahead forever. The 10 percent overweight gave her a lot of inertia.

We moved slowly northward, working up through Black Beach, Yellow, and White, Wrobleski patiently impatient with my caution—he would no doubt have preferred to start on White Beach and get it over with. But having had more experience, I was understandably more scared than he could ever be.

I learned a lot that day. The Terry Bull no longer rose to a wave while launching, she plowed through it. She was less prone to broach before a following wave. And when I was caught broadside by a roller in a suicidal attempt to turn around, she did not list—she took a turret-high wallop that buried me, stopped a ton of water in its tracks, and then sedately leaned to port, returned, and listed to starboard just in time to stop the next wave. On riding in to the beach she did not lift to the following wave like her lighter sisters, she let the water slap her stern and turret and give her more speed. She remained more nearly level and was in less danger of digging her nose in the sand and flipping over.

In a word, her weight and consequent inertia made her the most seaworthy craft in the group. I worked on my detailed report of the tests that night and saw it off to AGF with the morning mail.

The powers above were really anxious to get rid of those M8s. The ordnance people must have started work immediately after the interservice conference. Three weeks after I'd sent in my blessing on the Terry Bull ironmongery I was called by the ordnance captain to look over the latest arrival.

"I think we've got just what you wanted, colonel. Looks like a battleship."

It did, like a small battleship anyway. Or at least a gunboat. I borrowed a gunner from the 776th and with Wrobleski driving took off to the south edge of the sea firing range. I thought of starting the firing tests with reduced charges but feared the unspoken contempt of my fearless friend in the driver's compartment.

"Full charge, Corporal Benz," I ordered with a slight quaver.

"Full charge, sir?" he questioned.

"Full charge." Firmer this time. I searched the horizon for fishing boats that frequently crossed our assigned range. There were none.

"All right, you may fire when ready, Benz." Too bad his name wasn't Gridley.[2]

Benz shoved in the cartridge and closed the breech, then took his position as gunner. I hadn't brought a loader along because three of us trying to fight clear in case of a capsize would be more than enough.

"Target, sir?"

"Just elevate her ten degrees and let her rip."

She ripped, a hell of a blast compared to the sharp crack of the 37-mm. The tank seemed belatedly to remember she was supposed to recoil. She raised her bow a bit and solemnly bobbed a few times. The shell apparently tried to make Tokyo; at least I didn't see the splash between us and the horizon. I twitched Wrobleski's line for a full turn.

"Let's have one over the stern, Benz, and come down to five degrees elevation this time."

Benz cranked his turret around, sighted carefully at nothing, the howitzer coughed harshly, and the tank curtsied. This time I'd caught the blurred gray streak of the shell and saw the splash a mile out. Four to five seconds later we heard the faint boom of the burst. I pulled the line for a left turn and held it till we were broadside to the range.

"Now Benz, this is the one that may throw us. Life preserver tied fast?

A quarter blown up? OK, if we go over, this thing will be right upside down on the bottom, so don't try to get out through the turret. Push down, no, push up, to the bottom, shove to the rear, and pull down and out through the scarf gunner's hatch. Got it?"

"Can't I just stand up and push out of the turret as she's laying over, sir? Seems to me there's less chance of getting hung up on something that way."

"OK, if you think you can make it better that way and you won't foul up Wrobleski's lines. But you've got to be fast."

"Yes sir, I'll go out of the turret."

"Right. Now put another shell where you landed the last one."

He probably did. I don't know because I was too concerned with watching the roll. Funny. The howitzer blasted and the roll started, steadied, stopped at fifteen degrees (I should have wangled a clinometer from Captain Nielsen or Heinz), and swung back. Benz was poised on the edge of his turret like a baby bird about to take his maiden flight, then settled back in the gunner's seat with obvious relief. I wiped off some sweat, made a note, and pulled for a full turn.

"Last shot to starboard, Benz. Same elevation."

Just as Benz fired a swell caught us broadside. We didn't list much as lists go, but the additional ten degrees must have thrown the shell over the horizon. I began to worry about fishing boats again. But if they used the navy-prescribed routes they'd be safe.

I was startled, surprised, amazed, and considerably shocked when Admiral Buships arrived in a III Corps sedan and requested that I demonstrate the firing of the M8 howitzer-turret combination by our lone LVT that was so armed. He was still mad. Declined my offer of a cup of coffee, which is the lifeblood of the navy. Politely questioned the veracity of my reports on the seaworthiness of the howitzer-armed tank, and then we were both in a foul mood.

We jeeped to the beach where Northridge had assembled the tank in question. With Wrobleski and a full gun crew I invited the admiral to come aboard with me—we could stand on the deck behind the turret and have a good view of everything. He coldly refused. I gathered that he would never board such a misbegotten monstrosity. So he remained on the beach, skeptically observing our firing forward, starboard, aft, and port without capsizing, and defying the breakers while launching and landing without sinking or broaching. Apparently angered by the success of the demonstration, he declined my offer of lunch at the mess and sedaned to the airport, still mad.

Fast freights moved the M8 turrets to the Food Machinery Corporation near San Jose. Mr. Hait and his engineering crew mounted them on the

LVT (A-I) hulls and shipped them, a few to me and more to the docks in San Francisco.[3] The M5 turrets went back to the light tanks, surplus 37-mm. guns were built into the M15 antiaircraft combination, the erstwhile M8 half-tracks went to the armored infantry, and everybody lived happily forever after. Except Admiral Buships.

Dividing the Bay

We had preempted the first five miles of beach from the wharves in Monterey to the Soldiers Club on the cliff west of Fort Ord for the use of the Eighteenth Armored Group. Major Rathke divided this area into eight training beaches one thousand yards wide, depending on landmarks, each beach representing a normal tank battalion front. These beaches were named for the basic primary and secondary colors. We found that the surf was stronger on the unsheltered northern beaches so we started our people driving on Blue Beach, next to Fisherman's Wharf, and only on calm days did we venture to challenge the breakers on Brown Beach under the Soldiers Club.

With our ignorance of nautical rules of right of way, plus the slow steering response and great inertia of our machines, we created havoc with the traffic of the fishing fleet when we were operating from Blue Beach. The fishing boats were continually going out to catch fish or coming in to unload their catch at the canneries. Only the expertise of the skippers and the comparative agility of their craft saved them from serious collisions while wending their way through a cloud of fifty armored vehicles making their maiden voyages between Blue Beach and Punta Piños, commanded and driven by men who had seen the ocean for the first time a week before.

On venturing to sea as far north as Black Beach in the center of our sector, we encountered more confusion. Captain of the Port Nielsen would telephone or charge out in his launch with the request that we clear the area since it was required by the navy for torpedo practice firing. We would then squeeze southward with considerable disruption of our training program.

A small white-painted target ship would steam through the area we had vacated. Then a destroyer on the horizon, an unseen submarine, or a flight of low-flying planes would launch practice torpedoes at the ship. The target ship skipper, hoping that the torpedoes were set deep enough to run under rather than through his craft, would watch the wake and signal hits or misses. All very interesting and entertaining, but it sure played hell with Major Rathke's carefully coordinated training program.

Brigadier General Moore, chief of staff of the Ninth Army, telephoned. "The navy is holding a conference at their headquarters at the navy yard in San Francisco tomorrow at 1000. The subject is the partition of Monterey Bay between the army and navy for training areas. Since you are most concerned you'll be the army representative."

"Right, headquarters, navy yard, San Francisco, 1000. I'll be there."

Another call from Captain Nielsen an hour later. "Good morning, colonel. I'm calling from Frisco. We're setting up a conference for tomorrow at 1000 on the division of Monterey Bay for training purposes. Ninth Army tells me that you will be the senior army representative."

"Why yes, I just got the word myself. I'll be there."

"And what is your date of rank?"

"December 29, 1942."

And how many officers will you have with you?"

"None."

"OK, thanks a lot, colonel."

It was going to be a hard 130-mile trip at the prescribed rate of thirty-five miles an hour so I borrowed a sedan from the camp commander.[4] It came with a T-5 driver who had been a native of San Francisco. He advised an early start.

The lad knew his former hometown well, but had not anticipated the logjam of security checks at the navy yard. Instead of a leisurely quarter hour of introductions, coffee, and chitchat before the show opened, a navy lieutenant rescued me from the shore police and ushered me into the conference room at precisely 1000.

Captain Nielsen grabbed an elbow and urged me forward. "Commodore Chrisman, this is Colonel Triplet of the landing tracked vehicle group."

"Welcome aboard, colonel, we were beginning to worry about you."

The speaker didn't look at all worried, just irritated. He was a medium-height, plump, ruddy, white-haired officer who would do well as a department store Santa Claus if he could relax his cold, grim cast of countenance. He wore the broad bright bold bands, epaulets, and silver stars of a commodore on his blue uniform. Looked like the cards of the conference were stacked against the army.

"It was the low suspicious nature of your security people that held me up, commodore. Sorry I delayed you."

"Think nothing of it. Colonel Triplet, I believe you know Captain Nielsen. This is Captain Hageman, destroyers, Captain Bingham, subs, Captain Britton, air, and Lieutenant Ford," introducing a quartet of capable, khaki-clad officers, the first with a badly bruised cheek, the second wearing dolphins, and the third sporting pilot's wings on his chest.

I was seated on the commodore's right at the badly scarred, varnished oak table. Captain Nielsen and the aviator were on my right, while the bruised destroyer lad glowered at me across the table. The submariner and Mr. Ford were on his left. An ash tray, scratch pad, a chart of the southern third of Monterey Bay, a quartet of varicolored pencils, a protractor, and a parallel ruler were neatly arranged at each place. A steward distributed mugs of coffee with a creamer and sugar bowl for any weakling among us. My first sip explained the apparently melted varnish rings on the table. I reached for the cream.

The commodore tapped the table with his Annapolis ring. "Gentlemen, the navy is responsible for the control of water training areas at or below the mean low-tide level. This conference is now in session to determine an equitable apportionment of Monterey Bay between the army and navy for training purposes. The army is concerned with the training of DUKH and LVT units. The navy uses the bay for torpedo practice firing by destroyers, submarines, and torpedo planes. These requirements have sometimes conflicted.

"Colonel, we would like to have you state the requirements of the army for the use of Monterey Bay."

I woke up and realized that the ball was in my court. "Commodore, gentlemen, I am required to train and dispatch three LVT tank and three LVT tractor battalions to the Pacific theater of operations by December 10. Two battalions were sent last week, four are still in training. DUKH battalions are expected to arrive from time to time but I have no schedule for them at present. Their requirements will be similar to ours and we will accommodate them within the army area.

"We need to train these men under the roughest conditions possible without undue loss of men and machines. Monterey Bay has one sheltered area in the crook of the Punta Piños peninsula. Our water driving training must start in that area since our men are totally inexperienced both with their machines and sea driving.

"As the units become experienced they move north where the surf is higher. We have found that the farthest north we can make landings without unacceptable casualties is this point." I put a red "X" on the beach below the Fort Ord Soldiers Club.

"We need a water range with a safety zone of ten thousand yards with a firing line five hundred yards from the beach.

"Therefore our total requirements can be met by assigning this area for the use of the army." I lined out a quadrilateral with parallel sides extending fifteen thousand yards from the Soldiers Club on the right and Fisherman's Wharf on the left on an azimuth of three hundred degrees magnetic. The resulting figure covering five by five and one-half miles looked greedy even to me. I passed the marked chart to the commodore, who winced and passed it on to the destroyer officer.

"Your opinion please, Captain Hageman?"

"Commodore, this assignment of the most favorable area to the army would seriously handicap us. It would force us to use the roughest parts of the bay at all times. That is satisfactory from our viewpoint in shooting— we will probably be shooting in earnest under similar conditions. But it will be rough on the target and recovery crew. I recommend that the navy retain full control of the bay and assign specific areas to the army on a day-to-day basis as requested, provided they are not required for navy use."

"Captain Nielsen, I'd like to have your comments."

"Commodore, the assignment of areas between army and navy is not and should not be part of my duties. In my opinion retaining full control and requiring army to request areas on a daily basis would be impractical. Army requires daily training at sea and on the beach, our torpedo people require occasional use of those waters on no firm schedule. Therefore I believe a division should be made.

"I will, however, have to reserve a channel through the southern area for the use of the fishing fleet, regardless of whom it is assigned to. A channel one thousand yards wide from Fisherman's Wharf past Punta Piños will be required for their use."

"Captain Bingham, please state your opinion," requested the commodore.

"Sir, if we always have to shoot north of the area requested by the army we may have difficulty with porpoising torpedoes in rough weather. I recommend that the change be made in the present arrangements. Give the army the whole bay if they want it, with the proviso that we have priority when we're sent down there to shoot."

"Captain Britton, give us the air arm viewpoint."

"I agree with Captain Bingham, sir."

"Mr. Ford, let us know what the target and recovery people think about it."

"We like fairly calm water, commodore. If we always shoot north of this line the colonel drew we'll have the danger of porpoising, the recovery will be difficult at best, and we'll lose or break up torpedoes in that rough water. And those torpedoes cost $10,000 apiece.

"Give us the north half of the area the army wants and we'll always be able to handle recovery without loss or damage."

The commodore doodled a sloop and started on a battleship. Then he dropped his pencil and turned to me. "Having heard the opinions of these officers, colonel, do you have anything to add to your former statement?"

"Yes sir, I do. I am quite in sympathy with Lieutenant Ford who brought up the problem of recovery in rough water and the consequent cost of

$10,000 per torpedo lost or seriously damaged. We also have difficulties in heavy surf with tractors that are valued at $25,000 and our tanks that cost $35,000. Also, putting the GI insurance value on the men, the tractor crew is worth $30,000 and the tank carries $70,000 worth of men.[5] Both machines and men are vulnerable in rough water and the bill for a lost tank could be over $100,000.

"Considering replacements for losses, the machine can be replaced by the factory assembly line in a week but it will take twenty years to replace the crew. That's all I have to say, sir."

The commodore glumly completed his battleship, sketched the conning tower of a sub, drew the swirling wake of a torpedo between them, and sketched a fan-shaped explosion amidships on the dreadnought.[6] He decisively reached for his protractor and parallel ruler. Placing one edge on the Soldiers Club and the other one thousand yards north of Fisherman's Wharf, he firmly drew two lines well out to sea.

"This is it, gentlemen. The boundary will be as an azimuth of 305 degrees magnetic through the Fort Ord Soldiers Club, army south, navy north. Captain Nielsen will be responsible for the safe layout of firing ranges for the army and for a passage for the use of the fishing fleet.

"That is all, gentlemen."

He pushed back his chair, rose, and left the conference room as we jumped to attention. As he cleared the door Captain Hageman muttered bitterly. "Goddamn desk navigator!"

"Drydock swabbie!" agreed Bingham with feeling.

"How about having lunch with me?" invited Britton.

I did.

"Those torpedo planes are quite impressive, coming in low and fast as they do," I remarked as I carved into the steak. "Wish we had some planes to buzz my boys—give them a bit more realism."

"D'you mean you'd like to have planes buzz you, flying low?"

"Sure would, show my young men that those AA machine guns aren't mounted on their craft just for decoration."

"Well, our married fighters like to fly at thirty feet but the bachelors fly real low when they get a chance. But most of the time we get below one thousand feet we get reported and the admiral raises blisters on us. Are you sure you want us really to buzz you?"

"Certainly, it's the only way we can get used to swinging our guns on fast, close-in targets."

"OK, I'll talk to the admiral. When would be a good time to set it up?"

"We have a landing exercise every Thursday morning with all available battalions. Rendezvous two or three miles out at 0900 and landing at 1000."

"I'll see what I can do about some fighters or attack bombers."

At that moment I saw Commodore Chrisman enter the dining room with another officer, a tall, skinny, stooped captain. But no, he wasn't Chrisman. He was a plump, ruddy, white-haired copy wearing the four stripes of a captain.

"Hmmm, I see Commodore Chrisman has an identical twin," I remarked, nodding toward the distant passing couple.

"Oh no, that's Chrisman all right."

"But he was a commodore an hour ago, and—"

"Oh yes, but commodore is just a temporary grade, a captain is made a commodore on special occasions or when he is in command of two or more ships, or is needed to chair a conference. Chrisman was promoted by special order yesterday when the admiral found that you outranked him by three months. He was demoted an hour ago."

"Damned clever, you navy folks!"

The landing exercise next Thursday consisted of a feint at Monterey, a ninety-degree change of direction to the left under cover of a smoke screen, and a landing of two tank-tractor teams on Yellow and White Beaches. The four battalions were to rendezvous three miles northwest of the Soldiers Club with all units and vehicles in the final attack formation relative to the objective. The change in direction would then be made on signal by each individual tank and tractor driver yanking his steering lever to the left. This would be much faster than wheeling the unwieldy thousand-yard-wide columns.

It was a beautiful day, clear blue to the horizon, slight swells and moderate breakers. At 0850 the platoons were circling in position in rendezvous, tank battalions with Brown Beach three miles distant on their left, tractor battalions on their right. At 0900 on Colonel Kane's flag signal all tracks began beating foam at eighteen hundred rpm as the group started the feint toward Monterey.

At 0920, Captain Chisholm with his smoke-canister-carrying launch began his passes at full speed between the group and Monterey. The white cloud spread fast and rose rapidly. At 0930 a second flag signal from the command tank, every commander yelled "Now!" and every vehicle swung left. The attack had changed direction toward the objective beaches, three miles distant.

"Let's go," I said to Sergeant Cole, and he passed the word to the driver. We had sabotaged the governors so that Terry Bull or Shark, running light with no ballast, could make a little over seven miles an hour. It was probably hard on the engines but I needed this speed to precede the group for two reasons. I wanted to test the surf immediately prior to the landing, and I was able to use the few minutes gained to drive to the top of a sand dune and get a good overall view of the landing.

We'd just started our drive toward the beach. I was looking back along the first wave of tanks behind us when Cole exclaimed with emphasis, "Good God! Look at that!" I looked.

I had dismissed my conversation with Captain Britton of the brown-shoe navy, assuming that his proposal of the week before was merely polite conversation or would take a month of coordination to put into effect, but here they were.[7]

A cloud, no, a wide and deep formation, of fighter planes was approaching from the east at three thousand feet. As they crossed the beach they were peeling off and screaming down at us. Cole, getting enthusiastically into the spirit of the exercise, grabbed the port .50 caliber, yanked the cocking handle, and swung the gun on a fighter that had leveled off directly ahead. He hastily changed his mind, dropped the gun, dashed to starboard, and pulled the radio aerial down, ducking behind the cab. I ducked with him—that propeller cleared our cab by a hand span.

The attacking Eighteenth Armored Group was being counterattacked by what the air force would call a wing of fighters—I don't know what the navy calls a swarm of forty or fifty planes like that. Now they were coming, looping, diving, and driving in individually like nest-defending hornets. Suddenly they were gone, rendezvousing at a more reasonable altitude over the western horizon. Two minutes later a squadron of light bombers hit us from seaward. They were playing with Stuka tactics, I suppose, diving individually from altitude and pulling up at water-riffling heights.[8] Only two dozen of them, five or six flights.

As the bombers took off and reformed in the distance northward we noted that another squadron of a dozen planes deployed in line at an apparent altitude below the level of the cliffs and dunes was winging in from the northeast. Torpedo bombers! They drove in on the left flank of the group, dropped their imaginary torpedoes a quarter of a mile distant, and zoomed for altitude over Monterey.

As Terry Bull topped the dune from which we had a good view of the landing, here came the fighters again, this time from the north, sweeping along the beach line in a column of flights, four or five planes abreast enfilading the landing and howling away while the next flight screamed down on the deploying tanks and landing tractors.

"Wow!" commented Cole, who was obviously impressed. "If those guys were in earnest they could take care of a good-sized Jap fleet."

That afternoon I telephoned Captain Britton and babbled my appreciation of his efforts. "Captain Britton? This is Triplet, amphibs. I want to thank you for the naval air show you people put on this morning.

Magnificent! Scared the hell out of my boys, terrified me. You must not have any married men in those outfits, they were all down at wave level. We are especially complimented by your torpedo squadron attacking like we were a line of battleships. Please present my respects and thanks to the admiral. How about next week?"

"Glad you liked the show, colonel. Our people certainly enjoyed it. But never no more and I don't think I'd better give the admiral your message."

"Why not? We deeply appreciate his cooperation and—"

"I know, but I've been standing on the carpet ever since noon while he's been getting phone calls and telegrams from outraged citizens, the mayors of Monterey and Pacific Grove, and the governor of California. The governor demands a written explanation of the mass buzzing of Monterey by the navy and the admiral gave me the job of writing it. He's just not in the mood to hear any more about joint navy-air-amphib operations with your people—forget it."

When our fifth and sixth battalions had reached the point of proficiency that I felt would reflect credit on themselves, the Eighteenth Armored Group, and the army, I wrote another of "those damned letters" to army ground forces. I stated that the troops I had been directed to train had been dispatched or were ready for shipment. I therefore requested movement orders for my group headquarters to proceed to the Pacific theater of operations to command them in action.

The answer was frustrating. The requirement was changed. At least six more battalions, three of tanks and three of tractors, would be required, and the Eighteenth Armored Group would remain at Fort Ord to train them.

Six more battalions came and went. I repeated my request for active overseas service and the AGF answer was practically a carbon copy of the first, more LVT units were needed in the island-hopping campaign on the Pacific front. One cheering thought—my young men must be doing well for MacArthur since he wanted more of them.

So we received and trained the next contingent of surplus tankers and tank destroyers in seagoing tactics with their unfamiliar amphibious machines. As I began to receive their port calls I again pointed out that I had trained and dispatched twelve battalions and had six more on the way. I urged that it was high time that the group be sent to take charge of this unique force to ensure continued training, adequate maintenance, and proper tactical use in battle.

In October 1944, I got the answer—a kick below the belt. There was no requirement for an LVT group commander in the Pacific campaign. LVT units were attached to the landing forces as required and no overall LVT command was needed. Two more battalions would arrive at Fort Ord for training in late October and the Eighteenth Armored Group would train them for use as reserves or replacements.

I normally strongly disapprove of officers who play politics and make personal pleas to higher-placed friends for favors, but the situation was desperate. Here it was, a quarter to 1945, the war was passing me by, and AGF was telling me that I was to wither on the vine at Fort Ord, a safe six thousand miles from the nearest enemy. To hell with army ground forces. And MacArthur.

There was one friend who might help me out of this impossible situation, Major General Alvan Gillem, my first battalion commander of twenty years before.[9] I wrote him a personal letter stating the circumstances in full. Since I was not required as a group commander in the Pacific, I requested that he use his influence to have me sent to the European front where I might be of value in command of armored, armored infantry, or other combat units. Should have descended to this level long before—it got results. I received the orders that I'd been hoping for during the past two years.

I turned the command of the group over to the very capable executive, Lieutenant Colonel Northridge, packed my new war bag that Fiona gave me as a going-away present, and kissed the family good-bye for the third time. Fiona drove me to the airfield in her ancient Lincoln Zephyr and wished me "good hunting."

The poets and romanticists say that the emotions are affairs of the heart; the realists assert that the brain is the organ principally involved. Both are dead wrong. Love, hate, anger, happiness, all emotions are centered in the stomach. Fiona was waving her scarf as the plane swept down the field, and I felt like my tummy had been jerked out by the roots and stomped on.

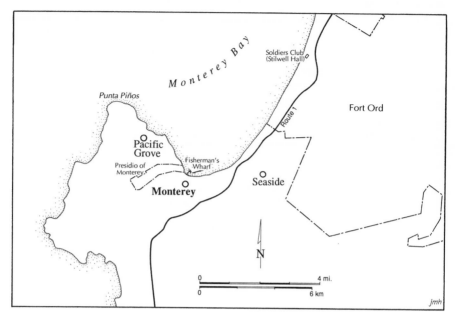

▲ Montery and vicinity.

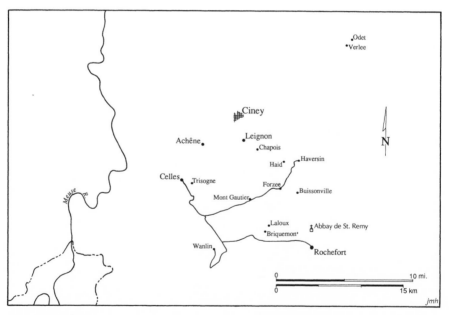

▲ Ciney et al.

95

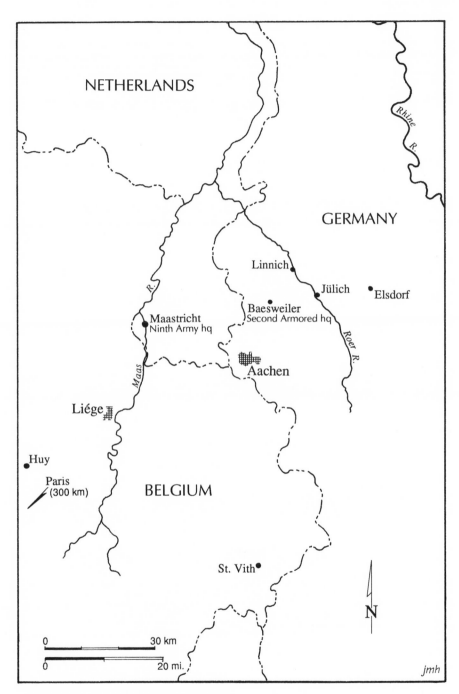

▲ Netherlands, Belgium, Germany.

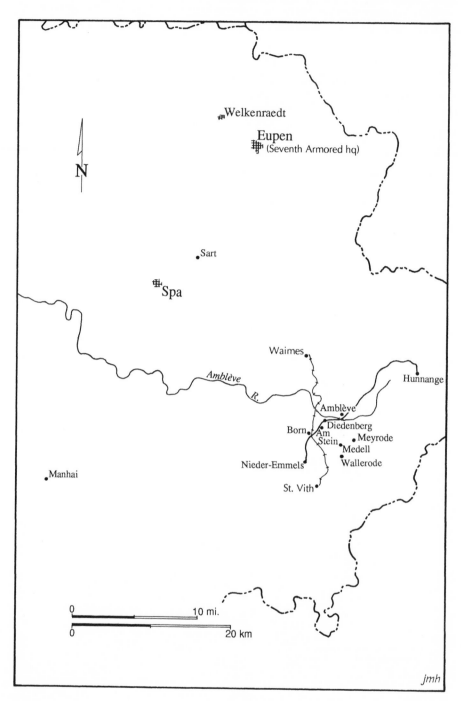

▲ Hunnange.

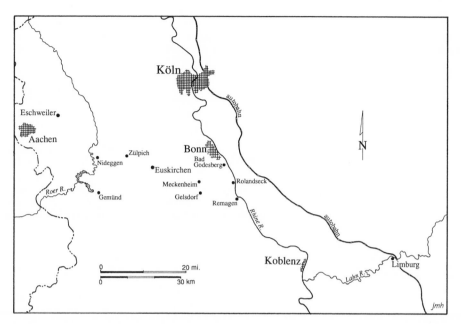

▲ Remagen to the autobahn.

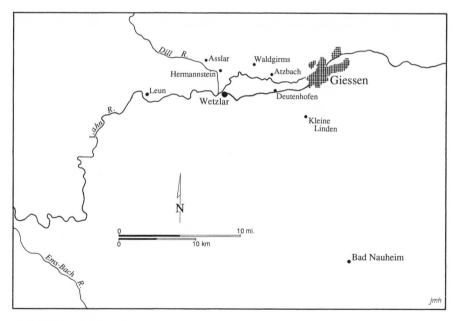

▲ On the Way to Giessen.

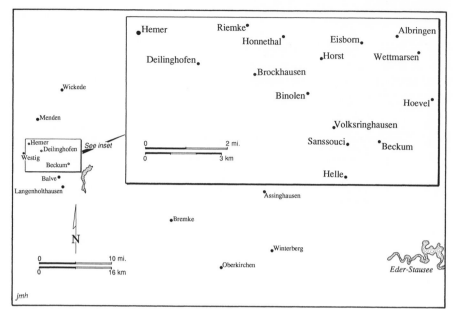

Hemer   Riemke
Honnethal   Eisborn   Albringen
Deilinghofen   Horst   Wettmarsen
Brockhausen
Binolen   Hoevel
Volksringhausen
Sanssouci   Beckum

Helle

Wickede

Menden

Hemer
Deilinghofen
Westig   *See inset*
Beckum
Balve
Langenholthausen

0   2 mi.
0   3 km

Assinghausen

Bremke

N

Winterberg

0   10 mi.
0   16 km

Oberkirchen

Eder-Stausee

jmh

▲ To Hemer.

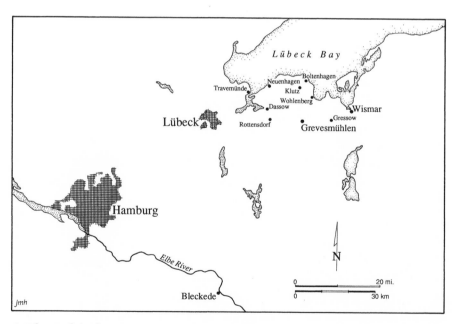

Lübeck Bay

Boltenhagen
Neuenhagen
Travemünde   Klutz
Wohlenberg
Dassow
Gressow
Wismar
Lübeck   Rottensdorf   Grevesmühlen

Hamburg

Elbe River

N

0   20 mi.
0   30 km

Bleckede

jmh

▲ The Baltic front.

▲ Test section, Infantry Board. Left to right: First Lieutenant O. J. Allen, Captain I. R. Clark, Major Triplet, Major H. G. Sydenham, Lieutenant Colonel H. M. "Count" Melasky, Major E. A. Chazal, Captain J. W. Hammond, Captain W. C. Rutherford.

▲ Infantry Board, test section in rear. In the front row is Brigadier General Bradley, fifth from left. In back is Major Triplet, seventh from left.

Testing. ▶

Major General Wogan congratulates us on our promotion.

▲ General Wogan, center, congratulates the just promoted Colonel Triplet. Fiona holds the eagles she is about to pin on her husband's uniform, the eagles' heads facing to the front.

▲ Amphibious tank on an M5 chassis, modified by the Food Machinery Corporation.

▲ Amphibious carrier, M5 chassis, modified by the Food Machinery Corporation.

▲ The great mogul.

▲ Snow scene.

▲ A Sherman in the snow.

▲ Attack.

▲ Infantry moving up with the tanks.

▲ American soldiers were not issued snow uniforms. They improvised, taking clothing from German dead, otherwise requisitioning bedsheets.

▲ General Hasbrouck planning the next move. The officer at right is General Clarke's replacement as commander of CCB, Colonel Joseph F. Haskell.

▲ Prisoners.

▲ Captured Germans in retreat, photo taken from an American tank.

War was not respectful of
religion. ▶

▲ Road scene, an M4 Sherman.

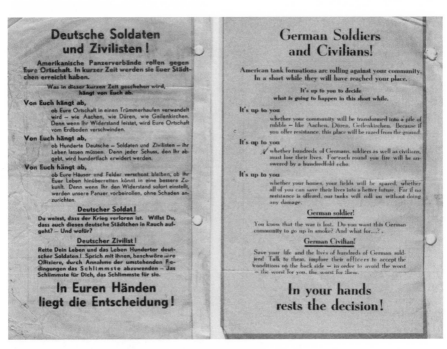

▲ An effective combination of force and leniency.

▲ Hanging out the white laundry.

The bridge at Bleckede
across the Oder. ▶

End of the war: sailing on the Baltic. ▶

▲ The commander of CCA atop his cleaned-up command tank, an M5 Stuart, ferocious in appearance, harmless in battle.

▲ The colonel and his staff. Fourth from left, Colonel Triplet; to his right is Lieutenant Colonel King.

Colonel Triplet with his modified M-3 submachine gun, "Betty Boop." ▶

▲ Colonel Triplet.

Eight.

To the Second Armored

Paris

Had an amazingly easy and uninterrupted flight to Washington, considering that it was winter weather in 1944. On landing I told a taxi driver I wanted to go to the War Department, now in the newly built Pentagon.[1] We wound around curve after curve gradually approaching this concrete monstrosity—looked like we were never going to make it. We finally slid into an underground opening and there I was, unloaded at the foot of a long, wide ramp that led one story from the concourse to the first working level.

Miles of corridors, hundreds of rooms, a regiment of officers flatfooting from here to there like an army of confused ants, each carrying a briefcase, folder, or sheet of paper to validate his absence from his post. In the offices were five thousand secretaries typing the papers for the officers to carry. Three-wheeled bicycle messengers trundled more papers from room to room, filling in-baskets and emptying out-baskets. It certainly was a far cry from the ancient two-story War Department building on Constitution Avenue that had been sufficient for winning the last four wars.[2]

By dint of numerous inquiries I finally located personnel assignment and got my orders. Priority for a flight at 2200 that night, destination Paris. That was encouraging and complimentary—Eisenhower evidently needed me right now.

While fighting my way out of that concrete maze I was hailed by Colonel Chrisman, whom I had last seen when we were lieutenants in the Fourteenth Infantry, jungle hounds in Panama fifteen years before. Since it was quitting time for the general staff, he insisted on giving me a personally conducted tour of Washington. I insisted even more firmly that I wanted to see Lee, who had come to the nation's capital to assist in the war effort. We compromised. He drove me to Lee's address, a rather large residence that had been converted to a boardinghouse for secretaries. The suspicious old battle-ax who apparently ran the place on the lines of a female monastery put me through a searching interrogation. Finally declared that I probably wasn't a cradle-robbing old lecher and reluctantly called Lee.

My eldest pride and joy appeared as glad to see me as I was to find her. I suspected that she had found the big city a bit less romantic than she had pictured, and was probably homesick. Chrisman again insisted on giving us his short tour of Washington, and since Lee had seen little of the place and I little more, we accepted briefly. After gawping at more imposing white marble buildings than we were interested in seeing, twenty seconds per gawp depending on traffic, we excused ourselves as soon as courteously possible.

During a seafood dinner on the highly advertised Potomac waterfront I received very clear "vibes" that the young lady was quite disillusioned about her independent life and regretted leaving California.[3] Be it ever to my credit that I didn't tell her to give it up and go home. She's a stubborn kid and would have stayed in spite of hell and high water if I'd put it that way. So I went on about how Fiona was now left lonely and helpless and it would be nice if she'd go back to Carmel and take care of her mother. Later I learned that she had done just that.

A final wordless hug and shoulder pats at the airport, my vocal cords seemed to be paralyzed, and the chartered civilian plane with matching hostesses and upholstery took off into the black night.

The only incident I recall about the flight was the dollar-bill poker game. While my seatmate was pursuing one of the stewardesses, a nicely turned-out WAAC captain paused beside the vacant seat. "Is this seat taken, colonel?"

"Ah, yes, but move in. You're a lot prettier than the old goat that was sitting here and he'll be busy for some time."

"Thanks. I just had to get away from that poker game, my luck is running low tonight."

"Poker game? Where do you find room on the plane for poker?"

"Oh, two people can play, I mean dollar-bill poker."

"Never heard of it."

"No? Here, I'll show you. Do you have any dollar bills?"

I inspected my thin wallet. Yes, I had four dollar bills. She dived into her shoulder bag, pulled out a well-padded purse, and just happened to have a dozen or so. She pulled down her lunch tray and squared off the pile of bills. I followed suit.

"OK, now we each cut our stack." We did.

"Now look at the serial number on your top bill, and select the best five digits to form pairs, threes, fours, fives, a full house, or a straight."

"OK, I've got a full house, nines and sevens."

"That's a good hand, but I lucked out with five sevens. Too bad. Let's try the next one." She regretfully dropped my bill in her bag.

My four fives looked good, until she pointed out her four eights. So it went for the next plays.

"That's all the dollar bills I have." And I returned my wallet to my hip pocket.

"But I can change a five or ten for you," and from the shoulder bag she removed a handful of loose ones. "Or we can play with fives or tens," she offered. "I have to give you a chance to get your money back. Your luck is sure to change."

"I have other plans for my fives and tens. But thanks for the lesson."

"Oh well," and she left to charm the navy commander five seats ahead on the other side of the aisle. Two minutes later he was reaching for his wallet.

I tried reading my paperback thriller but couldn't concentrate on the story. By God. That WAAC had laid down four sevens, four eights, four nines, and a nine-high straight and she'd dropped her winnings of my low-numbered bills into her shoulder bag and then offered to give me change from her culls. Seemed such a nice girl too. Oh well.

Awoke at the second dawn to see the meticulously manicured fields of England's farms sliding back under us. Daylight found us over the white-capped chop of the Channel, still no sign of the war, but I began wondering about the possibility of German fighters in the area. Would they shoot down a civilian plane? Probably, and rightly so. And what would I do? Not a damn thing to do but ride her down. Then put on the Mae West and swim if I was lucky. My morbid musings were interrupted by a stewardess making an important announcement that proved to be a determining factor in my future military career. "We will land at Orly in an hour, where you will be able to have a hot breakfast, so breakfast will not be served on the plane." It wasn't, and the coffee urns were completely dry.

That young lady was the first of several people who were responsible for my championship speed record in getting to the war.

When we debarked at Orly our request for the promised breakfast was curtly denied. "Just get on the bus, you'll have breakfast in Paris. No, there's no time for coffee, just get on the bus."

When we unloaded at the Palais de Somethingorother, the depot head-quarters, it was nearing 1100 and all hands were suffering from the time change, with the mild headache, dark brown taste, belly pains, and foul disposition characteristic of two days of plane travel and semi-starvation. My brief conversation with the depot chief of staff was less than satisfactory. He was a sharp young light colonel of (wouldn't you know it?) the class of 1935, very efficient and inhospitable. I spoke for the group of my fellow passengers. "What we would most appreciate, colonel, is breakfast."

"No, the hotels stop serving breakfast at 0900. It is now 1100. You will be able to get lunch at 1200."

"Well, how about some coffee?"

"No coffee. You can't get anything, not even a cup of coffee, without a ration card. Here's your billet assignment, Hotel Quelquechose. This is a sketch map of your hotel and your restaurant. You'll eat at the restaurant Comprendezpas, using this ration card. The card is good only at your assigned restaurant. This is your taxi chit. Give it to a taxi driver at the entrance and he will drive you to your billet. After that you walk."

"Walk? Can't I call in for a sedan or a jeep? I'll want to—"

"No. I've got a battalion of full colonels in this depot and barely enough transportation to keep the platoon of generals off my neck. Colonels walk."

"OK, I'll use taxis."

"I'm afraid not. Every taxi you see in Paris is chartered by us, running on our gasoline, and for official business only. They drive only for the chits issued by this office. They get caught taking money and they're out of a job."

So I taxied to the dreary, frigid four-story hotel where the overcoated, fur-hatted, and gloved clerk assigned me to a double room on the third floor. The open-work cage elevator was of course "desordrée," so the scrawny little porter and I carried my military Val Pac and musette bag (yes, I carried the eighty-pound war bag) up to the top story—the French don't count the ground floor.

Found that it really was a double room. It had a double bed, and somebody's plunder was already stowed on the left luggage stand. OK, I dumped mine on the right side and started for breakfast at 1145.

According to my caffeine-starved interpretation of my mimeographed sketch my restaurant should be six blocks from the hotel, partially around two circles. As usual on circles I must have taken the wrong exits, but in the tenth block I saw a restaurant with American officers homing in on the entrance. I had found it.

A smartly uniformed young military police lieutenant was standing at the door checking the arrivals. "Your ration card, sir."

I found the card among the confused crud of movement orders, hotel assignment, and sketch map. He gave it a brief look.

"Sorry, colonel, your card is for the Quelquechose. This is the Laissezfaire, for company-grade officers. You go back down this street to the circle, left around the circle to the second exit—"

"Lieutenant, I haven't had a bite or a drop since Iceland, and I'm going to have breakfast here. Here is my identification card and this is my billet assignment. Make a note and report me to the depot commander for direct disobedience of his orders if you like."

I think the young man was a bit disgruntled, but he scribbled in his notebook and let me pass with no further conversation.

I had a scanty but delicious lunch served by a waitress with a face and figure like Jeanette MacDonald and hands like a professional wrestler.[4] Funny, I didn't notice those powerful pink paws until she was clearing away the custard dishes. Good lunch, little but as the Germans say es schmeckt.

Versailles

Fortified by the third cup of coffee, I took a long walk around the area, broad avenues, traffic circles, and streets almost empty of cars, small parks, and the four-story buildings all of the same height as Napoleon had ordered so long ago.[5] Made a lot prettier city than the skyscrapers and high-rises of our country. Finally found my way back to the hotel, where the clerk handed me a message: "Report to depot headquarters without delay."

The snotty little squirt behind the desk appearing to be slyly pleased said, "Oh yes, Colonel Triplet. The general wishes to see you," and led the way into the sanctum sanctorum.

The fattish, mottled brigadier wasted no time. "Colonel Triplet? Ah yes, the provost marshal reports that you entered the wrong restaurant, refused to obey my orders as given through the military police, and directed the MP lieutenant to report you for doing so." The young man had certainly lost no time in making the report.

"That is correct, sir. My last meal was in Iceland yesterday and I didn't care to follow the rather confusing directions put out by your staff to get my next one."

"That is no excuse for disobeying my orders or your belligerent attitude. You seem to have a very short fuse. Aren't you happy here?"

"No sir. I've been in the military service twenty-seven years and the reception I've gotten in France so far is the coldest welcome I've ever received on a new assignment as a soldier, cadet, or officer."

"There's a war on, colonel. I've got over four hundred field-grade officers on hand and can't hand carry you like they do stateside in peacetime. Since you don't like Paris—Briggs, cut orders for him to Versailles."

"Yes sir. Today's train has left, but I'll have him on it tomorrow."

Back to the hotel, where I found my roommate snuggled down on his half of the bed in a "mummy bag," the sleeping bag that I'd developed while on the Infantry Board "for the use of front-line infantry soldiers." How had he latched onto one of those feather-filled luxuries?

His face emerged from the hood. I had known him at Benning, an undersized, scrubby, politically minded type with a repertoire of filthy jokes and a low alcoholic tolerance. Forgotten his name, so I'll call him Colonel Scrubbs, and how in hell had he made light colonel?

Anyway, he greeted me as though I were the prodigal son and was exuberant at having just located a job. He'd been in this repple-depple for more than a month and was weary and worn down by the local life of licentious luxury.[6] Now he was going to be assigned as executive officer of a rest and relaxation area near Paris.

"I'll take you over to see Colonel Albright tomorrow. Good friend of mine. Personnel officer. He'll find a good job for you if anyone can."

I visualized Colonel Albright flicking through his file of vacancies: "Ah yes, the CC of bordello 17 on the West Bank has been recommended for relief due to overwork and battle fatigue. How would you like this assignment?"

So I declined Scrubbs's kind offer to use his influence in high places in my behalf. "No, thanks. I'll wait for an infantry or tank unit. But I would appreciate your help this evening in finding the restaurant where we're supposed to eat."

He guided me to the Comprendezpas that evening. The décor was superior, the food was wonderful, but the calories would add up to a maintenance diet for a midget and none of the staff resembled Jeanette MacDonald. I was surprised to see Colonel Johnson, late commander of the Thirteenth Armored Group for ground training, at the next table. He had left the Thirteenth to win the war in Europe two months before, and his news was depressing. "Yes, I've been here six weeks now and not a nibble. There's no chance of getting out of here unless a colonel gets killed and with the war bogged down for the winter colonels just aren't getting killed fast enough. Six weeks in this frigid hell hole. Paris, the pleasure capital of the world. Ha. The pleasures of Paris with short rations and no heat get mighty cold after the first months. You're going to Versailles? Well, that's one step ahead, lots of luck."

Scrubbs suggested that we go out to see some of the reviving night spots, but after two days on a fully loaded slow plane I was tired clear down. Left him at the restaurant drumming up a party and returned to the hotel and to bed. Goddlemighty it was cold, stone cold, like going to bed in a walk-in refrigerator. Cocooned myself in all the blankets and quilts available and shuddered off to sleep.

Crash-clatter-bump! No, it wasn't a bombing raid, it was just Scrubbs falling through the furniture and charging into the wall, bringing down a large framed and formerly glassed painting of the Eiffel Tower. He picked himself up, unscratched by the shards of glass, and as he disrobed gave me a blow by blow account of the wonderful evening he'd had—wine, women, and music.

The wine I could believe, he was really tanked. Finally found his way into his sleeping bag, zipped it up to his chin, turned squarely on his back, and started snoring, a particularly unpleasant, gargling, rasping snore.

Further sleep was impossible with that going on. I tried poking him.

"Snaasrloh! Wha— Huh? ———Hahnhrk!"

I shoved him on his side so his mouth wouldn't drop open. It worked until I was just off to sleep again.

"Harrgl!" He had sagged over on his back again, sounded like he was drowning. If I only had a roll of wide surgical tape, but I didn't. Thought briefly about putting a pillow over his face until he stopped breathing, then thought of a more humane line of action.

I got out of bed, went around to his side, took a firm grip on the hood of his mummy bag, and pulled him to the floor. Dragged him out the door and parked him against the wall in the hallway lying comfortably on his back. During these maneuvers he hadn't missed a beat, sixteen welkin-ringing snores a minute.

I went in, locked the door, and had a wonderful night's sleep until 0600 when someone started hammering on the door. I opened up and was faced by the overcoated night clerk and porter supporting the shuddering frame of my skivvy-clad roommate between them.

"Thees Colonel Scrubbs, he ees enn these chamber, no? Yes. He ees ron about the hotel in search for the chambre de bath—he say he want the room of the bath. You take heem, yes?"

I took him. Or rather I stood aside and let him lurch purposefully toward the bathroom that he had so urgently tried to find. When he emerged five or ten minutes later he looked much happier but was still confused. As he was trying to snug down again in the mummy bag that the porter had recovered from the hall he was trying to rationalize his actions.

"Jesus, musta been drunk. Why'n hell d'I do a damnfool thing like that? Bunkin' down in th' hall."

He still doesn't know.

Making the 1300 train to Versailles was much more important than lunch, so I skipped the soupe du jour avec croutons and spam à la Quelquechose and settled for a thimbleful of heavily watered cognac at the railway station bar. Boarded the train for a window seat the moment it stopped. It was a weird string of second- and third-class coaches, all of which had been badly beaten up and seldom repaired during the past four years. Some of them had obviously barely survived strafing by Stukas, P-38s, Me-109s, and P-47s. All windows were closed and immovable, but enough of them were broken to clear the air of cigarette fumes and to admit the coal smoke and cinders coughed out by the antique locomotive. We had a full load of the Free French army in weird combinations of British, French, and American uniforms. They were a lively lot, eating, drinking, gambling, and shouting incessantly. It wasn't a restful trip.

We were late in starting, and the train halted three or four times for extended periods in open country, apparently so the crew could paste the locomotive together for another three-mile spurt. It gave me a lot of time for introspective thinking. Maybe the brigadier was right, maybe I had been a bit belligerent, perhaps my fuse was a little short, missing a couple of meals wasn't a valid reason for declaring war. And I'd certainly started off on the wrong foot with everybody I'd met in Europe so far. I'd have to take a firm grip on my temper in future and take a more kindly view of my fellow crusaders. I even regretted my brutal treatment of roommate Scrubbs. Yes, and I'd even try to like these loud-mouthed, obnoxious, supercilious, half-drunk French bastards I was cooped up with. No, no, that was too much, I could never like a Frenchman.[7]

So in this very Christian frame of mind I debarked at the station serving the Versailles concentration camp, pardon, replacement depot. But I was hungry again, so I was polite but firm with the T-5 jeep driver–guide. "Never mind the reporting in to headquarters, where's the mess?"

"The third building over there, sir. But you are supposed to—"

"Just take me to the mess and dump my gear at the BOQ, if you please. I'll report in after supper."[8]

"OK, sir, but the CO said—"

"Thanks a lot, corporal."

I dismounted and entered the mess where four-score young men were industriously stowing away their viands. I noted that the portions seemed adequate, probably because the mess did not have to split the ration to support a hotel staff and their immediate relatives. A few bus girls, no waiters, a cafeteria, so I went forward to the counter, picking up a tray and tools.

"We stop serving at 1800, sir," firmly announced the surly mess sergeant with impeccable military courtesy and obvious pleasure. I glanced at my watch, 1814. Oh oh, here we go again. I dropped the tray, vaulted the counter, and confronted the apparently apprehensive sergeant.

"[Illegible] and tell the commanding officer that he is to report to me at once."

The man did not break into a gallop as I had requested, but he did shuffle away at a reasonable speed, so I turned to the openmouthed cook who had been cutting up a hindquarter of beef for tomorrow's stew.

"Gimme that knife," I requested, and took the blade from his paralyzed fingers. He shrank away while I inexpertly hacked a goodly two-pound slab from the posterior portion of the mid-thigh.

"Fry that, rare, and warm up something to go with it," I asked, and he turned out a very nice meal, anything to humor this starving maniac.

Front Line Unit

I was well into my steak, eggs, and home-fried potatoes, when a very fit-looking colonel of engineers took a seat across the table. The mess sergeant was back in his domain behind the counter, conferring sotto voce with my cooperative cook, both staring wide-eyed in our direction. "I'm Colonel Raynes, depot commander," the big, sandy-complexioned colonel announced. "I understand that you wanted to see me."

"Triplet. Yes, I do. I don't like the way I've been received here. When I arrived three hours and fourteen minutes late through no fault of my own your mess sergeant announced that I would get nothing for dinner. Here's a copy of my orders, directing me to report to the Versailles R.D. It's your responsibility to see that new arrivals are fed and bedded down, and I suggest that you orient your mess crew. That's why I sent for you."

"Ah yes, Colonel Triplet. The general telephoned me about you. You seem to be unhappy with the replacement depot system. How would you like to go to a front line unit?" The question was apparently asked as a threat, as the German Oberst would ask the infanterie Leutnant, "Do you want to be sent to the Russian front?"

"That's what I came over here for. I'm two years late already."

The colonel seemed taken aback by my reply, but recovered nicely. "All right. I'll start inquiring about a slot for you, and tomorrow you can draw any clothing and equipment you need. My S-4, Major Burns, will pick you up here at breakfast."

And so he did. The major was a short, well-muscled, bouncy ball of fire, a vivid redhead. He was astounded by my order for immediate processing. "You sure must have a drag with the top brass, colonel. A replacement usually takes a week to a couple of months before he gets an assignment. But you went to the top of the list last night and I'm holding a place for you on the courier run tonight."

"I hadn't heard about the courier. Where are we going?"

"Oh, didn't Colonel Raynes tell you? It's Ninth Army, somewhere up in Holland."

Ninth Army, oh yes, General Simpson and the class of 1924. By God, I did have friends in high places after all. OK, I didn't disillusion Major Burns. Having friends in the top brass responsible for my preferred progress toward the front was more believable than the real reason, a thwarted appetite and consequently poisonous disposition.

I drew a helmet, pistol, web equipment, and map case. I bought a pair of combat boots, but couldn't get overshoes; they didn't have my size.[9]

I needed a new long overcoat but was a bit short of funds, and hoped that my ancient short overcoat would hold out until payday. If it didn't I could draw a field jacket. But I'd sure keep my eye out for a pair of overshoes when I joined the Ninth.

On returning to my billet I found my orders to Ninth Army in Maastricht, Holland.

The courier proved to be a three-quarter-ton truck carrying bags of mail and unclassified crud, a trio of infantry lieutenants, and me. Everyone else called it the courier—I called it Raynes's Revenge.

All through the frigid night we zigzagged hither and yon through rain and fog, stopping briefly at innumerable headquarters, dropping off a sack of this and taking on a bag of that. And on through a miserable day with a short halt in midmorning for a brunch. The driver and his supercargo assistant spelled each other at the wheel, the passengers endured.

The next afternoon on arriving at an imposing chateau in Luxembourg the supercargo sergeant announced a rest stop. Hurrah. We had supper at 1500 and went to bed. I was pleasantly surprised to be assigned to a very well-appointed guest room, where I took off my boots and dropped unconscious in the depths of a featherbed.

Up at 2200, breakfast, and we resumed our travail, our tour of France, Luxembourg, Belgium, and Holland.

About 1100 on December 16, I reported to General Simpson, who had his headquarters in Maastricht. He had been my onetime boss on the West Coast when I was turning tankers and armored artillery units into armored amphibians, and was gratifyingly glad to see me. Moore, Mead, and Hundley were still the working members of the Ninth Army staff.

At lunch the guest of honor was General Bonesteel, who had been a member of the B Board (Buckner, Butcher, Bonesteel, and Baker) that determined the fate of cadets who were chronic offenders against the restrictive regulations of the Military Academy in the early twenties.[10] He entertained us with his version of my case when I had accumulated a total of 308 demerits (300 was the allowable limit) on the first day of June Week, immediately before graduation. Instead of discharge for disciplinary reasons, the board voted to convert ten demerits to punishment tours. So I marched back and forth across the south area throughout June Week while my bride-to-be was entertained by my erstwhile friends. I graduated with 298 demerits (a record), an imposing set of blisters, and a young lady who felt neglected. The board had found it most amusing, and present company did as well. I didn't.

The soup course was interrupted by the *aka-put-a-put* sound of a one-lung motorcycle engine approaching overhead. All hands except

Bonesteel and I, who were both new arrivals, froze and listened intently. The sound stopped immediately above us. General Simpson laid down his spoon, patted his lips with his napkin, folded it, and placed it beside his plate. "Gentlemen, I suggest we adjourn to the hallway," he remarked, and leisurely led the procession. I was mystified but unquestioningly followed suit. A vague feeling of panic caused me to step on Bonesteel's heels, since I was the last man in the column, just like a herd-bound horse. We grouped in the hallway and waited.

"Buzz bomb," announced Hundley for my information.[11]

The windows rattled, the house quivered, and a sullen boom announced that the bomb had landed some distance beyond. We filed back and finished an uninterrupted meal.

After lunch General Simpson told me about my assignment. "You'll go to the Second Armored Division. You know Ernie Harmon, don't you? He's asked for a cavalry colonel to command a tank regiment, but there just aren't any cavalrymen available at present. Then your name came up. You have been in tanks for some time before the amphibs, according to your records."

"Yes sir, tank school 1929–30, Second Tank Regiment 1930–32, Sixty-seventh Infantry (medium tanks) 1934–36, Thirteenth Armored Division trains 1942–43, Forty-fifth Tank Regiment 1943, Eighteenth Armored Group (amphibians) 1943–44."

"Well, you should know as much about tanks as a cavalryman. The cavalry didn't get interested in armor until they had to turn their horses out to pasture in 1935. So we'll send you to the Second. Moore should have your orders cut by now. Good luck."

Hundley had a jeep standing by, and I was off to Baesweiler, where the command post of the Second Armored Division was located. We entered Germany, my fifth country in forty-eight hours. On crossing the border it was evident that German resistance had stiffened. The towns and villages were completely ruined, just burned-out walls and piles of rubble remaining. The CP in Baesweiler was located in a large tunnel that had been improved as a bomb-proof command post by the Germans.

General Harmon had been a drawing instructor at the Military Academy in the twenties and recalled me as being one of his more inept students in mapping and military sketching. I recalled him as the small, dark major who x-ed out my most serious mistakes and erasures, critiqued my sketches in a voice like a ton of coal rattling down a metal chute, and gave me a passing grade in spite of my obvious lack of talent. He talked over my past experiences and told me to take a few days to get acquainted with the division in general. "They're a fighting lot of sonsabitches, lots of dash and go. Captured and cleared the west bank of the Roer last week, lost fifty-four tanks. The Forty-first Armored Infantry is manning the Roer River line now, while the tank regiments are refitting and resting. We'll probably cross the Roer in the near future, so I want you to take a good look at the crossing points and at the Linnich-Elsdorf area."

At the evening mess I was seated on General Harmon's left, with the general and special staff officers ranged on each side of a long table in the tunnel. The moment Harmon entered the mess he went through an amazing personality change. His gravelly voice dominated, no, it was the conversation, and every sentence included one or more unacceptable forms of speech, adjectives and adverbs that would be unacceptable not only in an officers mess but suicidal if used in a waterfront saloon. A sample:

"Wells, you incompetent sonofabitch, have you got those replacement tanks up yet?"

"Thirty-one have been processed and distributed, sir. Ordnance says—"

"I don't give a good goddamn about ordnance. You light a fire under your a— and get those tanks."

"Yes sir" was the answer, with a slight smirk.

"Ellwood, I saw your draft of that letter to army and sent it back for a complete rewrite. You're a weaseling bastard, Ellwood, and if you can't —— I'll get somebody that can."

"Yes sir." And Harmon's wit was rewarded with a painful smile.

I do not propose to reproduce any of Harmon's conversation in full. I'll just say that while I have associated with soldiers, merchant seamen, bums, and hoboes, I have never heard such a constant stream of insulting and filthy language, the like of which would have cost him blood in any other environment. By the end of the meal I had a growing pain in my belly and I was wondering what the penalty would be for busting the nose of a major general. But the chief of staff and I were spared.

Later that evening I was still wondering about the reason for General Harmon's way of talking in public; was he trying to make his staff feel at home, prove that he was just one of the boys, show that they were close enough to him to eliminate the need for courtesy, or demonstrate what a vocabulary of bad words he had?

Ah yes, I had it. He had been a protégé and disciple of General Patton, who had the mistaken impression that soldiers and Reserve officers were only able to understand and were favorably impressed by earthy (profane, obscene, and filthy) language. He had been a good pupil, succeeding in reaching the same depths as his idol.

At the mess that evening the general was in a festive mood. We were entertained by thrilling and bloodcurdling tales of adventures, heroism, and derring-do. The incidents recited by Harmon in his soldier–Reserve officer vocabulary far exceeded anything I'd ever experienced in World War I—all we'd ever done was charge machine guns on foot. Just "let's go" and we went, mostly at a fast walk.

"—so I jumped up on his tank and said, 'Goddamn you sergeant, you yellow-bellied bastard, haul your a— up on that ridge and get your goddamn gunner on those tanks.'

"Then he turned around and shook his fist under my nose and said, 'Get your a— off my tank, you sonofabitch!'" (The sergeant had my complete sympathy at this point.)

"Well, any sergeant that can call a major general a sonofabitch to his face must have a lot of guts, so I got off his tank and he pushed up there and shot four Mark IVs with six rounds."

By the end of the meal I was doubtful if I could ever measure up to the speed, gallantry, and cavalry dash of the Second Armored Division, and I was certain that I could never call a sergeant tank commander a yellow-bellied bastard.

Nine.

Taking Command

Look Over

Early next morning I was taking off in the rear seat of an L-5 artillery observation plane to look over our front lines, the Roer River bridge, and possible crossing points, the German front, and the probable objectives of the next attack—Linnich, Juelich, and Elsdorf. I'd been briefed on the plan of attack the night before—infantry crossings, engineer bridges (the bridge still standing would probably be destroyed or too heavily defended and in any case would funnel our attack), and assault by infantry-tank task forces. The plan was compete in detail, all except the date.

"Why can't we have a date and time of attack?"

"It depends on the First Army taking control of the Roer River dams upstream in their area."

"What have they got to do with us?"

"There is a lot of water impounded in those dams. Suppose we start our attack while they're still under German control. The Krauts open the sluices or blow the dams at the right time, when a third or a half of our force is across the river, a fifteen-foot wall of water boils down that steel-banked channel, we lose our bridges and they wipe out everybody on their side while we can't do a damned thing to help them. We could lose a lot of tanks that way."

"I see, obvious, we wait on the First Army."

Yes, I could see the difficulties of the Roer crossing in this area. The river appeared to be a mere trickle but the banks looked like a miniature Grand Canyon from our three-thousand-foot altitude and the switchbacks on the approaches to the lone bridge confirmed that they were steep. Why hadn't the Krauts blown the bridge? They left it in place as a tempting bait to the trap, of course.

I could see nothing of the Forty-first Infantry positions on the west bank, and not a sign of the German outposts on the other side. Camouflage discipline on both sides was excellent.

"See that Mark IV, colonel? He rammed through the back of that farmhouse. You can see the gun sticking out the window—that house right in the center of our turn."

"I see the house, the one that looks like a tornado had gone through it, but damned if I can see the tank."

"OK. I'll drop to a thousand," and we spiraled down to within three hundred yards so I could get a good look. Next time I'd think before I talked.

"See it now?"

"Oh yes, yes, I see it." That was a damned lie. I still saw nothing but a pile of wreckage but anything to get away from there.

"I got that one yesterday. About the third salvo and she went up like a Roman candle. Wanta take a look at the Linnich-Elsdorf line now?"

I certainly did not want to see the Linnich-Juelich line from this altitude. As an infantry-tanker, a ground-oriented soldier, hanging up there in plain sight of the invisible German army was horrifying. But if this carefree young idiot could do it—so I lied again.

"Yes, I'd like to see their rear areas. But I think we should get a little higher, get a broader view."

"OK, I'll take her up to five again."

As we spiraled up over Linnich, I wondered about the callous unconcern of this suicidal maniac. "By the way, don't the Germans ever bother you?" I asked.

"Nah, they're scared to shoot at me."

During my experience with the Germans of the World War some twenty-five years before I had generally found that they weren't scared to shoot at anything or anybody and usually did. So I kept the subject open. "Why? You're not even carrying a pistol."

"Any time one of the bastards shoots at me I drop a battalion of artillery on him and if that doesn't settle him I can borrow two or three more battalions to pulverize the area."

"Oh, I see." Again I hadn't thought. When a rifleman or machine gunner was answered by eighteen to seventy-two cannon directed by an observer with a bird's-eye view he would be reluctant to expose himself to such retaliation. Like swatting a fly with a sledgehammer.

We continued cruising while I compared the map with the ground, the road net, and the ruins of the three villages below. Still couldn't see any signs of the enemy. Even tanks and trucks must be concealed under nets, in ruins, or have haystacks built over them.

A sudden series of rough air bumps tossed us about. I thought that perhaps the Jerry gunners weren't quite as scared of us as my young friend believed. And for some reason this sudden turbulence frightened my pilot as well as me. He straightened out with full power, shook his fist toward our own lines, and shouted, "Goddamn you bastards! Watch where you're shootin'!" He explained his outburst. "Those sonsabitches (apparently our own artillery observers) ought to be able to see that we're in their trajectory. Last week one of our ships just blew up and another one came back with a 105-mm. hole right through the fuselage. Damned carelessness."

I agreed—criminal carelessness.

A tinny voice over the radio: "Oboe King William from Peter Zebra How—Oboe King William—over."

From the pilot—"Peter Zebra How—this is Oboe King William—send your message—over."

Voice: "Oboe King William—enemy aircraft in your area—over."

Pilot: "Roger on your message—out."

He stood the plane on one wing.

"Say, colonel, would you like to look around and see if there's anybody behind us?"

He sideslipped and dived to a ground-grazing level and hedge-hopped toward the friendly side of the Roer while I strained my neck trying to look over both shoulders at once.

Voice: "Oboe King William from Peter Zebra How—Oboe King William—over."

Pilot: "Peter Zebra How—this is Oboe King William—send your message—over."

Voice: "Oboe King William—all clear in your area—over."

Pilot: "Roger on your message—out."

We zoomed up from our hedge-clipping level to a more comfortable four thousand feet and resumed our patrol of the German lines.

"Let me know when you're ready to go back to the field, colonel."

"Oh, I don't want to cut your observation mission short."

"My only mission is to show you everything you want to see in the area."

Dear Lord. The general's directive that I was to accompany an artillery observer on an observation flight had completely misled me. Instead of being a deadhead passenger I was supposed to be directing the flight. Ten seconds later we were headed for home.

The CO of the artillery battalion came up as I was getting my fear-weakened legs under me again.

"Congratulations, colonel. I'm reporting you as having qualified for one-fifth of a Distinguished Flying Cross."

"A Distinguished Flying Cross has the lowest priority on the list of medals I covet, major. I'll never make it. Scared the hell out of me. I'll do my reconnoitering in future on tracks, wheels, or my own flat feet."

Next day, escorted by a captain of the G-3 staff, I cruised about the division area, looking over the defensive outposts of the Forty-first on the river, observing the Jerry lines from our forward CPs, getting acquainted with various commanders, and inspecting the German armored vehicles that had been destroyed or captured the week before. I was impressed by the massive simplicity of the German Tiger tank, well-sloped heavy armor, the powerful 88-mm. gun, and the wide track. The neat lines of the Panther with its sloped armor and muzzle-braked 75-mm. were even more attractive. The Panther tracks appeared to be 50 percent wider than those of our M4s.[1]

"This one looks like it could move as well as shoot," I remarked.

"Yes sir. The Panther is probably the best tank built. It's fast, agile, and has a low ground pressure. Diesel engine, so it doesn't explode if a fuel tank is hit—gives the crew a chance to get out. Frontal armor sloped so that we see our shells bounce off. That high-velocity 75 will go through our apron or turret on the M4, and the muzzle brake shoots the smoke to each side so the gunner can shoot as fast as the loader can shove the ammunition. The only way we can take a Panther or a Tiger is to keep him interested in front and sneak a tank or tank destroyer around to hit him in the side."

We also visited a tank destroyer unit that was quite proud of their new equipment, the high-velocity 76-mm. guns mounted on the turretless M4 chassis. The tank destroyers had come a long way since I first mounted a 37-mm. gun on half of a truck axle welded to the frame of a four-wheel-steered jeep at Benning in 1942. And since the major role of tanks appeared to be fighting other tanks, in my opinion the tank destroyer was really becoming the best tank.[2]

Ardennes

On December 18 the principal topic of discussion in the mess was a large-scale raid that the Germans were making in the Ardennes against the Twenty-eighth and 106th Divisions. It wouldn't amount to much, of course, just annoying, and might interfere with leaves to Paris. The raid might be a strong feint to cover a large-scale attack across the Roer against the British or the American corps immediately on our left.[3]

Next morning General Harmon assigned me to the Sixty-sixth Armored Regiment. "You'll take over from Cross. He's been in command since Barker was killed last week. Cross is a Reserve officer but he's a damned good cavalryman. I'll have him stay with you for a week to show you around."

I moved to the regimental command post at Elsdorf, where I was welcomed by Lieutenant Colonel Cross. He was a tall, languid, washed-out blond welterweight wearing a bored expression and the ubiquitous yellow scarf of the Indian-chasing cavalry.

Damn. I wish I'd brought a scarf, either the infantry blue or the green one I was planning to make regulation wear for the armored amphibians. But come to think of it, the armored force colors were blue (infantry), yellow (cavalry), and red (artillery). Mix these three colors and you get black (armored force). I'd keep my eye out for a yard of black silk and start a new fashion.

Cross and I spent the day visiting the units of the Sixty-sixth, getting acquainted with their commanders. I wanted to get the feel of the general tone of the regiment. They all talked a most convincing game, but noting their indiscipline in maintenance, supply, and dress, I wondered. The same was true of the regimental staff officers whom I met at work and in the mess. There were many yarns about past heroic derring-do and too much talk about the invincibility of the Tiger tanks and the penetrating power of the 88-mm. gun: "—hell of a clank. Went right through that M4, through the half-track behind it, wrecked a jeep and kept right on going," was a typical description.

That night we were called to CCA headquarters where I met Brigadier General Collier, a small, sour, apprehensive-appearing brunet.[4] Also present were Major Evans, a chunky, sleepy-looking blond who commanded the second battalion of the Forty-first Infantry Regiment, and a captain of tank destroyers, both attached to CCA for combat operations.

Collier briefed us on the current situation. The German feint was continuing in the Ardennes with a view to drawing units from the Ninth Army southward to reinforce the First Army. The main attack was expected against the British sector north of us, with the probability that the enemy would break through and cut southwest across our rear areas toward Aachen or Liége. It was generally believed that the Germans would secure the left flank of their drive by seizing the steel manufacturing towns to our rear.

The probable mission of the Sixty-sixth (less two battalions, with the second battalion of the Forty-first Infantry attached) was to counterattack and capture the slag heaps of steel mills that might be in the hands of the enemy. These slag heaps by their height dominated the flat country for miles around and would give the possessor the advantage of observed artillery fire to the extreme limits of range.

Next day Cross, Evans, Major Jones (commanding second battalion of the Sixty-sixth), and I toured the rear areas, visiting three large smelting plants. General Collier was right, the slag heaps were important, and the longer we studied them the more formidable they seemed. Visualize flat-topped mountains, one hundred to three hundred feet high, the top being one to three city blocks in extent. The slope of the sides was established by the free fall of slag and ashes. The soft, sliding footing would be extremely difficult for foot troops and impossible for tanks— like quicksand. The flat tops of the slag heaps provided no cover and could be perfectly swept by machine-gun fire, so even when footing on the top was secured the clearing of the top would be difficult if the German garrison wanted to keep up the fight.

I gave up thinking about assaulting the slopes—the logical action would be to capture the smelter building, then attack the slag heap via the narrow-gauge rail lines used by the slag dump cars. I didn't like being confined to one approach, but it seemed to be the only solution, and supported by mortars and artillery and using a smoke screen would probably be economical.

That night, December 20, we were again called to CCA headquarters and we received our first intimation of the serious situation that was developing in the Ardennes. Collier stated that the raid in the First Army sector appeared to be building up. The Seventh Armored Division had been transferred from Ninth to First Army and had moved south to St. Vith. We would probably move into First Army reserve south of Huy, starting the next evening. Radio silence was ordered throughout the march.

At 1800 on December 21 my task force left our prescribed initial point and moved south on the prescribed route. The night was black, the temperature was way down, and the overcast skies dripped a heavy drizzle. The glow-worm gleam of the blackout light on the vehicle ahead varied in visibility from collision to invisible. With the radio silence the only knowledge we had of progress and of our units was gained by jeep patrolling, and after narrowly escaping the treads of a medium tank for the third time I stopped patrolling, much to the relief of my driver.

Our rate of march averaged four to five miles an hour—our speed varied from zero to a frantic fifteen miles per hour. In toto it was the saddest caricature of a motor march in which it has ever been my misfortune to take part.

About 1000 the next morning we closed on Odet and bivouacked, having made seventy-two miles in eighteen hours. Four miles an hour. We could have walked.

On checking over the units, I found Major Jones and his staff concerned only with the comparative softness of the featherbeds in the house assigned to them. I interrupted their research. "How does your battalion stand, major?"

"All present except 7 Company, sir."

"What are you doing to locate them?"

"Nothing—there's a radio silence on. All we can do is wait for them to show up."

"I know there's a radio silence on. But there are the provost marshal, the MP guides, and your own jeep patrols that you can send out to locate them. So let's stop testing the beds until you've located and led them in."

"Yes sir." He was obviously resentful of my unreasonable requirement—the missing tank company would show up sooner or later. But with half of my armor God knows where I'd be somewhat concerned. I was. He wasn't, but left to direct the search.

About noon a telephoned order directed me to be at the division CP at Chateau de Bouillon at 1400. On arriving I met Brigadier General White of CCB. I had met him at the First Army maneuvers in New York in 1935 when he was in charge of the cavalry's combat cars—three Christie tanks, siblings of our platoon, "Tornado," "Hurricane," and "Cyclone." But as a jeep in the cavalry is called a peep, a tank (basically an infantry weapon) was called a combat car.

When all combat and task force commanders were assembled in the war room, the S-3 began to brief us on the situation, but before he had finished his first sentence an officer entered and began talking excitedly to General Harmon.[5] The general called me, led me to an adjoining sun porch, and unfurled a map. "Triplet, boil down the road with everything you've got and grab Ciney—here."

"What is the situation there, sir?"

"I don't know but there's no time to waste. They're coming up from the southeast, through Rochefort. Grab Ciney and deploy across these three roads."

Speed seemed to be essential, so I cranked the nearby field phone and went through three switchboards to get S-3 at my task force. For security reasons my message had to be carefully worded. "S-3, this is your six.[6] Listen carefully and take this message. 'Boots and saddles!' " That ought to mean something to a cavalryman. "March order—tactical, heavy stuff leading. All hands prepared to move out immediately in same direction. Commanders meet me at the CP."

I left at a gallop, putting my winter gear on in the jeep. Then a study of the map, looking over Ciney, the routes I could take, the possible lines of enemy approach, and the defensive positions I should occupy.

On arriving at Odet, I began to get acquainted with the foot-dragging that was characteristic of veteran units and certainly of the Hell on Wheels Division as I observed it.[7] As I entered the bivouac area, instead of the readiness for immediate departure that I expected I saw the normal activity of maintenance, eating, and bedding down. Crews were not mounted and engines were silent.

Majors Jones and Evans were at the CP with the staff.

"Why aren't these people ready to move out, major?" I asked S-3. "Didn't you understand that I wanted them mounted up and ready to roll?"

"Yes sir, I gave them your message. But we aren't organized for a tactical march in task forces. And we could not interpret the order for all hands to move in the same direction."

I just couldn't believe what I was hearing. Never had I encountered such a total lack of initiative in officers. "Don't you have an SOP for task forces? And don't you know the same direction you've been moving in for the past twenty-four hours? And do you have to interpret 'immediately'? Now get to this—"

At this point General Harmon came on the phone. "Triplet, Harmon speaking. Do you have anything on the way yet?"

"No sir, I'm just giving the march order."

"Never mind the march order. Get going now. There are eight million gallons of gasoline in Ciney and a German column moving toward it. They must not get it. Now go."

It was a very clear order—didn't need interpretation. I resumed giving mine. "Jones, get your men mounted and wind up your engines. Lead them out on this road to the crossroad where I'll meet you. Lieutenant, follow the tanks with your destroyers. Evans, you follow the tank destroyers. I'll lead you into position and give you further orders in Ciney. Now take off and get under way, immediately."

The jeep driver and I threw our personal plunder aboard. The last word, about the headquarters. "Major, I'll be with the leading company. You bring up the headquarters at the tail of the infantry and set up at the main crossroad in Ciney."

Moved out to the crossroad, nothing in sight. Some tank engines were roaring in the village, but no column was being formed and our preparation to "boil down the road and grab Ciney" had stretched from "immediately" to an hour and a quarter. Went back to the tank battalion command post where I found Major Jones giving his company commanders and staff a five-paragraph field order complete with questions and administrative details. Most commendable in a tank school tactical problem. But not now. "Jones, get your people onto their tanks and meet me at the crossroad, now."

"Yes sir. F Company lead out."

Captain F said "Yes sir" and departed at a run. This young man was one of the very few rays of sunshine in an otherwise dark period. I regret that I never learned his name.

Boiling Down the Road

With things starting to commence to begin to move I returned to the crossroad, and five minutes later the leading platoon of F Company rolled up and I took off toward Verlee, Havelange, and Ciney at twenty miles an hour, the top reasonable speed for M4 tanks. Any faster and the rubber tires would heat up on the bogies, probably blow out, and I'd wind up short of the objective with a lot of barefooted or crippled tanks.

The terrain was a series of low, rolling hills, with small clumps of woods scattered along the route. Good tank country and good ambush country too.

Leading the column by a quarter of a mile or so in my jeep, waving them up to speed, I recalled the German tanks I'd seen littering the Baesweiler area and wondered what the hell I'd do if we bellied up to a Panther when we topped the next crest. God knows where the German column would be after all this delay. And what in hell was I doing out here acting like an infantry squad leader? As a regimental commander, presently task force commander, I couldn't run this outfit from the rear, like pushing a strand of well-coiled vermicelli.

Through Havelange into Ciney at last. We'd beaten them to it.

I ordered Captain F to deploy on the line Hill 300-Ferme de Tersot a thousand meters south of town. Caught Major Jones and directed him to deploy his remaining company on the high ground across the Leignon and Fays roads. The tank destroyer platoon was held at the crossroad in Ciney as our reserve to support either attacked flank. The rifle companies with their split-up portions of the heavy weapons company were dispatched to join their opposite numbers of the tanks, and headquarters was established in the town square. Forming balanced sub-tank forces on the fly like that is something I didn't want to do in the future, and I intended to make a change in my staff after this brouhaha, get somebody that didn't have to have orders interpreted and who would start action on his own.

But now we were fairly well deployed with Task Force Jones on the right and Task Force Evans on the left, no Germans in sight, and I could breathe easier.

Radio message to Big Six, "In position."

The division provost marshal rolled into the square with a platoon of tanks that he had brought over from the division area and that would be a most welcome reserve.

I would have preferred to deploy farther out from town and hold out a real reserve, but considering that I might have to fight on any or all of four routes of approach I had to spread them close initially. I'd pull out a reserve platoon with supporting infantry from the unengaged force as soon as the situation developed.

At 1630 an officer of the G-3 section of CCA jeeped into the square. "General Collier directs you to seize Leignon, this village three kilometers south of Ciney," was the message.

Jones was holding the road fifteen hundred yards from Leignon, so I directed him to move part of his force into the town and ordered Evans to move abreast via Trisogne. Both movements to start at 1700.

Just after this order was issued a British major reported as the liaison officer from a British tank brigade. "We're on the Spontin road just west of Ciney," he said. "Four battalions of Churchills."

"We're going to move forward a bit (pointing the moves out on the map) at 1700. Glad to have you with us. What are you going to do?"

"Oh, we will no doubt drop back a few kilometers and regroup," which no doubt they did. At least we didn't see any British tanks at any time during the Ardennes. But that was all right with me. The flat, square-cut Churchill looks too much at first fear-glazed glance like a German type to be safe. There was a very real danger that with the British operating near us considerable unfortunate shooting might take place between allies. With the British falling back to regroup, we would be at liberty to shoot at anything that moved to our front or flanks.

I moved out to join Evans's force and checked on Jones by radio. Orders—reconnaissance—reports—more orders—more reconnaissance. Delay, confusion, inertia, objection, and reclama. First "there is a whole lot of stuff in that town." Now "it's getting too dark to move in." Finally, an hour late, both forces were on the way, Jones entering Leignon and Evans on the high ground one thousand yards east of and overlooking the town.

Came 1900. Jones seemed to be making no progress, so I directed Evans to move his force in and secure the eastern half of the village.

"Yes sir, but the tanks can't go in there without infantry, and the infantry are all back there," indicating the rear of the column where the riflemen were asleep in their half-tracks.

"Well for Chris—they're your men. Get them up here with their tanks and get your outfit underway."

So F Company of the Forty-first was dismounted, brought forward, briefed, and dispatched in advance guard formation down the road toward the village that maintained a menacing black silence.

About this time, 2000, two cannon shots crashed in Leignon and sprays of ricocheting red tracers arched through the sky. Shortly thereafter Jones reported that he had arrived in the center of town and had destroyed a German roadblock. I moved in with Evans's riflemen, met Major Jones at the railroad crossing, and inspected the nearby roadblock. It consisted of one 75-mm. antitank gun sited at the main four-road junction just south of the railroad crossing. The Germans had fired at our leading tank and missed. The tank had fired a shell and a couple of quarts of machine-gun bullets at them and missed. Rifle patrols reported the town clear of Germans.

The bloodless battle of Leignon was over.

I called General Collier. "We have the objective."

"Good. Now move on down the road through Chapois and Haid and occupy Forzee. Hold those two road junctions immediately northeast of Forzee."

"What is the enemy situation?"

"No definite information on the enemy other than the Rochefort column and the group you ran out of Leignon. But if you meet resistance you can call on the —th armored artillery for support. Their observer should be reporting to you by now, and the battalion will displace forward as required to cover your advance."

I assembled the commanders, gave them the situation and the mission, and prescribed the order of march—Task Force Evans, tank destroyers, command post, Task Force Jones. Evans to put out an advance guard of riflemen. All other infantry to be in carriers and following the tank they support or riding on the tank.

The artillery observer joined us, we finally got started at 2100, and passed through Chapois without incident. I waited at the Chapois road junction until Evans's force had cleared and the destroyers had passed. When the headquarters vehicles showed up I left the jeep and mounted "Tar Baby," the M5 light command tank, and told the driver to push up to the point, passing as he could. This wasn't nearly as dangerous as it might seem; preceded by the infantry of the advance guard, we averaged one and one-half miles an hour with tanks and other vehicles merely idling forward in low gear.

We had passed the Ferme de la Happe and Tar Baby was pulling up to the leading platoon leader's tank when both tanks ahead halted. "What's going on, lieutenant?" I asked, keeping my voice down on a level appropriate to the vanguard.

"Don't know, sir, the doughs passed the signal to halt."

I pulled down into the turret and turned on the fifteen-watt bulb for a look at the map. Ah yes, the riflemen were reconnoitering Haid, a village that started three hundred yards around the road bend that we had just passed. Since we had made slow but steady progress since leaving Leignon, I did not want to interfere unnecessarily and waited more or less patiently. Dead silence except for the murmur of idling exhausts.

There was a sudden volley followed by a steady rattle of small-arms fire from the advance guard. The leading pair of tanks fired several rounds straight down the road ahead from their side-by-side position. The rifle fire sputtered down and fizzled out.

"Driver, pull off to the side so we can see what's going on."

We pulled out of the road and up on a bank where I was able to see a Volkswagen, a Kubelwagen, and a truck blazing between us and the first houses in Haid. Silhouetted against the flames a small double column of Germans was stumbling toward us, most of them with their hands clasped on their heads, others supporting wounded between them. Thirty-six total. Two more German vehicles were apparently abandoned in Haid.

F Company of the Forty-first was deploying astride the road on the forward slope, taking cover along a stone fence on the left and in an orchard on the right. They had done well in this skirmish. The scouts of the point squad had heard a motorized column approaching in time to warn the advance party. Captain F had deployed his men in the roadside ditch on the right and directed them to lie still and hold fire until he gave the command. The Germans driving without lights had unsuspectingly moved ahead until the lead vehicle was no more than fifty yards from our first tank. Not until the German advance guard was well within his net did the captain shout "Fire!" The resulting blast was annihilating. We had lost only one man, Captain F himself, a caliber 50 machine-gun bullet through the thigh from one of our tank-mounted guns. But the loss of one of our three best officers in the outfit really hurt.[8]

Unfortunately, the German column had been much too long to be really hurt—we'd captured only the advance guard. The growl and snarling of engines and the clank of steel tracks could be heard from the village ahead. I called Evans and Jones up. "Evans, you've hurt them and scared them badly. Sounds to me like they're backing up. Now is the time to push ahead and hit them while they're off balance."

"But sir, I've been checking on F Company and they're not in shape to go in there in the dark. Maybe if the captain hadn't been hit—"

"Jones, then you can deploy, leapfrog Evans, and turn them out of Haid. We'll have the artillery do some blasting while you're getting set."

"Colonel, my tankers just aren't about to go in there at night, finding mines by running over and exploding them and Panzerfausts shooting out of the windows, and the doughs wouldn't want to move in without the tanks right with them.[9] These men haven't rested or slept for forty hours or so. It's almost midnight now. Give them six hours and they'll be ready to go to hell and back by dawn. I recommend that we settle down till daylight and get some rest in the meanwhile."

Actually it wasn't all that dark. The night was clear and cold, fearfully cold, the nearer houses in the village and the threatening mass of woods on our left flank could be seen from our position. I made one more effort. "We give the Krauts six hours to dig in and it will take the whole damned division to dig them out."

"But we'll be able to shoot when it gets light and we'll have the artillery to dig them out, sir," reclaimed Jones.

"And the men are tired, awfully tired," added Evans.

So it went. It was the reverse of the Infantry School saying, "A soldier can always advance one more step and fire one more shot." It rather confirmed the General Staff School statement that "There are more tired commanders than tired soldiers."

Well, this wasn't the Infantry School—it was the fiery, dashing, cavalry-indoctrinated armored force of fightin' sonsabitches according to General Harmon, and the only way we were going to move into Haid was for me to drive them in at pistol point or draw pistol and clear the town myself—either solution being ridiculous. I gave up.

"We settle down here. Get your vehicles off the road and deploy your infantry, Jones, with security to your flanks. Evans, your riflemen are in a good position on the military crest to cover the town. Deploy your tanks to cover them. And see that mass of woods over there, four hundred yards left flank? Outpost that. And send out a patrol to see what actually is in and beyond Haid. Arrange security. The rest sleep as much as they can. Reveille at 0430. We move in on them at 0500."

"Yes sir," they chorused.

At this point I noticed a ragged movement to the rear by the riflemen on the left of the road. "Evans, get your people under control." I didn't wait for him. I swung up on Tar Baby and spoke to the driver. "Driver, move out into the field on the left where those men are moving back." He drove to where a cluster of men were moving up the slope to the rear. "Halt right there. Who's in charge?"

The riflemen huddled on the friendly side of Tar Baby and a tall young man with a carbine came up from the left flank. "Lieutenant Blank, sir."

"Lieutenant, did you have orders to fall back?"

"No sir, but the men felt too exposed on this forward slope and want to move back behind the hill so they will be protected by the tanks. We can hear tank tracks clanking down there in town. There's a lot of stuff in there."

Major Evans came up at that point, so I turned the matter over to him and wheeled Tar Baby back to the command post. There was a rattle of machine guns to the rear—by God! The Krauts are throwing a right hook into us! I directed the driver to move back to Jones's CP. The firing stopped as abruptly as it had started. "Jones, what was that firing about? Are you under attack?"

"No sir. Nobody seems to know. All my lot say it sounded in a different direction. I personally think somebody just got spooky and cut loose a few bursts and won't admit it."

I learned more about it days later at division headquarters when I checked on our claim for thirty-six prisoners in that skirmish. The graves registration officer was most bitter about it. "Why don't your people just line 'em up if they're going to shoot 'em?" he asked. "Making them run like that and droppin' 'em all over the landscape just makes a lot of unnecessary work."

Ten.

They've Got a Lot of Stuff in There

Forzee

My command tank, Tar Baby, was an M5 light. The armor was bullet proof, but anything bigger than a .50 caliber would go through her as though she was built of tissue paper. The turret was cramped, containing a gun that we would never use, a radio that I loathed, ammunition racks, and sharp corners that gave the crew bone bruises when we scuttled from cover to cover at a gallop. With a full crew of five she was the epitome of togetherness.

She had had a minor operation sometime in the dim past, probably during the African campaign, and certainly in warm weather. A hole had been cut in the bulkhead between the engine and fighting compartments, allegedly so that the fan would draw the powder smoke rapidly from the turret when the breech was opened to eject the fired cartridge case. A good idea. In hot weather, that is.

But now the result was that a goodly part of the air that cooled the engine whooshed down through the turret hatch and cooled me first. Riding in Tar Baby in the winter was like sitting in a jolting refrigerator equipped with an internal attic fan. One suffered from hypothermia from this built-in wind chill even at a standstill with the engine idling.

As soon as things quieted down I'd take her back to ordnance and have that bulkhead patched or replaced. A better idea, could some of the air flow be reversed? Hot air from the engine flowing out through the turret would make travel even in Tar Baby delightful. I'll have to see ordnance about that.

I had the three commanders up to the headquarters half-track at 0100 and issued orders for reveille at 0430, move out at 0500, order of march Jones, tank destroyers, Evans. The move would start before daylight, but the hoarfrost that was forming gave excellent visibility.

The road beyond Haid ran like a bowling alley through the defiles formed by high ground on either side, and Major Jones proposed that he send out foot patrols flanking the advance guard to prevent surprise. Since the alternative would be interminable delay while the leading tankers searched every bush with binoculars before moving, I agreed, with the proviso that patrols be relieved frequently. It would slow our advance to a crawl of a mile an hour but would obviate the possibility of ambush.

When they left to brief their officers I tried to get some sleep. Impossible. The temperature was way down and after shuddering half an hour in the track I left and climbed into Tar Baby. The tank seemed to be even colder but I endured it for a couple of hours, then got out and walked to restore circulation. Found a winterized jeep parked in the ditch, nosed up near a tree, with the plywood door open. Thought it was Jones's jeep. I'd seen him with one of the fully enclosed types. So I climbed in and closed the door, being careful not to wake the sleeping driver. I wanted to see Jones again before he leapfrogged Evans and would wait for him here.

I must have dozed for a while, came to, and by considerable peering at my phosphorescent watch saw it was 0415. Still no sign of Major Jones. It was almost time for reveille anyway, so I'd wake up the driver and ask him where the major was apt to be. I reached over to tap him on the helmet, but he wasn't wearing a helmet. It wasn't hair I was tapping either, felt like a bowl of oatmeal that had been kept in a refrigerator overnight. My God. It was brains. Now that my eyes were fully open I could see the line of 7.62-mm. holes across the scarred windshield and the crushed hood of the jeep, pushed in when the driver released the wheel and the vehicle jammed into the tree and bounced back.

"Excuse me." Asinine, but automatic reaction.

I climbed out and went forward to the track.

"Major Evans says his patrol reported that Haid is clear, sir," reported S-3.

"Good. So we won't have to go in shooting after all. Major Jones was notified, of course?"

"Yes sir, and the artillery registration was canceled at 0400."

Jones's force shoved through Haid in deployed formation just to be sure. I was disappointed to find only four burned-out half-tracks and staff cars and very few bodies showing as a result of our midnight brawl. The enemy had had "a lot of stuff in there" as shown by the tracks but had pulled out, with the exception of four scared but cooperative deserters who appeared, hands on heads.

I should probably have blasted the village with artillery immediately after the ambush of the vanguard, whether or not I knew it was occupied by the enemy. But I still don't like to destroy Belgian real estate or kill friendly civilians unnecessarily.

The advance was slow, the vehicles idling in low gear, and the foot patrols beating the bushes on the threatening slopes. It was a far cry from the teachings of the armored and infantry schools and for that matter very different from the élan of the combat troops of the World War.[1]

The advance guard point reached the junction with the Forzee-Haversin road at 0900. The long ridge of Hill 340 ran westward to the right of the junction. Forzee lay just over the ridge.

I pulled Tar Baby out of the column and followed by a platoon of tanks deployed fifty yards behind had the driver creep forward until I could see the roof of a house in Forzee and a steeple. "Stop."

I climbed out of the turret and stood up to get the best possible view; a head barely above the skyline shouldn't attract attention. Yes, there was Forzee, a small—no, good-sized—village.

Crack! Sounded like a stick of dynamite and exploded by my right ear. I looked around thinking that a tank behind me had fired. But no, they were backing hurriedly. Two more cracks in rapid succession in the distant left front, a tank in the advance guard platoon jumped backward six feet and a second shuddered and came to a halt, both crews were piling out and scurrying for cover. All vehicles all along the line were backing up. The foot troops had flattened or disappeared. Mortar bursts were mushrooming among them.

I then realized that the first crack had been a high-velocity shell aimed at me or at Tar Baby's turret. I had heard many 7.52-mm. bullets traveling by my ear at twenty-seven hundred feet per second but this one was probably a 75-mm. or larger, tearing a hole in the atmosphere one hundred times as big, just as fast, and close enough to wind-burn. I dropped into the turret. "Driver—back up." He backed fast. He'd heard it too and already had the gear in reverse, just waiting for me to get down off my perch.

The mortar fire was apparently not observed, the bursts wandered here and there without apparent reason, what we used to call "in God we trust" shooting, just smearing the area. I got on the radio and called Jones, Evans, Lieutenant Artillery, and Sergeant Destroyers to join me at the CP.

"Lieutenant Destroyers is out on reconnaissance, sir," the sergeant reported.

No one had seen where the antitank shells came from, just from somewhere in the direction of the village, and the mortar shells were apparently dropping straight down, so the mortar position couldn't be located.

"Well, gentlemen, it looks like we've found them. They don't have much strength or they wouldn't have fallen back this far—they would have come out and hit us. Now we're going in after them. We'll do it like this."

"Task Force Evans (less one infantry-tank platoon in reserve) to occupy the right (west) part of town to the church (exclusive).

"Task Force Jones to occupy the left (east) part of town to the church (inclusive).

"Reserve—one infantry-tank platoon from Evans and tank destroyer platoon.

"Jump-off line, this ridge, form up in turret defilade.

"Task Force Evans's heavy weapons company lay a smoke screen across the front of the village at zero hour minus five minutes. The breeze is favorable to blanket the town.

"Artillery to register on that clump of trees on the west end of the ridge and be prepared to support on call if resistance warrants it. We don't want to pulverize the place unnecessarily.

"Four riflemen to be mounted on each tank, the rest follow their tanks in their carriers.

"Zero hour 1000.

"Questions?"

There were none. Just a soggy silence. At that point Lieutenant Tank Destroyers returned from his lone reconnaissance along the ridge of Hill 340. "Colonel, I've spotted a Panther over there near the road junction just northeast of town. I'd like to take one of my guns over there where I can hit him from the side."

"Go with it. You'll save us a couple of tanks if you can hit him."

He called up one of his destroyers and guided it into position behind the crest on the right.

I gave the commanders a final word. "At 0955 smoke screen. At 1000 everybody starts and moves in fast. The sooner we get into town the less we'll get shot at. Now move out and get your people in position."

Lieutenant Destroyers was moving slowly ahead of his gun, easing it cautiously into position until the muzzle cleared the crest. A minute of pointing and consultation. One flat, powerful crack, then a column of black smoke appeared over the crest to the left, a series of muffled explosions, a display of pyrotechnics indicated that the Panther would bother us no more.

I wished I had twenty more men like Lieutenant Destroyers.

The attack or rather the movement went off very well. At 0955 the white phosphorus clouds began to slope and spread along the Haversin–Mont Gautier road just short of Forzee. At 1000 the tanks and tracks surged forward, galloped down the slope, and plunged into the cloud. We rocked across the banks and ditches of the main road with the riflemen clinging to handholds on the rear decks, then down the slope of a meadow and into the village, first through thick, white smoke, then a heavy fog.

The town was completely fogged at first, gradually fading out to a white haze. We blundered about breaking fences, through backyards, crushing outbuildings, and trying to avoid the houses. Small tank-infantry teams were moving jerkily through the lanes, the riflemen darting into and out of houses and barns, the tanks swinging their guns but without firing. We owned the town. We had thrown our Sunday punch and hit a vacuum.

Out and Back

As Tar Baby reached the church that I had designated as the command post a rapid cannonade opened from the high ground to the left rear. I called Jones. "What's the shooting about? Have you found any opposition?"

"There's a lot of vehicles getting away toward Buissonville and those woods to the south," he replied.

Lieutenant Artillery and I fought our way out of the haze, up to Jones's vantage point where the northeast breeze had cleared the smoke. By that time the fleeing Krauts had reached cover. Not a thing in sight, not even a wrecked target truck. It appeared that the gunnery of the Sixty-sixth Tanks needed improvement. But since Jones assured us that "there's a lot of stuff in there," Lieutenant Artillery called for fire on Buissonville and the woods on the high ground two kilometers southeast of us, Mont Gautier, Bois de St. Remy. When the salvos began to crash into the targets, I went back to the church where the staff had set up the command post and sent a report to CCA wrapping up what information we had to date, about as follows:

> We had captured Forzee and cleared the town by 1035. Losses two tanks, no personnel. Destroyed two Mark V tanks. Enemy personnel losses unknown. Four enemy tanks retreated into the Bois de Halleux, five hundred meters east of Forzee. Some enemy vehicles had retired into Buissonville, others into the Bois de St. Remy and Mont Gautier.

General Collier called. "Division has a squadron of P-38s in the air. Can you use them?"

"We already have artillery on both areas and the town—but yes, we'll call for the squadron to work them over too."

S-3 called CCA air liaison who called division air liaison who called the squadron leader. That took time. I went out to my observation post in the southeast of the village, where I could get a clear view of all three targets.

Then the sky was full of those funny double-tailed planes throwing streams of .50 caliber tracers through Bois de Halleux, Buissonville, and Bois de St. Remy. I couldn't see what they were shooting at but got their report via roundabout channels that there were "lots of enemy vehicles" in those areas. I doubted the veracity of that statement. There evidently weren't enough enemy to hold their attention because one flight swept down on Forzee, preceded by a crackling swarm of bullets that plowed one garden and ricocheted from the stone walls of the houses. I dashed back to the CP and asked CCA for God's sake to call off the close air support.

While we were planning the defensive and outpost systems, General Collier rolled into the area. He hauled me over the coals for using the church as a command post, which as a card-carrying atheist I thought was a bit unreasonable, since the church was large enough, centrally located, not currently in use, and slightly warmer than it was in the vehicles, but I got my crew out, nonetheless.

When we had cleared the sacred portals, Collier gave me two more missions. I was to hunt out the enemy tanks in Bois de Halleux and send a force through Bois de Hautmont to occupy Laloux.

I directed Major Jones to take and hold Laloux with his force and told Major Evans to comb the enemy out of the Bois de Halleux. Halleux was so low-lying and marshy that while the wide-tracked German tanks could make it, our narrow-tracked M4s would helplessly bog down. So Evans posted his tanks where they could detect and fire on any enemy movement while teams of auto-riflemen and bazooka gunners patrolled the area to force movement.

Luckily from our point of view the escaping enemy hadn't stopped in the woods and our patrols found it clear.

Busy as a bird dog the rest of the afternoon visiting Evans's thinly spread outposts (he had spread his force to defend the whole village since Jones had pulled out), visiting Colonel McDonald who had moved his Fourteenth Armored Cavalry Group into Haversin on our left, and securing the cooperation of the mayor in arranging billets for our men.

Late in the afternoon the CO of the third battalion of the Sixty-sixth came over to inform me of my current job. "We're moving up on the Trisogne-Haversin station road and are going to take Buissonville. I'd appreciate it if you would help us with direct fire on any targets we scare out of town."

While we were talking the P-38s returned and really concentrated on Buissonville with tracers and incendiaries. Several houses started to burn and the future occupant was wild. He dashed to his jeep, twisted the dials, and called division G-3 (air). "Get your goddamn trigger-happy flyboys out of Buissonville. They aren't killin' any Germans, they're just burnin' up the houses. We gotta have them houses to live in."

This message of course did not get through to the squadron leader until his planes had fully unloaded and gone and Buissonville was fully aflame. However, the wholesale arson about which he had complained may have helped, since he got into town after dark without a cross word and found that the Krauts had slipped away. He was also able to mine the two bridges immediately south of town and post two outposts to ensure that the Germans couldn't destroy them and he, if it proved desirable, could.

The mayor had been most cooperative about billeting the troops. He had placed the headquarters staff in his house and the houses next door and given us his dining room as a combined war room and mess, while he and his family moved to the cellar. Most Belgians within the sound of gunfire wisely retired to the cellar until the war moved out of hearing.

I inquired about Jones's progress and received the anticipated answer, "they've got a lot of stuff in there." To hell with it. So I went up to the master bedroom, pulled a featherbed over my frozen frame, and dropped unconscious.

Staggered down to the war room–dining salon and was greeted by Major S-3. "Merry Christmas, colonel. Task Force Jones just reported that they've occupied Laloux and found the place clear of Krauts."

That was good news. Better yet, the mayor's kitchen had been taken over by the headquarters mess crew and the C-ration breakfast that they turned out was a big improvement over tossing the contents of a packet of instant coffee over the tonsils and washing the bitter brew down with warm water—if one had remembered to hang one's canteen on the exhaust manifold of the jeep (tank) (half-track). Otherwise, the canteen was frozen solid and one made do with saliva.

Message from General Collier, "Send a section of tanks to General White, CCB, at Achene."

It seemed that the Krauts, having run into opposition on the Rochefort-Ciney road, had tried the Rochefort-Wanlin-Celles and been stopped by CCB. The Germans were running out of fuel and CCB had surrounded the bulk of the Second SS Panzer Division. They were having a field day maneuvering around the immobilized German tanks and sniping them from favorable positions. The night before, Christmas Eve, our troops had ceased all firing at 2300. The PW interrogation crew, all former German Jews, with a battery of loudspeakers turned at full volume, had serenaded the entrapped Germans with a soulful rendition of "Stille Nacht, Heilige Nacht" at 2355. At the stroke of midnight they had wished the enemy Froeliche Weihnachten and every gunner in the division yanked his lanyard and every mortar in CCB spat out its hell.

It was a nice haul. The count of German equipment destroyed and captured proved to be in excess of all expectations, a nice Christmas present for General Hodges and Field Marshal Montgomery. But this anticipates the future—back to the grim present.

About 1500, CCA radioed General Collier's order to take Mont Remy, which is covered by the Bois de St. Remy, and to hold the road net in that area. I was afraid of that, had been anticipating the move, and foresaw an awkward operation.

The Forzee-Rochefort road led straight through the woods over the high ground of Mont Gautier. Range to the woods proper was two kilometers. Halfway between the village and the woods a small stream called the Rau de Vachaux crossed out front from left to right under a bridge on the road. On the right (southwest) side of the road it appeared wide and from the growth of vegetation was probably marshy. Left of the road on the higher ground the streambed seemed to be narrower and the approaches certainly dryer. So we would attack on the left until the stream was crossed, then oblique right to straddle the road for the push through the woods.

So we would mount up under cover of the houses in Forzee, drive out in the meadow across the road in two columns, assault and support, individual vehicles face right on command and the lines move out with all practical speed, using marching fire on the edge of the woods. When the stream was crossed we would oblique to the right until the right infantry-tank team was on the right of the road, last push through the woods to the far edge facing Rochefort.

The heavy weapons company from positions in Forzee would support the advance by overhead fire on the edge of the woods until fire was blocked by friendly troops, then move forward and join us on the objective. The destroyer platoon was to move out at the tail of the support (left) column, overmatching the advance and firing on appropriate targets of opportunity, joining on the objective. The artillery was to fire on the near edge of the woods until our troops approached, then walk a barrage up astride the road ahead of our advance.

I explained the plan of action to the officers concerned, interrupted frequently by General Collier coming in on the radio asking how far we had gotten, hadn't we gone yet, and when were we going?

So a spotty plan, a hasty briefing, and at 1600 we mounted up and boiled out of town, the mayor and his family and assorted townsfolk cheering and waving just like a Class B movie. Being better acquainted with Belgians now, I realize that they didn't give a damn if we won or got shot to pieces, they were just glad to get rid of us.

We moved from the cover of the village, crossed the road into the open field, faced right like a chorus line, and started down the slope toward the stream at a good clip. The tanks were firing with their gyro-stabilized guns, the mortars were coughing out their shells, and heavy and light machine guns were inching along the objective woods. Two salvos of eighteen simultaneous bursts of the 105-mm. shells had exploded at the optimum sixty feet above the target area. It looked like a good show.

Then a German tank broke from cover in a clump of woods just beyond the bridge, heading for the main forest beyond. Our attack came to a screeching halt as each tank stopped and all gunners began shooting at that scuttling, tan-colored target. Maybe the light of the early dusk was poor, perhaps our lads were nervous, perchance they just couldn't shoot. Anyway our tracers registered shorts, rights, and lefts while that yellowish-tan blot ran straight for the right corner of the woods, no evasive action, just pouring on the coal.

"Lead him, lead him," I found myself shouting, and a hell of a lot of good that did.

With a final derisive wag of his broad, square-cut, and most vulnerable tail the target tank disappeared behind the shelter of the tall timber. That meant I'd lose two or more tanks trying to dig him out later.

"General Collier on the radio, colonel," reported my operator, totally unconcerned with the outside world.

"Tar Baby-6 here."

"Tar Baby, break off your move. Pull back to your outpost. Report to my CP immediately."

"Roger on your message. Wilco. Over."

"Immediately."

So I rogered once more and put Tar Baby into motion to contact Evans and Captain E personally—the formality of call signs, recognition, and radio conversation just take too much time.

I woke my sleeping jeep driver and we started back to Forzee. As we approached the road junction leading north into Haid, I saw a large half-tracked vehicle coming toward us—something odd about the silhouette, a Kraut personnel carrier, and told my driver, "Pull off! Pull off!"

The lad queried "Huh?" and continued on a collision course. At a distance of thirty feet in front of us the German turned toward Haid while we swerved to the left and skidded past him with no change in speed. Scalloped bucket seats—empty—yes, Kraut.

"What did you say, sir?"

"Didn't you see that German half-track?"

"Was that a—oh my God!" He had expressed my feelings exactly. The mystery of the lost Jerry was never solved. It was never heard of again.

Amazing how much easier it is to get the outfit stopped and started to the rear than it is to move them forward. They did move back in good order, sections alternating in moving and covering those silent woods across the stream. The artillery was silent and the heavy weapons ceased fire. It was completely dark when we reached Forzee. The citizens of Forzee did not cheer us on our return.

Eleven.

Defeat

Bois de St. Remy

I was completely burned up by this peremptory and I believed dangerous change in our plans just as I'd gotten the outfit going. It looked like the Bois de St. Remy was occupied only by a handful of Krauts and in half an hour we could have taken the area with little or no trouble. Later it might and probably would be different. However, I didn't know the big picture and would probably find out more about it when I met Collier at the Chateau de la Libion.

I found CCA headquarters very comfortably dug in at the chateau, but Collier in a morose mood. He first worked me over for recalling the section of tanks I had loaned to CCA—which was a mystery until I remembered my order. "Pull in your outposts. I want to make this move at full strength." My staff, Major Evans, or Captain K had taken that to mean the detached section. I'd have to be careful to give orders that couldn't be misinterpreted. General Collier went on.

"A battalion of the Thirty-third Infantry Division will arrive at midnight to relieve the second battalion of the Forty-first. It's their first experience in combat so be careful with them. The second battalion of the Forty-first will report to CCA at Leignon.

"Push ahead on the right and occupy Franceaux and Briquemont by dawn. There's nothing in there and we want to tighten up in that area. Block that road. Keep your main force dug in at Forzee. Questions?"

"Yes sir, we would have had the Foret de St. Remy in another half hour. Why were we called back?"

"We didn't want to take a chance on your getting cut off."

Ah yes. Field Marshal Montgomery's touch, fall back and regroup, don't get cut off. He evidently hadn't recovered from the boo-boo he'd made in Holland when he'd dropped his paratroops too deep into enemy country and couldn't shove the armored units in over the dike roads fast enough to join them.[1]

About 0100 on December 26 the attached battalion pulled into Forzee in trucks. One company was sent to the third battalion of the Sixty-sixth at Buissonville and one went with Jones's guides to join him at Laloux. Evans's crew spotted the newcomers on outposts and in billets. And took off to the war in the northwest.

During the night Jones cautiously moved on and occupied Briquemont but held off on approaching Franceux because there was "a lot of stuff in there." There may have been, but come daylight it was all gone and

148

his untried infantry and veteran tankers were able to move in without a harsh word.

Just after dark the night before, Evans had sent a patrol to look over the stream, Rau de Vachaux, across our front, and had reported that it was thoroughly frozen. That took a load off my mind and simplified any future move we might make toward Rochefort.

That morning was spent in visiting outposts and inspecting the field fortifications being dug for the defense of the village. The digging and camouflage were being done halfheartedly as usual—American soldiers just won't dig willingly until after they get shot at. I directed the major to have his officers directly supervise, and feared there would be little improvement unless the Krauts threw something at us.

About 1000 on the day after Christmas, I received a Spidex message from General Collier directing me to "take Bois de St. Remy at once." Pulled out yesterday's aborted plan, dusted it off, and with three changes briefed the commanders concerned.

Since the Rau de Vachaux was frozen solid we would attack straight ahead astride the Rochefort road.

To ensure that we arrived on the objective without being hit with aimed fire the mortars of the battalion (including those with Jones's force) would lay a smoke screen on the edge of the woods. I also asked the third battalion Sixty-sixth to smoke the detached point of woods just south of Buissonville to obviate any chance of accurate enfilading fire on our lines.

The attached battalion had two companies, one rifle and one heavy weapon, and was not equipped with armored personnel carriers as the Forty-first had been. There were far too many to mount on the company of tanks—they would have to accompany the tanks on foot, except for four or five men per tank.

The artillery action would be as before, TOTs on the edge of the woods followed by a barrage astride the road ahead of the troops as called for.[2]

I was careful about explaining this plan in great detail. It was to be the first action by this battalion and had to click. They had to win their first fight.

To ensure plenty of time for the plan to percolate down to the privates, I set zero hour for 1300.

In the meantime I dashed over to Buissonville by jeep to see the CO of the third battalion Sixty-sixth. Scuttling along the road in broad daylight some thousand yards from the woods was a real test of the position. If I got there and back without getting shot at, there just weren't any Germans over there. Oh well, it would be a good live training maneuver anyway.

Major Third Battalion (what was his name?) met and led me into the cellar of the burned-out shell of his command post. I could understand his hatred of the close support given us by the flyboys of the army air forces. "Carefree bastards" was the kindest word he had for them.

I showed him on the map, then pointed out on the ground, exactly how I wanted him to screen our left flank, and he put his mortar crews on the job.

Then to horse and back to Forzee where there were scenes of confusion as the riflemen mounted their tanks and the other troops moved into their initial positions under cover of the houses and barns of the village.

I had been considerably relieved by my unscathed trip to Buissonville and on climbing into Tar Baby opened a K-ration.[3] As I chewed off a chunk of cheese I overheard a remark from one tanker to another, "Guess everything's going to be all right, the old bastard's hungry." That gave me to think—the appetite of a commander is evidently a practical gauge by which the troops estimate their chance of success, and ever after that went to war being seen by as many of the men as possible, having my lunch en route. Always the cheese—the scrambled eggs or veal loaf is apt to crumble or spill if your hand shakes under fire. But American cheese—even if you drop it, it can be dusted off and never loses its cohesiveness.

Actually I shouldn't have been out there, should have been back in the mayor's dining room letting the major run his show or cheering him on by FM radio. But I never did trust radio reports or the execution of radio orders. So I went along for the ride and to get involved if necessary.

Once more we boiled out of town with the townsfolk waving us on. Had a feeling of a second viewing of a John Wayne film—this was where I had come in.

Everything worked like a charm until we crossed the stream and started up the slope toward the smoke-screened woods. I was idling along with Tar Baby at a restrained two miles per hour among the first platoon of E Company when one of the smoke-throwing mortars got off the beam. Half a dozen rounds of flaming phosphorus burst among the riflemen. They didn't panic—just seemed to regard it as a nuisance, brushing the smoking particles off themselves and each other, and keeping on the tempo of the advance. I was calling "mortars—cease firing, out the mortar fire, you're firing short" without benefit of call signs or recognition, but in the meantime all fire of both mortars and artillery had been lifted. We were approaching the edge of the woods.

The riflemen were fanning out to lead their tanks into the fog-filled woods while the tanks fired bursts of .50 caliber over their heads. The heavy .50 goes a long way through light timber, making a fearful racket with every branch it strikes.

The left flank was first to enter and, glancing that way, I had a bad moment—a tank was burning, flames bursting and twisting above the engine compartment. Damn. Then as the tank waddled through a clear spot I saw the fluorescent red recognition panel that every vehicle had tied down over the rear deck had been torn loose at one end and was blown about by the hot air louvers. Hah.

Now if these lads just avoided shooting each other in this white-hazed woods we had it made.

Tar Baby angled off to the right where we'd repeatedly missed the German tank yesterday, looking for a soft spot, finally plunged into the woods. Then things got tough. We tried to push through alone, but a light tank just isn't equipped to deal with those trees on an upgrade and we had to fall in behind an M4 that was making good progress, preceded by a small group of riflemen. Angling out a bit farther to the right, we struck a small lane that paralleled the main road and started up the slope with better speed.

Seeing a dead German by the roadside, I halted Tar Baby and dismounted. It would be interesting to know whether he had been killed this morning or yesterday. Nudged his foot a bit with my foot and got the answer—he'd been cooling off overnight. Comforting, maybe there weren't any Krauts in the woods today.

But at a trail junction at the top of the hill flank we passed a still burning half-track personnel carrier and the smell of burned meat assured us that there had been Germans in the woods after all.

We angled over toward the main road, a short-strength rifle squad, Captain F in his tank, Tar Baby, another M4 on the flank, and two aid men, a very assorted crew. Tar Baby became hopelessly bellied on the root system of an overturned tree, so I dismounted and told the sergeant to get a tow-off and bring her up to the crest when he could, then went forward to join my gang.

The tanks had ceased their overhead machine-gun fire shortly after entering the woods. In the smoke-hazed confusion, keeping direction was difficult and maintaining a line was impossible, so to prevent accidental casualties Captain F had ordered a cease-fire at identified enemy targets.

Both of the M4s were in trouble with the larger trees of the higher ground. Captain F dismounted and joined me in following the rifle squad. As we reached the flat crest of the ridge, eight Germans broke cover from practically underfoot and dashed off through the trees like so many deer, no, like a flock of snipe. Our men, apparently stricken by buck fever, let them make several jumps before they started firing. I panted up to where they were firing near the abandoned rifle pits, picked up a carbine, fully loaded, and as the Jerries zigged and zagged I helped them on the way with the contents of the magazine. Like a shooting gallery, but with very animated targets.

The Germans disappeared on the down-slope, apparently unscratched. The marksmanship as well as the gunnery of this modern army. I was examining the sights of my carbine when I noticed the squad leader beside me, very pale, perspiring and eyeing me oddly.

"What's the matter, sergeant, you hit?"

"Oh, no sir. You know, colonel, I sure wouldn't have had the nerve to do that."

"Do what?"

"Pick up that carbine and shoot it."

"Why, didn't one of your boys drop it?"

"No sir. It was lying right there when we got here."

Then it was my turn to pale, perspire, and palpitate. After hearing and teaching about booby traps for three or four years, I seize the first opportunity I see to detonate one. The fact that the scared Krauts had abandoned their weapons and that one of them left his honestly loaded trophy was immaterial. My bull-in-a-china-shop lack of thought was most embarrassing and frightening.

I started to the east toward the main road junction, which I estimated to be a hundred yards distant, where the CP would be organized. About that time, however, there was a rattling burst of rifle fire to the south and Captain F and I started toward the sound of the guns. Maybe we had found some solid opposition.

After snooping ahead four hundred yards I began to feel very silly; the idea of this young man and I playing cowboy and Indian through these woods with nothing but a couple of pistols was ridiculous. I should be back with Tar Baby reporting our position to Collier, and he should be reorganizing his tank company.

"It isn't necessary for you to come out here, captain," I said, intending to remind him that he had a company to take care of. He interrupted. "No sir, but I've got just as much right as you. I'd like to see what's up there too."

I thought of turning back but now that the firing was close I'd feel even sillier, so we pushed ahead. The trouble was we didn't know who was shooting at whom, where, or why.

We came to the south edge of the woods at the Rochefort road. The open ground beyond ran down a slope fifteen hundred meters to the Ferme

Abbaye de St. Remy to the southeast, and two kilometers to Rochefort to the south.

Just across the road a squad of our riflemen had cornered some Germans in a log barn or hay storage, had set the barn afire, and were pumping bullets through it from all angles.

Farther down the road following a jutting angle of the woods, the remainder of their platoon was enthusiastically attempting suicide by attacking a machine-gun nest just north of the Abbaye. The gun was yammering at them with no effect and they were firing back but at twelve hundred yards.

Recalling General Collier's admonition about limiting our attack, I yelled at the helmetless red-headed lieutenant. "No, lieutenant. Halt. Cease firing. Fall back here."

But he was in a berserker rage and even my hog-calling voice didn't get to him, so I had to dash out and personally convince him by repeating my order.

"But sir, that gun right down there—we can take it right now."

"Get down here, lieutenant, and listen. That gun is over a thousand yards away with a perfect field of fire. You start down there and not one of your men would make it. You don't have to win this war by yourself. Now pull your men back and I'll get the artillery on that gun."

He reluctantly obeyed. I wished I had five thousand like him.

While I started moving his men I dashed back to the burning barn, but it was all over. The Germans had tried to make a break (or surrender) and there they were, piled up as they came out the door, no weapons. Deliver me from the bloodthirsty enthusiasm of an American recruit in his first battle. Went back up the road to the crest where the major was to set up his CP. Captain F called my attention to the broad tracks of a Tiger tank that had apparently pulled hurriedly out of the position in ambush covering the four-way road junction. I was glad that I'd cautioned my people to stay off the road.

The haze of smoke was drifting slowly south and as now up to our position. Sections, squads, and stragglers, tanks and foot troops, were blundering through the foggy woods in all directions, trying to find their units or commanders. And finally the battalion commander and one of his captains joined us. I recognized him as commanding E Company, the unit that had been hit by the short-falling mortar fire.

"Captain, please give your men my apology for the mortar fire that dropped into them by mistake. How many casualties did you have?"

"I haven't had any casualties so far, sir. I've gotten all present reports from all platoon leaders and they—"

"Good. But tell them it wasn't intentional anyway. I'm going to look into it and assure you that it won't happen again."

"If you don't mind, colonel, I don't think I'll tell them anything. They don't know but what that's the way it was supposed to be."

"By God, you're right, captain."

The major was getting his force well in hand, outposts, defensive position, and rolling reserve laid out, so I left him with it. Returned toward the place where I'd left Tar Baby hopelessly hung up and found that the sergeant had wiggled her free and maneuvered her up to the area where we'd fruitlessly fought the battle of the galloping gray ghosts. I mounted up. "All right, sergeant, let's go home. Should be able to follow the trace where those mediums have eaten through."

Never was I more mistaken. For an M5 light to follow an M4 medium through woods is difficult; to try to backtrack on that trail is impossible. It's also dangerous. Every tree and sapling that had been pushed over during the forward movement remained sloped in that direction at about ten to thirty degrees, just the angle at which medieval infantry used to slant their spears to receive a cavalry charge; each of these treetops, splintered trunks, and limbs becomes a lance, threatening to decapitate the tankers in the open turret. We could button up and be unable to direct the driver (and risk the chance of a Panzerfaust from a bypassed and dedicated German) or get off the trail and force our own way. We took the latter course, cutting our way straight downhill through and over the trees parallel to our former trail.

It was getting dark, visibility limited to twenty or thirty yards, when I saw movement among the trees a short distance on the left front. Jittery about Jerries who may have been bypassed, I swung the turret machine gun in that direction, told the driver to stop, and called, "Who's there?" The answer was a bullet cracking by my ear and an outraged voice, "You damned fool. Can't you see that's one of ours?" So I took my finger off the trigger. A sergeant came out of the brush.

"Sorry about that trigger-happy recruit. Anybody hit?"

"No, close miss but we're OK. Why are you posted back here?"

"We aren't posted, we're lost. We're from the support platoon and supposed to join up with the company somewhere around here. Do you know—"

"Just keep pointed uphill, sergeant. The battalion CP is at the top. You can't miss it." Don't know why I tacked on that last absurd statement, but everybody who gives directions does it.

At the command post I learned that the Buissonville task force had captured Havrenne, east of our Bois de St. Remy, and had shortly thereafter beaten off a counterattack made by an understrength battalion and a dozen tanks, nine of which were destroyed. Couldn't help wondering about that report; must have been a very understrength battalion—the main German strength was south and west of us. Everything we'd encountered was tissue-paper thin.

C-rations and hot coffee for the men tonight, wonderful. A sharp contrast to thawing out a K-ration or melting fragments of chocolate of the D-ration with saliva, as the lads out there in the woods were doing.[4] But my guilty conscience did not interfere with my appetite. And the mayor's featherbed was luxurious. A very nice war.

Shadowboxing

During the frosty morning of December 27 I visited the battalion in St. Remy, went with the major around the outposts, and directed a contact group to be placed between this garrison and Jones's task force on the right.

We then made tentative plans for the capture of Rochefort if it were required. The town was built at the junction of a north-south and east-west road and its capture would probably be required to limit German movement. It lay astride a stream flowing from east to west just south of the east-west road.

Our best approach appeared to be the envelopment of the west flank, moving the infantry-tank team under cover of the forest a thousand yards to the right, fifteen hundred yards south, and attacking Rochefort from the west. Cross the stream and take the south half if feasible.

The tank destroyers and heavy weapons would support the attack from the forward edge of the Foret de St. Remy, having perfect observation on the flank of any resistance. The artillery could be placed precisely in front of the assault troops with no possibility of endangering them by firing short.

While approaching the town, if a crossing point or bridge could be found the team would cross the stream and take the southern half of the objective as first priority. This should discourage the northern part of the garrison and make clearing the town easier.

If no crossing point could be found, clear the north bank and use artillery to eliminate opposition on the south bank.

It was a damned good plan, and the major called up the commanders to brief them for the possible attack.

It was 1530 when I was called by General Collier. The message was simple—"Take the road center at Rochefort at once." So here we go.

I passed the word to the battalion commander, mounted my jeep, and galloped to the CP, expecting to find the tanks and rifle companies on the way. But the best-laid plans of mice and men—

Due to the winter cloud cover it was black night, and there were valid disadvantages to the plan we had made that morning. The movement through the woods to the right, to the left, and to the left again would be difficult in darkness. Tanks would be useless for combat; they could only follow the foot troops, alerting the enemy by the sound of their engines. The supporting fire of destroyers and heavy weapons without daylight observation would be chancy and probably dangerous.

The major recommended that the attack be made frontally. Two rifle platoons in assault, one in support. The enemy was not in force, the move would be only two thousand yards straight ahead, and our men while able to keep in touch could be covered by darkness.

"If" and "if only" are the two most futile expressions in the English language, and normally I never use or think about them. But in this case if only I had not approved the major's plan of action, if I had insisted on the original right envelopment, it would probably have taken all night to move into position, but the assault would have been made with full force and with ideal supporting fire at dawn. But that is useless speculation and a disregard of the disagreeable facts. I did approve the frontal attack.

"OK, major, you're the one that's doing it. Let's get the show on the road."

He had already pulled the tanks forward with the destroyers to the edge of the woods. But they would take no part in the action unless enemy tanks were encountered. He directed Lieutenant Artillery to have the artillery battalion prepared to fire on the town, particularly on the road junction, on call.

The heavy weapons company was to site mortars and machine guns to fire into south Rochefort after resistance developed.

To protect the right flank of the attack from the possibility of enemy tanks moving from the southwest toward Rochefort, a sergeant and a squad were sent on the proposed route of our enveloping attack to lay a daisy chain of mines across the road and to cover these mines from positions nearby during the attack.

Yes, it might work.

During the attack of the day before, overcoats and overshoes had been worn or tied readily available on the tanks. The riflemen had in many cases been considerably fatigued on this account, while some overcoats had been abandoned. Since this attack would be over within a short time, overshoes and overcoats would be left in squad piles and brought forward after the objective was taken.

Company commanders were given the plan of action and departed into the woods to put it into effect.

The major, his staff, Lieutenant Artillery, and I did Swedish exercises, walked about, and thrashed our arms to keep the blood circulating. Trying to see the town was fruitless, even from our ideal observation point.

The movement into position appeared to be interminable. The night was black and cold, very cold.

Radio conversations between the major and his commanders even in veiled code brought up unforeseen delays and difficulties.

The troops were moving into position late, lost, confused, and cold. A hoarfrost began to form and visibility became a little better. Absolute silence from the enemy, the town, and our troops. At long last, at 2100, the major reported that the rifle company was moving out.

By God, they actually were moving, advancing out of the woods in skirmish lines, with two platoons in assault position and one in support. It was too bad that they had taken so long to get started because the frost was heavy now. They were silhouetted against the white background, discernible at three hundred yards.

"Good visibility," remarked the major. "Now they can see what they're doing."

"Yes, I'm sorry to say. So can the Krauts—if there are any over there."

The support platoon faded into the night. Complete silence, looked like it was going to succeed without trouble.

But I'd had that happy thought too soon.

A machine gun rattled into action somewhere in the northwest out-skirts of Rochefort and the *plirrrrrp* of Schmeissers was heard from the same area. The German tracers illuminated the frosty field with a pink glow. There were Jerries over there, about a dozen. There was no answering rifle fire.

"What progress are they making?" I asked the major.

"They are pinned down by heavy fire. Can't make a move."

"Have your assault platoons commence firing and move out with marching fire. There's only one gun in action."

The major gave the order. But got the answer that the captain was afraid any shooting would draw fire.

"He's getting shot at now with everything the Krauts have. Tell him to answer it."

No action resulted. Our people evidently preferred to be passive sil-houetted targets, and nothing could persuade them to answer the fire.

Our OP was also being honored by a few stray rounds and a burst now and then, and by watching the tracers I believed that we could put the gun out of action by dropping a load of TNT two hundred yards beyond the point where the tracers were igniting. I called for the artillery observer.

But he was gone. Going back to his tank, I found him inside and ordered him out to the knoll.

He protested that he had to be in his tank to operate the radio.

"Well, bring your tank up where you can see the target or bring your remote control box up there. I want you where you can direct fire."

Returning to the OP, I asked the major to call up his heavy weapons company commander. When the captain appeared, I pointed out the probable position of the gun as indicated by the tracers. "Just follow down the line of tracers and spear everything one hundred to three hundred yards beyond the point they ignite, and you'll silence him. Put your mortars and machine guns on it. You'll know when you're close because he'll stop firing."

But both he and the major protested that they couldn't fire over the heads of our own men in such an unorthodox fashion, especially since we could not see either our troops or the enemy. They had never done such firing and didn't want to experiment. What I fear was the real reason, that our tracers would reveal our position, they didn't mention.

So I went back again and found my artillery man fumbling with his magic box and field wire. Leaving his sergeant to do the fumbling, I grasped him firmly by the wrist, towed him up to the knoll, and directed him to shoot a 105 battery volley a safe distance beyond the suspect gun position, then "walk" the bursts back this way until he got results.

No, he couldn't do it. He had no reference points, visibility was zero, map firing was too inaccurate, he'd never done that kind of shooting before, and couldn't shoot blind over friendly troops. I pointed out that the friendly troops might be endangered by his artillery but they were being killed by that machine gun so let's start shooting.

He called the fire direction center and God help us the artillery battalion commander backed him up, no firing except at the Rochefort road junction, on which they were registered.

During this contretemps the enemy brought a Nebelwerfer into play, dropping a dozen rockets into and around the OP area. The ululating screaming of the rocket sirens, even more than the explosive effect on their targets, truly qualifies them for their nickname of "screaming meemies." In company with everyone else on the knoll I went to ground and rooted my nose in the frost, knowing that every one of those screeching, howling, whistling things was dropping right between my shoulder blades. The screaming stopped abruptly with a rolling volley of soul-shaking crashes of high explosive.

The artillery observer took off for his tank and I ran him down again. "What the hell are you doing back here again, lieutenant?"

"Going to direct fire on that screaming meemie, sir."

"Then get up there where you can see where you're shooting and talk over your remote box. Did you locate the launches?"

"Not exactly, sir. Just the general area."

"That launcher can be anywhere within a mile of us, so drop the nonsense. If you're going to shoot anywhere, get that machine gun."

He didn't do any shooting, but he did stay up there during three more soul-chilling volleys that the Krauts fired at leisurely intervals—it takes time to load those things.

The battalion commander asked for permission to withdraw and re-organize for an attack at dawn, the men were freezing, immobilized as they were.

"They say they're pinned down," I objected. "If they can't make a move forward, how in hell can they move back?"

"Captain F says he can do it, and he's the man on the ground."

Well, if Captain F saw a way to disengage I was in favor of it, impossible as it seemed. I informed General Collier on the situation, asked permission to withdraw, and guaranteed that we'd have the town by 0900.

"What's the matter," he asked, "have they got a lot of stuff in there?"

"No sir. They've got a machine gun, a Nebelwerfer, and maybe two dozen men. But they're staying and our men won't move in at night. They'll go in at dawn with the artillery and tanks to help them."

"You can't do it. Keep pushing the attack."

The situation was bad—impossible. When "Lightning Joe" Collins had given the order to take Rochefort at noon the day before, the job could be done easily. When Harmon gave the order at 1400 it was still feasible since we could use our full strength. But at 1530, by the time the platoon leaders got their orders, it had become a night attack with no support, and with the men inexperienced in night fighting it was doomed to failure.

But Collier was under pressure from Harmon who was afraid of being relieved by Lightning Joe who was being pushed by Hodges and Mont-gomery, so we were ordered to keep pushing. Keep pushing? We hadn't pushed yet.

I had a number of options. They were all unpleasant.

I could go down there with the major, raise pistol, and holler, "Let's go!" in World War I fashion. And much good that would do.

I could snoop around and eliminate the gun crew myself, but at my advanced age I wasn't the snooper or sniper that either Sergeant York or I had been twenty-six years before.[5]

I could direct the major to withdraw and reorganize and have a fair court-martial before I had my buttons pulled off and my saber broken.

I could threaten the battalion and company commanders with court-martial for "failure to obey" and "cowardice in the face of the enemy" but my threat would appear inconsequential compared to that presented by the handful of persistent Krauts in Rochefort.

I could scream, turn purple, and have a Patton-like tantrum.

I could do nothing, just go back to the OP in Forzee and let the major handle it. Dear God, it was cold. I'd sure get myself a long overcoat come payday, and a scarf too—even a yellow one.

"Major, pull your men back to the woods. Have them creep or crawl. No man is to stand up, walk or run. Bring all the casualties with them. Get hot coffee up for them. Prepare to make that envelopment as we planned at dawn."

Then like Achilles sulking in his tent I went back to my jeep and ignored the radio. I was too busy framing my defense for the future court-martial.

The assault troops withdrew in amazingly good order, bringing their wounded with them. There was no interference by the enemy, who I suspected were running low on ammunition. God knows they had shot up enough of it.

Casualties—eighteen wounded, twenty crippled or frozen feet, amazing, normally there was one killed for every three wounded. The daisy-chain patrol added ten more frozen-footed casualties to the list.

Since this group was the only unit of the task force to accomplish their mission, I directed the major to write up a citation recommendation that the sergeant in command be awarded the Bronze Star.

Men shuddering into their overcoats and pulling on overshoes, three trucks up for the casualties, at last the boilers of sugar and creamed coffee from the kitchens in Forzee, and forming for the enveloping movement—

"Colonel—General Collier on the radio," said my driver who was monitoring the chatter over the air waves. Here it comes.

"Tar Baby-6, here."

"A-6 here. You are to occupy and dig in to defend the area where you were yesterday morning with your borrowed troops only. Assemble all of your own troops in the vicinity of your command post. Report to your command post for details. Do you understand?"

"Understood, sir, wilco. Over."

"Out."

Goddlemity, saved by the bell.

Got the major busy setting up his defensive position, started the tanks moving back to Forzee, and jeeped to the OP to find out more about the situation. The coded message gave details that couldn't be sent in the clear. We were turning the sector over to the Eighty-third Infantry Division with their borrowed units in place. The Sixty-eighth Tanks (less detachments) would assemble initially at Forzee. The Second Armored

Division would then assemble at a location to be designated later in army reserve.

So with our figurative tails between our legs, Task Force Triplet retired to the featherbeds of reserve troops, and so ended the most fruitless, exasperating, disappointing, shadowboxing battle experience of my career.

The division in general and CCB had done well, surrounding the immobilized Second Panzer Division and hitting their immovable tanks in their vulnerable tails. We in CCA had merely shadowboxed with "a lot of stuff"—the advance guard of the Rochefort-Ciney-bound column and the skeleton security force in Forzee, the Bois de Remy, and the dozen courageous Krauts in Rochefort.

My only consolation—I had pushed those gallant, dashing cavalry, "fighting sonsabitches," in spite of their foot-dragging reluctance, into moving between the Second Panzers and eight million gallons of gasoline.

Twelve.

To the Seventh Armored

Workshop and Wretch

At division CP, General Harmon handed me a radio message order from First Army to report to the Seventh Armored Division. "The Seventh is at Eupen, Triplet. Glad to have had you with us. You've had your fight. (And a hell of a poor excuse for a fight it was.) Best of luck."

And I was off into the frigid night, bound for Eupen. This was evidently what military historians call a war of movement, for me at least.

I should have bedded down and waited till morning before starting for the Seventh Armored. Driving through blacked-out traffic in snow on poor roads to a destination unknown to the driver is at best a hazardous sport. In an open jeep with windshield down it is also very uncomfortable.[1] We fought our way through suspicious roadblocks. Thank God that T-5 Carter was familiar with baseball games, baseball scores, and baseball heroes—I'd spent some forty-five years of total disinterest in the game and probably knew less about the Giants and Babe Ruth than Oberst Skorzeny did.[2]

After getting lost a few times we entered Eupen, convinced suspicious sentries that we weren't saboteurs, and entered the imposing marble and glass office building that was the home of Workshop, code name for headquarters, Seventh Armored Division, about 0500. The duty officer arranged a room, a cot, and a wonderful cup of coffee, so after the ice crystals in my blood had melted I settled down to make up lost sleep.

Finally came to life just before noon and after an eye-opener of well-boiled and aged coffee went to check in with the general. Found that the chief of staff was Colonel Ryan, my rear-rank plebe at West Point.[3] Ten minutes of "how's old so-and-so" and "do you remember when," during which I learned that Bruce Clarke, recently promoted to brigadier, commanded CCB. He was also in Ryan's class and had been a charter member of the B football squad with me for three years. Brighter than most football players, made engineer.[4]

Ryan escorted me in and introduced me to General Hasbrouck, the division commander. Hasbrouck was a tall, well-built, classically handsome, emotionless officer who gave me the impression that if stabbed he would bleed ice water.[5]

After a coolly courteous welcome he inquired about my assignments during the past four years. Then he asked me to tell him about the Second Armored, searching questions about morale and performance, seemed eager to hear any derogatory gossip.

I held back a bit on that one. Since my last real combat experience was twenty-six years in the past it ill-behooved me to say what I really thought about the cautious, reluctant, foot-dragging shadow-boxing I'd seen during the past two weeks. And I certainly hadn't learned how to cope with such veteran units either. Pushing them via telephone and radio had been a total failure, and going up front for a face-to-face confrontation hadn't worked much better.

So I just said that they were a good outfit with a wonderful reputation. A bit slower than I'd expected of the armored force in battle, due no doubt to the cautionary directions of Field Marshal Montgomery.

During lunch I got my assignment. "Do you know Bruce Clarke?" Hasbrouck asked.

"Oh yes, he and I butted heads for three years of football."

"Bruce has CCB. As assistant division commander he'd normally command CCA, but he prefers to stay with B. Do you know Tompkins, cavalry, nephew of the notorious Colonel Tompkins of the Seventh Cavalry?"

"No, I've heard of his uncle but never met this Tompkins."

"He has CCR."[6] A slight pause—

"I'm giving you Combat Command A—you can go down there and take over this afternoon."

A combat command—wonderful! The best job in the army!

In the light armored division a combat command consisted of the headquarters and headquarters company with the following units attached for normal tactical situations: one tank battalion of three medium companies and one light company; one or more infantry battalions; one tank destroyer company; one combat engineer company; one armored cavalry platoon of armored cars; one antiaircraft platoon of M-15 quadruple .50 caliber machine-gun mounts. A battalion of 105-mm. field artillery was normally in direct support during combat or if the command was operating out of range of the division artillery the battalion would be attached. When a situation required more strength, additional units would be attached from CCR or transferred from CCB. Divided into well-integrated task forces, a combat command, although small in numbers, could go anywhere and do anything. At least a force of more than one hundred guns of 37-mm. to 105-mm., armored and mobile, should be able to do so.

But no, the number of guns I had was not the deciding factor. The important factor was the men, their training, attitude, and morale. Although it hadn't been mentioned by either Ryan or the general, I knew that the lucky Seventh had been badly whipped at St. Vith and had been forced to retreat and later to retire from Manhai. It was the bitter gossip at the Sixty-sixth mess that the Seventh Armored knew how to get those new long-barreled guns: just run off and leave the tanks with the short-barreled ones.

Yes, the important consideration was not how many tanks and guns I had—I'd be most concerned about the men and their morale, particularly the esprit of the leaders.

And these men had been defeated twice already—

As I left the marble halls of Workshop, while passing through the lobby I saw an apparition pushing through the entrance. Looked like a plump, brown woolly bear—the light-brown caterpillars that prophesy a mild winter. By God, it was Bruce Clarke, Brigadier General Clarke, whom I'd last seen as a cadet twenty years ago. And now with a silver star welded on the front of his helmet.

"Hello, Clarke. Glad to see you. Congratulations on the star," with an appropriate handshake.

"How are you, Triplet. Heard you were joining us. Come over and see me this evening. I'm over near Spa."

"OK, I'll be there about 1700 or so."

"See you then," and he went on toward Hasbrouck's office.

As a cadet Clarke had always been stout; now he was fat, and the fur overcoat he was wearing did nothing to enhance his figure. Looked like a woolly bear, no, like a coonskin-coated college boy of the torrid twenties. But that's just my nasty, envious disposition showing. I'd have loved to wear a liberated fur overcoat in this weather, but I'd have to be a general to go nonregulation like that.

Oh well—

I mounted the jeep that Ryan had called from the division pool. "All right, corporal, let's go to CCA."

The CCA command post was a large, princely residence behind a wrought-iron fence. A sign, "CP Wretch," was posted on the gate. I checked in with the duty officer in the foyer and to my astonishment he asked if I wanted to see the commanding officer. Hell, I was the commanding officer.

"The commanding officer? Didn't division notify—"

"Yes sir, Colonel Rosebaum, right this way, sir."

"Why, ah, yes, I would like to see him."

This was news to me. I'd thought that I was sent to CCA because the CO had been killed or promoted and certainly expected that the staff would be apprised of my appointment. But when the lad led me into the library I found my old friend Dwight Rosebaum, whom I had last seen when we were both captains in the Sixty-seventh Infantry Regiment (medium tanks). He dropped the volume of pornographic French art that he'd been studying. "Triplet! What are you doing—"

"Rosey!—are you getting a star?"

"Me? A star? I've been recommended for a Silver Star but it'll probably turn out to be a Bronze."

"No no. I thought you must be getting a promotion. Where are you going?"

"Me? I'm not going anywhere."

"Well how come General Hasbrouck sent me over here to take over CCA? Wretch is the code name for CCA, isn't it?"

"Take over CCA? By God, first I've heard about it!"

The confusion was complete. There just wasn't room in a combat command for two bird colonels. Rosebaum got on the phone with Ryan and demanded to be put through to the general—"Yes, no matter how busy he is." Hasbrouck finally answered.

A short but justifiably heated conversation ensued, concluded by Rosebaum's directive, very inappropriate from a colonel to a general, at the fiery conclusion of which he slammed down the receiver. "That double-dealing, wishy-washy, treacherous, sneaky, underhanded sonofabitch. Cited me for a Silver Star and doesn't have the guts to tell me I'm being relieved, or why."

"Gee, Rosey, I'm sorry. I didn't know a thing about it. Nobody told me you were here and I didn't know I was coming here till twenty minutes ago."

"And I didn't know it then. That's one hell of a way to relieve a man, send word by his replacement. That cold-blooded, two-faced, back-stabbing bastard. So I'm off for the repple-depple. But before I leave I'll take you around to meet your commanders—they're a fine lot of men. I'll want to say good-bye to them before I go."

And in this awkward manner I inherited the command of CCA of the lucky Seventh Armored Division—and a more embarrassing situation I hope never to see. My sympathies were with Rosey.

A Fine Lot of Men

The executive, Lieutenant Colonel Rodman, was a small, blond, colorless, ineffectual type, totally lacking in force or initiative. The wispy blond mustache didn't help. The only picture of him that I can recall is when he was hunched on a stool before a fireplace in a farmhouse, rubbing his hands and staring into the flames, this when he should have been setting up our little war room and checking on the status of our units. He wasn't with us long.

Lieutenant Colonel King [Rodman's replacement] was a big, chunky type, heavy round face, small blue eyes, weathered ruddy complexion, and light brown graying hair beginning well back on a high forehead.

Seemed to be a positive, aggressive type. Two Silver Stars were indicated by the ribbons on his bulging chest. Colonel King had two appearances to which I was accustomed. Normally he looked like a jolly, ruddy English squire of the Dickens era. In battle, stick a pair of horns on his helmet and he'd be the perfect picture of a Scowegian berserker—with appropriate action. But his language under all circumstances remained oddly Victorian. With his tonsure-type bald scalp framed by long graying hair he resembled a normally benevolent bishop reluctantly recommending one of his flock for excommunication.

Lieutenant Colonel Wemple, known to his men as Rebel, commanded the Seventeenth Tank Battalion. He was of medium height and sturdy build with pale blond hair and complexion, oval features usually set in a serious, questioning expression. He gave the totally false impression that he wasn't quite grasping the conversation, briefing, or the correct situation. Shortly after VE Day, I attempted to recruit him into the Regular Army with his current rank and seniority. "I appreciate the compliment," he replied. "I'd like to, I like the army, but I'm afraid I'd better get back home and take care of Louisiana Oil."[7]

Lieutenant Colonel Rhea of the Twenty-third Armored Infantry Battalion was short, plump, round faced, dark haired, with unusually small hands and feet. He did not give the initial impression of being a combat infantryman or a warrior type. As I got to know him better during four campaigns I found that his performance ranged from inaction through heroism to foolhardiness. Kept me in a constant state of amazement. For instance, who else when informed that a large manor house was occupied by the enemy would drive up, knock on the door, tell the frightened maid to take him to the Germans, and return with his driver herding nineteen supermen? Then taking a small palace as his CP spend several hours playing classical music magnificently on the grand piano.[8]

Lieutenant Colonel Seitz of the Second Battalion of the 517th Parachute Regiment [attached to CCA] was one of the best soldiers I have known, and I have known a hell of a lot of damned fine soldiers. He completed three very hairy missions for CCA with never a question or word or complaint. I note that I was correct in my judgment. During his subsequent promotions to four-star general he commanded the XVIII Airborne Corps in which he served as battalion commander when I observed him in the Ardennes.

Lieutenant Colonel Milner commanded the 489th Armored Artillery Battalion, which usually supported or was attached to CCA. He was a tall, bulky blond with an outgoing personality who exuded confidence at every pore. We discussed his method of operation, with batteries necessarily emplaced some distance in rear of the task forces and open to an enveloping attack. "I should think that you'd want some infantry-tank teams for close-in protection," I remarked.

"Oh no, we've got heat (high-explosive antitank shell) and WP (white phosphorus shell). That'll take care of any tank they've got. And we have machine guns to beat off any infantry attack. Your task forces can go ahead and play games with the Krauts without worrying about us. We can take care of ourselves."

A very reassuring, refreshing type to talk to.[9]

Major Sorenson was the S-2 (intelligence). Middle-sized, blond, a pleasant conversationalist, he knew practically everything about the German army in general, and in common with everyone else from the private on outpost to General Eisenhower knew little or nothing about the current situation. In selecting a staff I would pick my men in order of importance: executive, S-4 (supply and evacuation), S-3 (operations), S-1 (personnel), surgeon, and—there's one I've forgotten, oh yes the S-2 (intelligence). The line troops sent a lot of information to the upper echelons but practically never got anything back; we always learned about the enemy on our front the hard way. Consequently, I felt that Sorenson was a good officer buried in an inconsequential job.[10]

Major Larsen, another lad of obviously Norwegian ancestry, was slightly built, thin faced, and very serious. He was the S-3 (operations) and had an efficient crew that he had trained.

Major Gruen, the S-4 (supply and evacuation), was another blond with a commonly anxious, hollow-eyed look, but surprised us now and then with flashes of humor. He could not be faulted for his worried look; he was responsible for the all-important movement of the trains, the truck convoys of gasoline, ammunition, and rations that were vital to the success of our operations. Considering what one courageous German rifleman could do to a truck convoy loaded with five-gallon cans of gasoline and 75-mm. tank ammunition, his customary apprehensive look was understandable. Incidentally, I learned that he was the crown prince of the American branch of the Gruen Watch Company.

Captain Hochberg commanded B Company of the Thirty-third Armored Combat Engineer Battalion. He was short, stocky, brown hair, blue eyes with spectacles. His men had among other duties the blood-chilling chore of mine and booby-trap disposal. Hochberg was quite enthusiastic about the bridges that he had just received. If he mounted it on the prow of an M4 chassis he could bridge a forty-foot stream or gully for the passage of medium tanks.

Captain Miller of the tank destroyer company was a tall, lanky type with Lincolnesque features, a confidence-inspiring man who spoke well of his new M10s with their 90-mm. guns.

A platoon of M15 antiaircraft half-tracks mounting .50 caliber machine guns in quadruple mounts was led by Lieutenant Cullen, a lightweight, middle height, sharp-looking brunet.

A platoon of armored cars from the Eighty-seventh Reconnaissance Squadron was commanded by a dashing young blond, Lieutenant Carraway, who was the epitome of the cavalryman, complete with yellow scarf and riding crop. I was happy to learn that the armored cars were not normally attached to the combat command since they were of little or no value for either combat or reconnaissance.

T-5 O'Hare was my jeep driver. He was of minimum height and weight with brownish hair, eyes, and complexion. Looked older than his age. Reminded me of an elf or gnome—no, the Hibernian version, a leprechaun.

O'Hare had a phenomenal road sense. He studied maps instead of paperbacks and chatted with other drivers about roads, landmarks, and driving conditions. Consequently, even when the division was on the move he could find any unit or CP by the most direct or practicable route. He could return in fog or blackout unerringly from the most complicated route.

"What did you do as a civilian, O'Hare?" I asked.

"I drove ten-ton tractor trailers, sir."

"Ten-tonners. That must be quite a chore."

"Oh no, they have power steering and power brakes. They're easier to drive than this crate. They're a lot more comfortable too, better sprung, and there's a bed overhead right in the cab. I never get a bed nowadays, have to sleep on the floor if I'm lucky. Gee, I'd sure like to have a bed."

The conversation ended at that point. If there was a bed available in the command post area it was going to be mine.

Speedy, Esprit, and the Poet Laureate

Yes, O'Hare knew where CCB was located—on the road between Sart and Spa, not much of a road but we could make it. After nine miles of ruts and snow we found the small but luxurious manor about 1720, perfect for a short drink and dinner.

Clarke was enthroned behind a large desk in the study. He rose, greeted me without enthusiasm, indicated where I was to sit, and we sat.

I had anticipated a lot of "do you remember when" and "what became of old so-and-so." More to the point, I expected to get a few valuable tactical and psychological tips on handling a combat command in the Seventh Armored. Neither conversation developed. A bit of trivia and then the only bit that I remembered. "If you want to speak to me personally or need help ask for Speedy, that's my code name." Speedy, Clarke informed me.

"OK, Speedy it is. I don't think I have a personal code name so I guess I'm just Wretch-6."

And that was about it—no invitation to the mess, no introduction to the staff, no drink, not even a cup of coffee. The unworthy thought occurred to me that he had invited me over just to establish the pecking order.

So when the silences became longer and more oppressive I took my leave and jeeped back to the warmer and friendlier clime of CCA.

Damn, forgot to ask him how he got that fur overcoat.

I found the esprit of the Seventh to be high. This was surprising, since they had been forced to retreat from St. Vith and then were defeated at Manhai. They were proud of the fact that it had taken six German divisions to whip them. They seemed to feel that they had won the battle, especially since they had retired while heavily engaged without major losses.

The Seventeenth Tank Battalion took pride in the performance of one of their light tank crews. I reviewed and approved a citation for Bronze Star medals for all members of the crew. Quite a wild yarn, but the burned-out carcass of the Tiger proved it. This is the story.

During the night retreat from St. Vith there was naturally a great deal of confusion. Columns were neatly formed and started on the prescribed routes, got lost, bumped into other columns, crossed, and lost coherence—a blacked-out, silent, logical chaos.

As the cold gray dawn gave a modicum of visibility the sergeant tank commander of an M5 light tank was puzzled by the odd silhouette of the tank he was following. It certainly wasn't the M5 of his platoon leader and it wasn't an M4. My God! It was a German tank, a big one, a Tiger! A Tiger lost and in our column, or were we in a German column?

Any man with normal good sense would have told his driver to halt, let that big bruiser get lots of distance. An American M5 had no business messing around with a German Mark V Panther, and even less with the dreaded Mark VI. But the sergeant didn't know that. He was supposed to shoot Krauts and here was a Kraut tank tail presented at point-blank range. So:

"Driver, that tank ahead, ease right up on his tail, close as you can. Gunner, tank straight ahead, AP, aim at his exhaust or louver, when I fire the machine gun, rapid fire."

They crept up to a yard behind the sixty-ton monster, yes, the man standing in the turret was wearing a Feldmuetze, so the sergeant gave him a burst. The gunner immediately began slamming AP shells at every possibly vulnerable point in the tail and back, hoping to find a weak point. The German commander slid out of sight into his turret.

The gunner had placed five fast rounds into the enemy stern before the surprised Germans were able to react. Then the massive turret with the long 88-mm. cannon started to swing slowly around to slap this impudent M5 into eternity. The 37-mm. continued spitting its AP with failing hope of penetration, but just before the 88-mm. was looking them in the eye a cloud of black smoke erupted from the outlet louvers, the Tiger stopped, and the black-uniformed crew boiled out.

"Over and above the call of duty." That stereotyped phrase required in any citation for bravery suddenly seemed absurd; it is the duty of any tank commander to destroy any enemy tank he encounters. But would any other man of my acquaintance make such a harebrained attempt? Would I? Hell no.

While making the rounds during a peaceful interlude, I dropped in on the headquarters of the Seventeenth Tank Battalion. Found Colonel Wemple and Major Dailey hugging a Kachelofen, a big tile-covered heating stove typical of this part of the country. They were being entertained by a capable-looking, sandy-complected T-5 who I'd just heard rendering a mountain-type ballad, accompanying himself on a guitar in a professional manner. "Please go on with the show," I asked. "I'd rather hear guitar music than listen to the troubles of the Seventeenth."

"Give him 'The Song of the Seventeenth,'" suggested Major Dailey. "This is Corporal Maugham, the songwriter and unofficial PRO of the battalion.[11] He composed this one about the outfit and I think it damned good. Let's have it, Maugham."

The lad launched into a ballad that covered the history of the Seventeenth Tank Battalion in verse from New York to St. Vith, sung to the tune of "Casey Jones." Pretty damned good. Gave me an idea. "I say, Corporal (technical fifth graders wear two stripes with a T and always like to be called corporal, so when I want a favor—), does making poetry come easy to you?"

"Yes sir, it's just a knack I have. It sure isn't a gift. I've got verses and rhymes running around in my mind all the time. All I have to do then is find a tune that will fit them."

"It seems to me that every man in CCA might like to have a poem like that to send to his folks. Could you make up a 'Song of CCA' telling where we go and what we do?"

"I sure could—"

Oh I'm a guy in CCA (strumming chords)
And have a lot of fun.
We screwed our way through England—
In France we chased the Hun.

"Something like that, sir?"

"Well, I don't think that bit about England would go well with the folks at home. But you've got the idea about the esprit and bragging all right."

"How about this one for starters?"

Oh we're the men of CCA.
You've heard of us, no doubt.
But once again we'll brag of how
We knocked the Germans out.

"Now you've got it, corporal. Put that one in your notebook and add to it after every action. I'll have Major Larsen's crew give you the dope on names and places, you put them into poetry, and you'll be published in five thousand copies."

"I'll sure work on it, colonel."

And so the poet laureate of CCA was designated and "The Saga of CCA" was conceived.

Thirteen.

Hunnange

Assignment

In the cellar where Workshop Forward was set up I found General Hasbrouck, the corps commander General Ridgway, and CCB's Brigadier Clarke. Ridgway was pacing like a caged lion, Hasbrouck was studying a map, and Clarke was looking mulish. Hasbrouck held his place on the map with a finger and looked up. "Triplet, I want you to attack this afternoon in coordination with CCB and take this part of Born east of the Waimes–St. Vith railroad."[1]

The devil got into me—I was hit by several of the seven deadly sins at once.

Envy. I envied Clarke his fur coat, his star, and the extra one hundred dollars a month that his exalted rank gave him.

Anger. Yesterday while battling for Diedenberg and Am Stein, I'd had to dispatch a tank-infantry section team two kilometers west on the Diedenberg-Born road to protect CCB's left flank. And I could not understand why Hasbrouck had to have me protect Clarke's flank—I was damned well able to protect my own.

Braggadocio. My young men had taken three hundred supermen as prisoners in the last two days. Why in hell couldn't Clarke take the alleged two hundred in Born?

Recklessness. By God if Clarke couldn't do it we could.

A flash of temper can get a man in a lot of trouble. "Yes sir, but it would be dangerous with two forces attacking toward each other, my people are a trigger-happy lot. I'd rather have CCB pull back and let us go through town shooting everything that moves without waiting to figure out friend or foe. Besides, my riflemen are mostly in German snowsuits now and there'd be a lot of sad mistakes. So if CCB will pull back and catch them when they run out I'll beef up Wemple's task force with another rifle company and he'll take Born."

Clarke objected. "We already have cleared the outskirts on the west and south and we'd just have to go in and take those houses over again. No, I'm against pulling out. If CCA can just—"

"Pull your people back, Bruce," decided Hasbrouck. "When can you attack, Triplet?"

Wemple's force on Am Stein was in an ideal position for the jump-off; the enemy had no tanks, so his fifteen M4s and five M5s would be enough. But I had to have time to reinforce him with a rifle company from Seitz's paratroops and a reinforced rifle company from Rhea's force. "It's near 1125—I think we can jump off at 1400, sir."

"1400—make it so."

General Ridgway had been an interested listener and now put in a word, studying the map. "There'll be a gap in this area," he said, pointing to the western edge of Born where the railroad headed for St. Vith. "Put something in there, colonel. I don't want a single one of those bastards to get away."

"Right, sir. I'll have Seitz put a platoon in these houses to knock off any stragglers."

"Good."

So with the approval of everybody except Clarke, I took off, thinking that I'd probably bitten off a hell of a lot more than I could masticate. Called Colonel King and asked him to have Colonel Milner and all task force commanders at Rhea's CP soonest. All hands were present by the time I reached Diedenberg.

"Gentlemen, we have the job of taking Born. Colonel Wemple, your force with two more rifle companies attached are to make the attack.

"Rhea, send Wemple your support rifle company reinforced.

"Seitz, you give Colonel Wemple a reinforced rifle company."

"The enemy is believed to be two hundred men, a small force, but they are fighting. No tanks and so far no antitank guns. Probably they have Panzerfausts.

"There are two obstacles. The Amblève River that winds along here with most of the eastern part of town on the south bank. Second the railroad embankment is impossible for tanks except directly north of the western part of town and possibly down here at the southern part north of this patch of woods.

"Now Colonel Wemple, I suggest a smoke screen just east of the eastern part of town, the breeze is from the north and will clear it for you rapidly. When the 489th starts the smoke, mount up and move in fast. Clear the east part of town. Then try the southern crossing of the railroad for your tanks. Time of attack 1400.

"I'll have Hochberg report to you with his bridges and mine-removal experts just in case you need them.

"And if you need more tanks Rhea's tanks will be available.

"Do you have any questions?"

"If I give up a rifle company and a tank company I'll have only one reinforced company and a light tank platoon to meet the counterattack the general is expecting," Colonel Rhea pointed out. "That isn't much to defend Diedenberg."

"You have a light paratroop battalion on your right, a paratroop regiment on your left, and three battalions of artillery behind you.

"Further questions? All right, Wemple, it's your show and you have a lot to do."

I jeeped back to Elvange, started Hochberg and his heroes up to Wemple, tried unsuccessfully to eat lunch, gave it up, and just quietly jittered.

About 1330 while mounting Tiger Bait, I received a message.[2] "Cancel your 1400 move." I canceled, the knot in my stomach relaxed, and I finally had lunch.

Later information revealed that CCB had about 1230 started through Born with mayhem, murder, and destruction and reported the place cleared at 1430, much to the satisfaction of Wemple's warriors.

In an amazingly clean cellar in Born, I found Generals Ridgway, Hasbrouck, and Clarke. Again Ridgway stood apart with the two hand grenades hooked on his jacket and his M-1 rifle, the other part of his trademark, standing against the wall nearby. Again Hasbrouck and Clarke were discreetly wrangling over an air photograph and map of the Born–St. Vith area. I was not briefed on the problem but gradually got the picture from the conversation. Actually the next hour and a half can be summarized in a repetition of the following three exchanges:

Ridgway: "I have to have Hunnange tomorrow."

Hasbrouck: "Bruce, you've got to take Hunnange tomorrow."

Clarke: "It's impossible. The Emma Rau is a marsh impassable for tanks without a great deal of preparation. It will take one full day to make the crossing. The Born forest is heavily garrisoned. It will require one day to clear that area. On the third day I can take Hunnange. It will be difficult. The snow is deep, my men have been consistently on the move for over forty hours, and they are in bad shape for lack of sleep, but we can do it in three days."

Repeat the above at seven-minute intervals. Dear Jesus, I was sleepy. But since I usually get in trouble when I talk I kept my teeth tightly clinched for well over an hour.

Finally, in order to help Clarke but mostly to settle this silly problem so I could go back to bed, I spoke up. "Bruce, you can make a shortcut, moving under cover of the railroad embankment along here, crossing the railroad at this grade crossing between the cut and fill. Then you will only have to cross the small eastern branch of the Emma Rau and run the Krauts out of the In der Eidt Woods. Then it's only a kilometer across open country to Hunnange. That way you'll bypass the Born Woods defenses, you'll have a smaller stream to cross, and you won't have to attack Nieder

Emmels, and the Born Woods and Nieder Emmels Krauts will probably [unreadable]."

"Hazardous." Clarke dismissed the idea. "It would risk the annihilation of the penetrating force and it would still take three days."

"If you can't take Hunnange tomorrow, Hasbrouck, I'll have the Thirtieth Infantry Division do it."

"You'll have to take Hunnange tomorrow, Bruce."

"I can do it in three days," said Clarke stubbornly.

Whereupon Hasbrouck leaped on me like a duck on a beetle. "Well, Triplet, you'll have to do it in one."

Hell's fire and corruption, I'd really put my foot in my mouth.

Ridgway was glancing from Hasbrouck to Clarke to me like a disgruntled eagle trying to decide which of us to bite first. Hasbrouck looked like an amateur gambler trying to fill an inside straight, Clarke's expression was mulish, and I suspect that I resembled a pole-axed cow.

"Can you do it, Triplet?" asked Ridgway, "get through that marsh?"

"Yes sir, we'll get them through if we have to push them."

There I go again, and little did I know how true that bit of braggadocio would be. I called King, "commanders meeting at 0100."

For a half hour we went over the detail of my plan that I had so unthinkingly proposed. That is, Hasbrouck and I did. Clarke just sulked.

General Hasbrouck, still obsessed with the fear of a counterattack from the Amblève-Wallerode ridge, wanted me to continue to screen the left flank from Bambusch to Auf der Hardt, a distance of six kilometers. However, I pointed out that if I had to guard that front against a possible counterattack my attacking force for taking Hunnange would be so weak that success would be doubtful. On the other hand, the 508th Parachute Regiment could continue to hold the Bambusch and Ebertange areas and garrison Auf der Hardt, releasing Seitz's battalion for the Hunnange job.

Second, I wanted to concentrate all my attention on Hunnange so I wanted to turn the 508th back to division control until the town was taken.

Last, if a German attack was made from the east the principal commanding points would be held by the 508th and any German force coming through the gaps to hit the flank of my column would be unfortunate—we'd be fully deployed for action.

Hasbrouck agreed, handed me the air-photo mosaic we'd been studying, and wished me luck. I mounted up and started for Elvange.

It was snowing again, hard.

Years later I learned how naive I had been during that miserable night. Actually there were three stars hovering on the verge of eclipse and to mix metaphors I was the poor damned chimpanzee that hauled their chestnuts out of the fire. The three generals didn't like each other; Ridgway was going to have Hunnange on the twenty-second of January or bust Hasbrouck to colonel, and Hasbrouck was so disgusted with Clarke that he would have relieved him except that Ridgway insisted that Clarke recapture St. Vith on the twenty-third, one month after he'd been run out of the town, figuratively rubbing his nose in it.

Quite a coil.

I found a very sleepy crew awaiting my arrival at the CP but they were thoroughly awakened when I stated that we would capture Hunnange that day. I asked Larsen and Sorenson for a rundown on the enemy situation before going into the plan of action. The information was meager. A patrol of one officer and fourteen men of Seitz's battalion had engaged four enemy half-tracks in the western outskirts of Medell. After machine-gunning the personnel and burning the tracks they had been attacked by a Tiger tank. They took cover in a stone house but had to leave by the back door when the tank started blasting the house to bits.

One of Wemple's outposts on Am Stein had been attacked by a combat patrol shortly after the snow had started the evening before. One man in field-green uniform had approached, hands up and waving one of our surrender propaganda leaflets. When challenged he called "Kamerad" and dropped prone while a dozen men in snowsuits behind him opened up on the outpost located by their "scout." There were no survivors except for the wounded scout who was so scared he was incoherent.

We were still getting considerable artillery and mortar fire from the Amblève area into Diedenberg and Auf der Hardt.

Little was known of the enemy except that they did occupy Amblève, Medell, Wallerode, the In der Eidt Forest, Hunnange, and St. Vith, but we did not know the units and strengths.

The snow was continuing to fall and the depth it would reach was unknown. Already it was deep enough to make movement difficult for the medium tanks with their duck-foot track plate extensions, and probably impossible for light tanks and half-tracks.

The railroad embankment between Born and In der Eidt was so high and steep that it formed a perfect antitank barrier. At one point a ridge ran down from Auf der Hardt to the railroad and the map and photograph agreed that a grade crossing might be made where the tracks entered the cut across the nose of the ridge.

Beyond the railroad the eastern branch of the Emma Rau appeared to be very narrow and could probably be spanned by one of our tank-borne bridges.

Southwest of the crossing the In der Eidt Forest was cut by frequent fire trails that would afford easy movement.

Beyond the forest an advance of one kilometer over the open fields would put us in Hunnange.

While I was outlining this situation General Hasbrouck came in with welcome news. "Task Force Brown of CCB has entered the Born Woods on the road Born-Moulinde-Nieder Emmels. He reports that he may be able to push through the woods in time to take part in your show, so I'm attaching him to CCA."

"Delighted to hear that, general. He can keep the Nieder Emmels Germans off our backs. Lieutenant Coombs, Colonel Brown's force is joining us. Set him up with frequencies and call signs in the command net."

I then gave the details of my plan of action.

Seitz would put a screening force over the railroad crossing, into In der Eidt Woods to protect Hochberg's engineers working at the railroad and Emma Rau crossings. Move out as soon as possible.

Hochberg's company of engineers was to start as soon as possible, coordinating their move with the paratroop screening force, reconnoiter the railroad and stream crossings, and get a bridge across the Emma Rau.

The main force would move out in column at 0600. Order of march: Seitz-Wemple-Rhea, Seitz from Auf der Heidt with men mounted on tanks and the borrowed half-tracks from the Twenty-third AIB should make the downhill run to the crossings long before Wemple's force, fighting the up-grade, could arrive.[3] Wemple and Rhea would move from Diedenberg with tank-dozers in the lead.

Task Force Brown was to drive through the Born Woods, pause at the east edge of the woods, and attack Nieder Emmels at the same time we attacked Hunnange from In der Eidt.

The 489th Armored Artillery would continue to fire on Meyrode and Medell while displacing batteries forward to the Elvange area to get within range of Hunnange. Colonel Milner was also to arrange for support on call from all division artillery. After making the crossing of the Emma Rau the four task forces were to deploy abreast, using designated fire trails, Brown in the eastern edge of Born Woods, Seitz in the right half of In der Eidt, Wemple in the left half, and Rhea in the southeast edge facing the Immelsberg Woods.

At the attack time to be announced later Brown's force would take Nieder Emmels, Seitz would occupy the eastern half of Hunnange, Wemple would take the western half of the town, and Rhea would occupy Immelsberg Woods.

By the time the orders were issued it was past 0200 so questions and discussions were cut to the essentials and the commanders left for a hard day of work.

The armored car would be impossible in the snow so I ordered the half-track to stand by for action at 0600. Tiger Bait's antenna had been replaced and she was my first mount, but I was taking no chances on my communications failing again.

Then, since I'd had three long days and a long one coming up, I turned the war over to Colonel King and the staff and pulled the featherbed up around my ears. There is never any situation so bad that it can't get worse (and usually does) so after a commander has done all he can he accomplishes more by getting himself in shape for the coming emergency than he does in continuing to jitter during the lull. A tired, sleepy, sick, or nervous commander can cause a hell of a lot of useless casualties.

Couldn't get to sleep until I'd staggered out to the war room and told King to attach B Company, 814th Tank Destroyers, in toto to Wemple's force. Following up his assault, they would be in perfect position to support either Rhea, Seitz, or with a short run Task Force Brown; I didn't think the enemy had enough tanks to make a serious attack but if they had—

Then off to the hours of anxiety nightmares—

Getting in Position

At 0500 I was up for coffee; no difficulty about getting it this time. Colonel King had all hands up and busy as bird dogs. There were no reports other than routine, which contrary to the proverb indicated bad news. Subordinates when having difficulties do not like to report them until they've tried to overcome them and reports flow in most frequently when everyone is making good progress. All force commanders were away from their command posts and all the executives reported progress being made, but I was skeptical enough to want to make sure.

Another foot of snow had fallen, making it thirty inches on the level, but the engineers had plowed the main road so Tiger Bait pounded down into Diedenberg in good time, trailed by the half-track.

The streets, lanes, and alleys of the town were crowded with tanks, infantry, half-tracks, and jeeps waiting (and anxious) to get on the way. Wemple's M4s had given up butting at the snowdrifts at the western exit, but progress was being made by the tankdozers. Rhea's men, pulled in from their outposts so they'd be in plenty of time to follow Wemple, couldn't move until Wemple cleared. The resulting congestion made one hell of a traffic jam, complicated by an occasional high-explosive shell from the direction of Amblève.

The move shortly developed into an advance on a single-tank front, the four tank-dozers in column leading up the two-kilometer slope to the middle between Auf der Hardt and Am Stein. The front dozer skimming the top foot off the snow would pile up a large bow wave. It would then turn off to one side, pushing its load of snow off the main route, the second dozer would then take the lead, followed by numbers three and four, while the former leader took place at the tail of the dozer column.

The plowing was painfully slow work and we barely made it. By the time we reached the crest three dozers were immobilized with burned-out or frozen clutches. But the remaining machine made easy work of the downhill slope to the crossing.

Seitz's force was moving down the slope behind the ridge toward the crossing and the first of his tanks had reached the railroad. Tiger Bait couldn't pass the dozer and was helplessly bellied when we tried, so I told the sergeant to bring her up when he could, and took off on foot down the slope.

The intermittent cracks of rifles and the high-pitched *plirrrrrpt* of Schmeissers indicated that Seitz's screening force was doing all right in the woods beyond the crossing point. His fourth tank was crossing the railroad as I panted onto the scene. The first two, loaded with paratroopers, were disappearing into the woods beyond. The third was struggling through the muck and mud of the Emma Rau and barely making it.

There was no bridge.

An air burst popped overhead. A mortar shell plopped instead of bursting at the stream crossing and emitted a cloud of smoke. Both were attempts by the enemy to register accurately for a concentration of fire on the crossing. There were occasional rattling bursts of 20-mm. antiaircraft stuff evidently fired from a considerable distance into the column struggling down the slope behind us. Heavy explosions indicated our held-up column on the slope above Diedenberg was catching hell from the German artillery in our left rear. And no bridge.

I saw Captain Hochberg plunging through the snow from the stream to the rail crossing and made a bad mistake. "Captain Hochberg."

"Yes sir."

"Captain, if you and I both live through this day I'm going to court-martial you for manslaughter. Where is your bridge?"

Much to Hochberg's credit he kept his temper. "The bridges are back there, sir. I hope they're still coming but with all that weight they're much worse off than the tanks in this snow. We had to do a lot of shoveling even to get them in the column. They're in Colonel Wemple's force near the tail and when they get here I'll put them in. But I'm afraid they won't be of much use; the ground is so marshy that the approaches will immediately become impassable. Our best bet is corduroy—my men are cutting logs to lay on the approaches and in the stream bed. I think we can make it that way."

He was absolutely right and I was thoroughly ashamed of my asinine outburst. "My sincere apologies, Hochberg, and I hope you'll consider my last remarks unsaid. One thing about the logs, if they're six to eight feet apart they'll do for the tanks. And build several approaches on this side only at first. We can tow them out. Pull off several tow cables, hitch them together, and post a tow tank on the firm ground beyond to lift them out. Post your engineer guides but you know what to do better than I do. On your way."

Another of Seitz's tanks was bucking over the railroad track. A sharp explosive *crack* sounded as it crept behind the other side of the cut. An antitank gun or a tank had been sited to enfilade the track, but the first one had missed. I stopped the next one until I caught one of Seitz's officers. "Lieutenant, there's a gun laid on this crossing. Post a reliable NCO here to halt every vehicle and warn them. Every tank and half-track is to jump across there like a bat out of hell, all the speed they can make. It'll be a rough ride but, oh yes, have infantrymen dismount and duck across individually. I don't want them thrown off."

"Yes sir, and when we're all across I'll pass the word on to the next column—I'll give the sentry a message to—"

"Won't be necessary, lieutenant, I'll tell Colonel Wemple myself."

I waded back to the half-track that had just crossed the saddle, and radioed Colonel King on the current situation. I asked him to have Milner's artillery drop smoke southeast of In der Eidt and west of the Wallerode ridge to get enemy observation off the crossing. The smoke was strangely ineffective—two days later I learned why.

In the meantime our vehicles continued to leap across the opening of the cut like the moving targets in a shooting gallery, and every time a tank jumped there was the sizzling crack of a high-velocity shell behind or overhead, but they were all misses. I suspect that the gun was located at such a distance that in spite of its velocity of three thousand feet per second and the doubtless superior reaction time of the gunner it just wasn't fast enough to catch such a fleeting target. Must have driven the Kraut out of his mind.

Hochberg's attempts to guide Seitz's few half-tracks through the marsh had miserably failed, with four of them hopelessly bogged at all angles, and his men were starting to tow one out. Those inferior imitations of a German invention should never have been born in the first place. I called the captain over. "Hochberg, the tanks are a necessity. Those half-breed abortions are a doubtful luxury. Let them sit here and rust or sink out of sight. Concentrate on getting the tanks across. I'll see that the tracks are stopped." I had my own track radio operator send messages to Seitz, Wemple, and Rhea: "Abandon half-tracks and shove them out of the way. Proceed on tanks or afoot."

Shortly thereafter the helpless tracks were ruthlessly pushed aside and ski-suited or white-sheeted infantrymen were hitching rides for themselves, their mortars, machine guns, and ammunition boxes on the backs of their supporting tanks. Those for whom there was no room followed afoot. The sight of a rifleman, his M-1 slung, shoving ahead with a mortar shell in each hand was proof of our parlous plight.

By the time Seitz's men had completed the crossing the Krauts had ranged in with a Nebelwerfer, affectionately known as screaming mee-mie because of the psychological effect the projectiles have on the unfortunate recipients. A Nebelwerfer fires volleys of up to a dozen 150-mm. rockets, each of which has a siren attached to the stabilizing vanes. These flights of rockets came screaming, ululating, and whistling into the crossing area, bursting with brain-jarring crashes but, due to the deep snow, with little casualty effect.

It was now 1100 and if any foolish gambler had offered me two bits for the whole confused command including my own frostbitten hide I'd have gladly taken the bargain. A third of my outfit was across the bog still bickering with the Jerries in the western corner of the woods, the Amblève artillery were still pounding at Rhea's force from the left rear, the antitank gun, mortars, and artillery (thank God they didn't have much of it) were slamming at us from the direction of Wallerode, and now these damned rockets were dropping in from God knows where. The crossing was getting churned up so badly at all points that we probably wouldn't get many more tanks across. It looked like we had drawn a broken sword and thrown the scabbard away.

Seitz reported his sector to be cleared, however, and Wemple's outfit was crossing now. The tanks plunged one by one into the marsh, the tracks would start to spin, then a crew of Hochberg's engineers would drag up and hook on the five-tow-cable line attached to one of the tow tanks standing on the solid ground beyond—then a slow, steady pull until the bogged tank got its feet under it on firm soil, unhook the cable, drag it back, and repeat about forty or fifty times.

The endurance of those engineers, cutting, carrying, laying, and re-laying logs; fumbling through knee-deep snow, ice water, and mud; hauling and hooking the two cables—their labors approached the su-perhuman. If this insane operation succeeded it would be due to the efforts of Hochberg's men to get us up to where we could fight. I could have done without one of the task forces, but the engineers were essential.

I had the headquarters half-track pulled across, since I could depend on its radio, and told the sergeant to bring Tiger Bait over at the tail of Wemple's column.

While I watched the towing operation, Colonel Rhea came up afoot to look at the situation and scout his direction of advance through the woods. "That artillery coming in from the rear is bad," he remarked. "First time I ever saw a shell kill the mounted rifle squad, the tank crew, and burn the tank. They sure hit the jackpot that time."

"I know, I've had the 489th doing counter battery firing in the Amblève area but they can't seem to silence the Krauts."

A flurry of shells and rockets started arriving at that point; we burrowed adjoining pits in a snowdrift and carried on our further conversation like a pair of jack-in-the-boxes, bobbing up between bursts. Rhea's snow-caked eyebrows and ears gave me my first good belly laugh of the day. He seemed almost as pessimistic as I felt. "This swamp crossing looks damned near impossible to me," he remarked.

"It damned near is, but you can make it. Hochberg's boys have the swing of it now and they'll get you across. If it gets worse and they can't, just leave your tanks and heavy weapons behind and come ahead with your rifle companies. Clearing Kninelsberg Woods will be a job principally for riflemen anyway."

"Can't we find a better crossing point upstream?"

"No, Hochberg's already looked."

I mounted the track and followed Seitz's trail through the fire lanes, finding his men somewhat bewildered but in good spirits. I stopped by a platoon who only knew that they were to "wait here." "Can you tell us where the Krauts are, colonel?" asked the rather scrubby-looking platoon sergeant. "We've run 'em all outa this patch of woods and the lieutenant's out looking for some more."

OK, if they were that interested. I spread my precious air photograph, pointed out where they were and where they were to go when Rhea's force was in position. They were very interested in Task Force Brown on their right and Wemple's force on their left. My briefing of these lads took almost ten minutes but the sincere thanks of the sergeant made me believe it was time well spent. I've never had a more interested audience.

We pushed the track forward until there was danger of its being spotted from Nieder Emmels, then I moved ahead on foot. Found Seitz and his company commanders at the forward edge of the woods looking over their objective. They were utterly reckless in exposing themselves, appearing totally indifferent to enemy reaction. I cautioned Seitz. "Colonel Seitz, your men have plenty of time before the jump-off and I don't want any of them killed unnecessarily on account of foolhardy exposure."

"Yes sir. You people keep behind cover and move slow and easy."

So with the respectful but secretly amused tolerance accorded to World War I veterans by the brash young warriors of today his lads became more circumspect about their snooping and peeking.

Both Nieder Emmels and Hunnange, each a kilometer distant, looked dead, no guns, no vehicles, no movement, and no smoke—which deceived no one. Any enemy positions were so thoroughly camouflaged with snow that Jerry could have had anything in that area, so we made the safe presumption that he did.

After hearing Seitz's final orders I returned to the track and found Tiger Bait panting behind her. A number of paratroopers were melting snow in their canteen cups at the idling exhausts for drinking water. All water cans were frozen solid. So was every canteen unless the owner had been foresighted enough to keep it warm inside his shirt.

We moved south through the principal fire lane to where Wemple was organizing for the attack and found his men still coming up. I had hoped to jump off at 1500 but that was hopeless. The possible advantage of surprise had long since disappeared, so we could afford to take our time and do it right. This was no time for a piecemeal or uncoordinated attack. I wanted certain success with the first dash. If any one of the forces failed, the reserve to be used would be the least engaged portion of the force that had had the easiest success, plus the 489th Armored Artillery Battalion and if necessary the rest of the division artillery. Chancy to put all our forces in the line, yes, but the mobility and strength of an armored command permits taking chances that would be unthinkable in an infantry brigade.

I mounted the track and Driver Sauer began wrenching the machine through the rutted snow, following the tank tracks toward the front. Beside the fire break lane ahead I noticed one of Seitz's lads sitting with his back against a pine hole, up to his waist in snow. A bloody bandage covered a goodly part of his bare right arm, forearm supported by the partially unbuttoned jacket in lieu of a sling. He seemed to be chewing or biting at something in his other hand, no, he was trying to open a K-ration package with his teeth. He grinned and waved the packet at us as we passed.

What a recruiting poster.

No, come to think of it, that picture in full color wouldn't draw many recruits for the infantry, but it would sure sell a lot of war bonds. I gave

Colonel King the current situation to be relayed to division, stating that we were planning on 1600 for the attack (subject to change). Then we went on to Task Force Wemple.

In a large brush-grown clearing facing the Hunnange-Nieder Emmels road I found a very reckless exposure on the part of Wemple's tanks and men getting organized for the attack. At the north end of the clearing I spotted five of the dreaded 88-mm. guns abandoned by the enemy and pulled the track and Tiger Bait in behind a couple of them for partial protection. Then I walked (waded) forward to see Colonel Wemple. His tanks were bunched altogether too close and Captain Britton was mounting his men on the tanks far too early. "Say, Colonel Wemple, let's get your tanks out of sight in the woods and tell Britton that we have an hour to wait. Let his men stand down and take it easy. Unless the Krauts are blind, we'll probably get shot at a little before we take off."

I found my pessimism to be warranted. Jerry began ranging on us with single artillery rounds and an occasional volley of screaming meemies. Not too effective but nerve-racking, as were the frequent messages relayed by King from division wanting to know about our progress. I could only reiterate that we were trying and would make it all right.

By 1530, I saw that Rhea could never make the 1600 deadline and that Brown probably could not. About that time General Hasbrouck called me direct, asking about the situation and reiterating that we must have the Hunnange crossroad that evening. He sounded desperate. "General Ridgway is threatening again to push the Thirtieth Division down from Nieder Emmelser Heide to take the town if we can't do it."

"No need for that, sir. Even if Rhea and Brown can't make the jump-off line I'll attack with Wemple and Seitz at 1700. They have enough force to take Hunnange and I can clear the other areas as troops become available, but I think they'll make it, and it will be a lot more economical if they do. Much cheaper to do the whole job at once with everything I've got."

"OK, you're on the ground—1700 it is."

Success

The next hour was a miserable eternity, Britton's riflemen huddling against tanks, destroyers, and tree trunks for partial protection from the harassing tree bursts.

At 1625, Colonel Brown reported that he was in position in the south edge of the Bois de Born and could jump off over the fifteen hundred yards of snow against Nieder Emmels at the time stated. Just as I had expected the Bois de Born Germans weren't about to try to cut me off—they had feared that they were about to be surrounded and had abandoned their position in the woods. So much for Clarke's fears.

At 1645, Rhea called about his troubles. "I've got less than half my tanks up here and don't think I can make it."

"Tanks would be nice but not at all necessary on that brush-beating job you have, Rhea. You attack fast with what you have at the time stated. Everybody rolls at the same time."

I had called for three TOTs (all shells exploding sixty feet above the targets at the same time) by division and corps artillery, the first volley at exactly 1700, and directed all forces to start rolling on the first blast. Artillery thereafter to be available on call by task force forward artillery observers.

As the second hand of my watch showed 4:59:59 a tremendous swishing overhead indicated that the 489th and her sister battalions were on the ball; a thunderous crash in Hunnange, Nieder Emmels, and Bois de Kninelsberg proved it. The anxious drivers jazzed their engines and Wemple's infantry-laden tanks and destroyers started to roll.

A second screeching overhead, a series of bursts on the objectives, and a volley of bursts over our heads caught us with their shower of steel splinters. Infantrymen were dropping or falling off tanks; the ones that dropped like bundles of laundry had probably been hit. The artillery officer crouching behind Wemple's turret was yelling into his radio, "Cease fire, short," Britton was standing up waving his M-1 like a baton, bellowing, "Mount up, let's go," and another volley showered us with tree branches and chunks of metal. It was hell with the gates ajar. As the British would say, it was bloody awful.

It took some doing on the part of Wemple and Britton to get them going again, but go they did. Fourteen tanks and a dozen destroyers lurched out of the woods in two ragged lines and took up the fire, blasting at every house, barn, bush, and snow-covered haystack, everything that could contain or hide a tank or gun in Wemple's sector was fair game.

The big picture was imposing, forty-five tanks on a mile or more of front, erupting like so many miniature volcanoes. It was the prettiest battle I ever saw. The erstwhile quiet winter scene with the bluish shadows of an early dusk emphasizing the white of the snow was cut through by white gun-flashes and crisscrossed with red tracers that cast pinkish reflections over the scene. Multicolored pyrotechnics fired by the German garrison calling for help or illuminating the front added to the show.

Once started there was no hesitation. All tanks were forging ahead, butting their way through the drifts, keeping up their marching fire, throwing lots of ammunition ahead of them as they moved. Every tank had an infantryman manning the .50 caliber antiaircraft gun, sprinkling fiery steel the breadth of the objective.

At this time I saw an example of the remarkably good shooting that was characteristic of the gunners of the Seventh Armored. A German tank or destroyer camouflaged in a white mound in the southern outskirts of Nieder Emmels hit one of Wemple's M4s. The tank exploded and burned—a fountain of white flame, burning tracers, and internal explosions. God damn. A hellish sight. But the red line of the German tracer had barely faded from the retina when one of our tanks and a tank destroyer in the second wave lanced a converging pair of shots that exploded the German vehicle. Yes, Wemple's gunners were good.

The headquarters track floundered forward through the drifts to the end of the clearing and the operator handed me two similar messages: "Brown to Six, am being fired on from left rear." "Seitz to Six, receiving fire from Task Force Wemple."

Hell and corruption. And that German that our people had just blasted was in Seitz's sector. Maybe some of Wemple's men are a bit careless.

"Caution Seitz about firing into Brown—I'll take care of Wemple."

Wemple's command tank was sitting in the plain two hundred yards out of the clearing. I didn't want to take the thin-skinned track or Tiger Bait out there and the interminable call signs and recognition formulas of the simplest radio message would take so long that I stomped out there afoot. Wemple started to dismount but I signed him to stay in his turret so he would be instantly available to his radio. "See that you're not shooting into Seitz," I yelled, but what with the tank engine idling rapidly and the general thunderous hubbub he couldn't get it, leaned way over, cupping his ears.

"Can't hear you, colonel," he shouted.

A handful of bullets streaked in from Nieder Emmels and crackled on the armor and I dashed around to the left side of the tank. There a high-velocity tracer, looking like a flaming football, cracked by close enough to scorch the paint on his turret and a mortar shell blossomed, so I changed my mind and floundered back again, Wemple leaning over the hatches trying to follow me.

"Wait, colonel," he bellowed, "I don't think it's very safe out here, let me back up a little."

That remark was a gem of understatement that I will cherish to my grave. To add to the comedy he backed up thirty yards (still leaving his tank a bull's-eye out on the snowy plain) and settled calmly down to hear Seitz's complaint with total disregard to the hell and hardware that was cracking and sizzling past him from all angles.

He started his checking but by that time the situation was clarified. Message from Brown: "We bypassed some Krauts. Clearing them up now."

The cease-fire called by our artillery observer hamstrung our artillery for further firing; every gun in every battery in every battalion had to be checked for elevation before another shell could be fired. But in spite of this handicap the attack forged ahead, the tanks and destroyers slogging ahead at full snow-butting speed, until the riflemen were jumping off their mounts and tossing grenades through the nearest windows.

The German defense caved in, improvised white flags fluttered in windows and doorways, Seitz's paratroops took possession of a Tiger tank that had been abandoned by its crew with the engine still idling. By dint of a good deal of butting, backing and filling, Tiger Bait pushed across the field to Hunnange. We set up the CP Forward in a small, relatively undamaged stone house where the Belgian owner immediately claimed that our men had his "rahddio gestohlen." I was not in the mood nor had the time, however, to give my sympathetic attention to this doubtless false plaint.

Message by Slidex code to Workshop-6: "We have Nieder Emmels, Hunnange, Kninelsberg. 1737, Wretch-6."

Fourteen.

Recapture of St. Vith

Loose Ends

There were a lot of loose ends to tidy up and the work would go on all night. I called King in the clear, to hell with the Kraut radio intercept. "Wretch-5, this is Wretch-6, send all half-track ambulances to your side of the Emma Rau crossing. I'll have our wounded sent to this side. Your stretchermen hand-carry over the marsh. We have Nieder Emmels so you can request Workshop engineers to plow the Born-Nieder Emmels road. Send fuel and ammunition refills as soon as road is clear for trucks. Send trucks and MP escorts for eight hundred prisoners. Request Workshop recovery vehicles to tow half-tracks out of the Emma Rau. Send half-tracks up via Born-Nieder Emmels road. Over."

"Wretch-6, this is Wretch-5. Received your message. Wilco. Over."

"Wretch-5, this is Wretch-6. Out."

That should be enough to keep Colonel King happily busy for [illegible].

So came to a fairly happy ending one of the damnedest, most confused military messes I'd ever been involved with. Two hours of planning, twelve hours of gut-bursting labor under impossible and hazardous conditions, and half an hour of combat. That morning it was hazardous, by noon it was hopeless, at 1700 it was in the hands of Mars, Minerva, and Thor, and thirty minutes later the show was a complete success.

Message: "Workshop-6 to Wretch-6. Return to Wretch CP rear."

I turned the local problems over to Colonel Wemple, reminding him to push the evacuation of the wounded on or in tanks, and to outpost our position. Then Wretch-CP Forward took off for that God-awful crossing. Tiger Bait got bogged up to her bow gun so I abandoned her, told the sergeant to get towed out when he could, waded across (my God it was cold, and how could the poor damned engineers work all day in that freezing gruel), and commandeered an engineer jeep to take me back to Elvange.

Found Hasbrouck, the division artillery commander, and Colonel Milner there with Colonel King. Hasbrouck was naturally delighted with CCA's total success, but was quite concerned by the report that we had been fired on by our own artillery at the jump-off. So were the artillerymen, and so for that matter was I. Those two volleys had cost us thirty men. It was quite a brouhaha for a few minutes of protests, accusation, reclama, and recrimination.

188

"It wasn't our guns, they all checked perfectly."

"All I know is that every time your volleys came over one volley burst over our heads."

"Did you trace the direction of the strike?"

"No, an air burst doesn't leave a trace of the strike."

"Didn't you hear the direction they were coming from?"

"Yes, from the rear."

"Couldn't they have been German guns; that battery near Amblève had been hitting you all day, according to your forward observer."

"Yes but that was all single rounds. They probably had only one gun. This was a volley, followed by a second volley."

"When you called a 'cease-fire' did you—"

"Just a moment. I didn't call a cease-fire. That was your forward observer and I presumed that your man knew his business."

Colonel Milner had retired from the discussion and had been doing some heavy thinking. He now put forward a theory that made sense. "General, gentlemen, I think I may have the answer. Every gun in division artillery checked for elevation. The German artillery, probably a battery, has been harassing CCA all day with single rounds during their approach march and with single tree bursts on Colonel Wemple's position in the woods according to Lieutenant Ames's statements. Why they used only single rounds we don't know, probably for conservation of ammunition. Let us suppose that all guns in the German battery were loaded and firing in turn. Let us also suppose that the German battery commander is an intelligent, fast-thinking type. In his position near Amblève he could hear our first TOT fired toward the Hunnange target. Having experience, having observed our methods, he anticipated that we would fire additional TOTs. I believe that he then commenced 'all guns' and, when he heard our second TOT 'fire!,' purposely gave our troops the idea that we were firing short."

"That is probably the explanation, Milner. There is no great difference between a posit (radar-fused) burst sixty feet above the ground and a tree burst in a sixty-foot treetop. It certainly fooled us and Lieutenant Ames. I'll spread the word."

So we had fallen for a damned clever Hun trick and put our artillery out of action for an hour.

Oh well—

Accompanied General Hasbrouck to General Clarke's CP in Born. Hasbrouck was full of zing and good humor since General Ridgway was off his back about Hunnange. Clarke was his usual morose, sulky self. The conference went on three times as long as necessary and I was sleepy unto death but kept my mouth firmly closed except for an occasional necessary "yes sir," "no sir," or "I understand." No more brilliant tactical ideas from me, not until I'd recovered from the last one.

The talkfest wound up like this: Clarke was to take St. Vith next day, the twenty-third of January, exactly one month after he had retired from the place. The attack would start at 1430. I would patrol vigorously toward St. Vith in the early morning. Turn Task Force Brown and Nieder Emmels over to CCB. Loan CCB my Task Force Rhea for the attack. Support CCB's attack by overhead fire from my tanks and tank destroyers. Fair enough.

By the time I got to Elvange it was quite late, so after passing the new directives on to the staff I had a belated lunch and went to bed, in earnest this time. Must have slept well, at least the Jerries blasted the roof off the house next door during the night and I knew nothing about it until I was told next morning.

Up betimes, directing the headquarters commandant to move the CP into Born, took the jeep and Tiger Bait and found the road into Nieder Emmels well plowed and beaten down by traffic. The day was beautifully clear and very cold.

Found Colonel King at the CP Forward in a flaming fury. Due to some of his tanks being bogged down, plus the refusal of the artillery to fire pending the check of elevations, Colonel Rhea had not fully occupied the Kninelsberg Woods the night before, and King had had practically to hand-lead him to the southern edge of the forest. King was recommending court-martial or at least Rhea's immediate relief and transfer. "If the Krauts had had tanks or guns in those woods they'd have enfiladed your whole line. And the log shows that he reported that he had 'occupied Kninelsberg.' He didn't say 'partly.'"

"All right, look into it and after this show is over we'll see what's to be done about it. What was the result of the patrolling?"

"Britton's two patrols reached the northern outskirts of St. Vith and returned with no difficulty, so CCB ought to have easy going into town. I've reported to division and CCB already."

"Thank you, King—now I'd like to have you go back and organize our new CP in Born."

Made the rounds with O'Hare and the jeep, less conspicuous than Tiger Bait and equally shell-proof. I found the men to be in good spirits, considering the weather, and in a winning frame of mind.

All task force commanders were assembling their tanks and soft-skinned vehicles behind houses, buildings in Hunnange, or under cover of the Hunnange-Kninelsberg ridge, anywhere to get them out of sight of the dominating high ground of Wallerode.

I visited Wemple, who had selected an isolated house six hundred yards from Hunnange for his CP. It was pretty hairy, jeeping along that blank-white landscape not more than a thousand yards below probable German observers, and I asked him about his choice. "I say, Wemple, don't you think this is a bit exposed for your command post?"

"No, it's a lot better than the place I had in town. We were getting shelled in there regularly, that's why I moved out here early this morning. Besides, this place has a nice cellar."

"Yes, but that wide open road between here and town, isn't that dangerous?"

"I don't know, sir, you're the only one that's made that run in daylight." Dear God. If we could only make it back.

Task Force Rhea, occupying the snow-drifted Kninelsberg Woods, had been fortunate in inheriting the excellent German dugouts and log huts, while the outposts had burrowed in and set up housekeeping like Eskimos. The most effective method of getting comfortable in snow and subzero weather was for two men to select a drift three or four feet deep, dig out a rectangular hole five by eight feet down to the ground surface, roof the forward six feet with cedar logs or limbs two or three inches thick, spread a shelter half over the roof, hang the second tent half over the entrance, and pile the excavated snow over the roof to the depth of a foot or more. Pine tips on the floor for insulation and bedding. The overhead logs gave protection against the splinters of tree bursts, a candle flame used for heating a K-ration would warm the place enough for the man off duty to take off his boots in comparative comfort, and the pine tips made a soft mattress. I noted that the man on watch in his two-by-five-foot snow pit usually had rigged another log as a seat. Ingenious.

The trip was quiet until O'Hare and I left the jeep to plow through a field afoot to visit an outpost at the south edge of In der Eidt under the observation of Wallerode heights. I had thought that two men, well separated, would not be considered a worthwhile target. I was wrong; some spendthrift Jerry observer called in three successively closer mortar bursts, and we pulled back faster than I would have thought possible. After ten minutes of perspiring and breathing heavily we went the long way around behind a ridge and made it unscathed.

About 1000 on January 23, I was back at the Belgian farmer's house we were using as a CP. Glancing out the window toward Nieder Emmels, I saw Brigadier General Clarke trailed by a trio of his officers dragging up the road toward the center of Hunnange. Afoot. Thinking that he would stop in for a cup of coffee or a briefing on the situation I checked on the coffee, cups, and chairs, and laid out our situation map on the table. All set.

But in vain. The big fur overcoat dragged by the "Wretch CP Forward" sign without missing a beat, and the overweight owner didn't even glance this way. Speedy was curiously not making a social or official call on CCA.

He must be mad at us.

Maybe we should have taken three days to capture Hunnange.

Attack

About 1030, General Hasbrouck called, "Wretch-6, this is Workshop-6. My boss wants to see the show. He'll be at your place an hour ahead of time. Pick out a good safe place where he can see the whole thing."

"Roger. Wilco. Over."

"Out."

OK, General Ridgway would be at my CP at 1330, and would want a safe observation post with a good view. I'd fix him up.

I went forward and found the ideal observation post on the military crest of the forward slope, immediately southwest of Hunnange where the Germans had dug squad trenches four feet deep during their siege of St. Vith. Perfect. The Germans are masters in the art of field fortification and these had everything—depth, good parapets, and inconspicuous location. They were laid out in the field halfway between the Hunnange crossroads and the top of the dominating knoll to the southwest, two hundred yards south of the road, and I feared that those areas would take a beating from artillery and Nebelwerfers when the attack started.

About 1200, Colonel Ryan called. "We've got a squadron of P-38s in the air with two-hundred-pound bombs that they want to unload. Can you use them?"

Good question. It was going to be Clarke's attack but until 1400, I was in charge of the sector, so—"Yes, I'll use them. I'll put my birdman on them now." I called my air liaison officer who was with Wemple's headquarters. "Division is giving us a squadron of P-38s. Direct them to unload on St. Vith. Have them smear any target they can see in town."

I left O'Hare with his jeep behind a building and walked out across the plain behind the ridge east of town where some of Wemple's tanks, destroyers, and "soft" vehicles were parked, waiting for the attack. The birdman joined me and we moved forward toward the crest of the ridge to see the blasting.

"Any minute now," the be-winged lieutenant assured me.

"Good, they should soften up the Krauts a bit."

"No sir, they'll annihilate 'em."

It was very comforting to hear this assurance from an expert. Although not commanding the attack, I had a vested interest in it since the Twenty-third AIB and the Seventeenth Tanks were taking part.

"Hyar they come" yelled someone among the parked tracks, and coming they were, from our left rear, neat five-plane flights in column at two thousand feet. A beautiful display of air power.

As the leading flight reached the prolongation of our line the planes peeled off successively and swept down on my vehicles, preceded by a storm of .50 caliber tracers and followed by the exploding fountains of two-hundred-pound bombs.

I floundered back to the nearest vehicle, jerked loose an identification panel, a fluorescent flame-colored rectangle two by five feet, and flapped it at them ineffectually. Others were doing the same. Birdman had regained his jeep and was yelling into his radio transmitter. But most of the lads had sensibly dived into cover on the friendly side of their vehicles or were digging prone into the snow.

The first flight having softened us, the succeeding flights finished the job of annihilation. Birdman was shouting at the squadron leader, using language that would ordinarily get him, a lieutenant, court-martialed, but still they came.

After unloading all their munitions the flights reformed and zoomed off to the northwest, well satisfied with a good day's work.

There were apparently no vehicles burning. I would probably get a horrendous "butcher bill" from the surgeon later. Thoroughly sick and disgusted, I started back toward my OP beyond the crossroad. Heard the diving scream of propellers behind me and being just then allergic to airplanes I glanced back. There was a lone P-38 dropping in from over Kninelsberg, doubtless the squadron leader who had belatedly recognized our vehicles and panels, probably coming over to waggle his wings and drop a note of apology.

But I was quite put out about his stupidity, damned if I was going to forgive, forget, and wave at him. I went stomping on my way, still mad. He ripped over at minimum elevation and immediately after he'd howled past there was a jarring thump as a two-hundred-pound bomb landed in a garden thirty feet away, a dud.

Close air support. Hah.

Of course I understand that the air force traveling at 250 or more miles an hour has a difficult time seeing the small picture we have on the ground. I know that the Germans also use colored identification panels in two-color combinations just like we do, and that day we might have been using the same code. And I had heard that bomb-loaded planes can't go back and land at their base without fully unloading their bombs somewhere.

But I also know that we asked them to hit St. Vith instead of Hunnange, that the two towns are two kilometers apart, that Hunnange is a small village at a simple four-way crossroad while St. Vith is a fair-sized town with seven roads and a railroad, that Hunnange is on a hill while St. Vith lies in a bowl-shaped valley, that our tanks, destroyers, and half-tracks bear little resemblance to their German counterparts, and that we were displaying the correct color code on every vehicle.

As for unloading their blasted bombs, they had all of Germany and a goodly section of Belgium to dump them on. Why us?

O'Hare, parked behind a building in the edge of town, gave me the answer. "Of course they unload on us, colonel. They've found that it's dangerous to strafe Germans. We don't shoot back, the Krauts do."

"By God, I think you're right, O'Hare."[1]

About 1300, CCB troops started moving into and through Hunnange deploying, with Rhea's task force, in town and behind the Hunnange ridge on a two-thousand-meter front. All of Wemple's tanks and destroyers and Seitz's tanks had crept into cover behind buildings or in turret defilade behind the crest. I had sent O'Hare back to the CP to intercept General Ridgway and guide him to the OP on foot—it was only four hundred yards and much safer than riding.

But about 1330 to my surprise, disgust, and horror, here came my wild Irishman skidding his jeep along the road on the crest with two other jeeps skidding behind him. General Ridgway and five of his staff dismounted and posed. I galloped up there. "Colonel Triplet, sir. I recommend we move down into those trenches, general, we're right on the skyline here."

"Oh, I don't think that will be necessary," says he, looking over the lines of soldiery, tanks, and destroyers huddled behind the houses or crouched behind the ridge.

"O'Hare, get these jeeps out of sight."

He jazzed his engine and skidded ahead to the cover of the next house, closely followed by the general's jeeps. I wished I could have gone with them.

The Jerries began slamming a few shells into Hunnange and the knoll, just as I had prophesied. Our artillery began tuning up, hammering the main road junctions and the roads beyond St. Vith.

At 1400 my tanks and destroyers crawled out from behind houses, crests, and shrubbery. They swung their turrets, waggled their guns, and opened a rattling hail of aimed fire on likely point targets all along the front. The destroyer behind the first building on our left lunged forward into the open, flexed its gun like a boxer limbering up in the ring, settled for three rounds, and fired. I was wroth at the idea of wasting expensive ammunition with such "In God we trust" shooting but followed the tracer and the sole remaining church steeple in town collapsed (hopefully with the German observers) when the shell burst. Damned good for a quick draw.

I was getting a stiff neck, starting to duck as usual for everything coming, passing, or going, but having rigidly to check the impulse on account of the general standing like a statue "influencing the troops by his example."

Finally a Kraut 75-mm. assault gun bracketed us with three fast rounds that were close enough, what the air force would call wide hits.

I tried again. "General, I've got a trench down there with good—"

"All right, I think we can move down there now," and we leisurely strolled the two hundred yards down the slope to my selected OP. I had to stay with him, it wouldn't have been polite for me to make it in track time as my twitching toes were yearning to do.

At 1430, CCB's armored infantry creaked to their frozen feet and started toward the town, plodding through the drifts with their tanks idling along with the first wave, firing as they moved. Successive thin waves of infantry followed. It would have made a good movie in technicolor with sound effects but if the Germans had had any strength it would have been very hard on the tanks that were moving at one mile an hour. Clarke would have done better to mount all the riflemen he could on his tanks and move in fast.

There was little resistance. Not more than two hundred prisoners were taken. But it was a good show. General Ridgway thanked me for the entertainment, mounted his star-flagged jeep, an M-1 at the ready, rode the skyline road out of sight. I relaxed and resumed my cowardly custom of ducking for everything that I heard coming my way.

Sometime later between campaigns General Ridgway gave a cocktail party for his commanders and staff. I recognized one of his young men as having been at my elbow at St. Vith. "You remember St. Vith, don't you—weren't you one of the silhouettes in that shooting gallery?" I asked.

"I sure do—was. That third round gave me a wind burn," he replied with feeling.

"Well, what's the reason for him standing out in the open like Napoleon at Austerlitz?"

"The general is very religious, reads the Bible and prays. You know, 'a thousand shall fall at my right hand and ten thousand at my left, but the arrow that flies by day shall not come near me.' He firmly believes that God will not permit him to be hit before Germany is totally defeated."

"Seems to me that may be all right for him if God is taking a personal interest in his welfare but I'm an atheist and it probably makes it tough on his staff and junior commanders who don't have that Divine Protection."

On reaching the CP, I put my feet up and mulled over Clarke's attack on St. Vith that afternoon. It had been carried out in the classic style of the battle of Cambrai in the Great War, infantry on foot accompanying tanks moving at a speed of a little over a mile an hour.[2] Suicidal.

If the Germans had had the right weapons and/or their usual pugnacity he would have lost a lot of men and tanks and one of his task forces he'd borrowed from me.

I believe that a modern armored attack should be made at the top practical speed, riflemen mounted on the tanks and all guns firing, followed by the rest of the infantry in armored carriers, in trucks, or afoot. But the winning principle is speed.

The enemy will be shooting as accurately and rapidly as possible throughout the attack. If he can shoot 15,000 projectiles while your attack moves toward the objective at ten miles an hour he will be able to fire 150,000 if you move in at one mile an hour. It's that simple, almost mathematical. If you lose 15 tanks and 150 men at one mile an hour you'll lose less than 2 tanks and 10 men if you move in fifteen times as fast.

Further, a rapidly moving target is harder to hit, the fire in movement will disturb the enemy, and the rapidly approaching menace will probably affect the enemy marksmanship.

So from all viewpoints the chances of economical success are increased and casualties of men and machines are reduced by speed.

I have heard that Clarke had stated that General Ridgway did not understand armored warfare. I began to wonder if Speedy did.

Fifteen.

High Ground

Getting Ready

Conference at division CP at Born. Hasbrouck was in good spirits, with no trace of the anxiety that had ridden him the last four days. General Ridgway was evidently satisfied with the recapture of St. Vith and had taken off the pressure; at least he wasn't present on this occasion. "Gentlemen, I want to introduce Colonel Parker of the 424th Regimental Combat Team, attached to the Seventh for this campaign."

The middleweight, lean, dark, and weathered colonel to Hasbrouck's left rear took a step forward and nodded, then took a chair at the far end of the semicircle. Hasbrouck resumed his briefing.

"The enemy still occupies the Bois de St. Vith, Wallerode, Keppelborn, Langterberg, Medell, Meyrode, and Amblève—all on dominating high ground overlooking our positions. What units and in what strength is unknown, but it is believed only expendable second-class units remain holding the flanks of the salient. We are to capture these positions tomorrow and push combat patrols two kilometers beyond this line. The dense woods and mountainous terrain beyond the objectives make the use of armor impracticable so from there on the Eighty-second Airborne Division will take over. Bruce, CCB will move through Prumerberg and push ahead a kilometer into the Bois de St. Vith on the right flank of the attack.

"Triplet, Task Force Rhea will revert to CCA and you will have Colonel Griffen's Thirty-eighth Armored Infantry Battalion and a 4.2 chemical mortar company attached. You will take Langterberg, Keppelborn, and Wallerode. Colonel Parker, you will capture Medell, Meyrode, and Amblève. We have plenty of time to accomplish this mission, all day tomorrow, and will be supported by a battalion of corps artillery. In order to concentrate the support of division and corps artillery for each attack I intend to have your attacks made at least at two-hour intervals. Two hours will enable each of you to clear your objective and send out your patrols. The question is in what order should the attacks be made? Think it over and decide the time you would like to jump off in each sector."

General Hasbrouck let us talk. Having stupidly talked myself into a bear trap about Hunnange a couple of days before, I maintained a heavy silence and studied the map. The imposing Langterberg-Wallerode ridge in my sector was of outstanding importance. Centrally located and standing three hundred feet higher than any terrain in our lines, it gave the Germans commanding observation over all of our division sector.

197

When we took possession it would require the German artillery, mortars, and Nebelwerfers to fire blind. The slope was also steep and the snow on those hillsides would practically preclude the use of armor. Yes, it would be primarily an infantry affair, a long, slow advance through knee-deep snow uphill all the way. Overwatch with tanks and destroyers and get them up if and when we could. Damn.

Finally Clarke spoke up. "I'll attack at 0600 and should be well into the St. Vith Woods by 0800."

I kept my dark silence and made notes, disregarding Hasbrouck's expected stare in my direction. At long last Colonel Parker asked permission to move at 0800. Good.

Then without apparent enthusiasm I took the leavings. I would attack at 1000.

That was just what I wanted, attacking with men well rested, time for visual reconnaissance, and superior visibility for direct and observed fire. Furthermore, CCB pushing ahead on the right and the 424th shoving in on the left would put my opponent well out on a salient, lower his morale, and obviate the possibility of flanking fire on my men. Last, it would permit my use of artillery support for a longer period if necessary. Although my lads had the toughest job, I felt that these conditions would give us success with the fewest casualties. Selfish of me, but remembering Hunnange, I wasn't feeling charitable.

At the CP in Hunnange, I found that Colonel King had had a rough night. He complained about the screaming meemies, of which the Germans apparently had an inexhaustible supply. One flight had removed most of the roof of the command post. "Played hell with the ceiling too. If this stuff thaws we're going to have to move."

"OK, King, get another CP after this meeting, one with a cellar this time. And tomorrow night we'll move into the best house in Wallerode."

The commanders were all present. Wemple of the Seventeenth Tanks, Rhea of the Twenty-third Infantry, Seitz of the second battalion of the 517th Parachute Regiment, Hochberg of B Company of the Thirty-third Engineers, and Lieutenant Colonel Griffen of the Thirty-eighth AIB. Colonel Griffen was a tall, well-built, colorless, competent-appearing blond type. I'd never worked with him before, but he and his battalion had a good reputation.

I distributed the marked maps that Major Larsen and his crew had worked up for this show and gave the group the division picture, including the respective times of attack for CCB, the 424th, and CCA. Then I went into the details marked on their maps.

"Colonel Rhea, from your present position in eastern St. Vith you will move up the slope to the northeast and take Wallerode. We know that as of last night there were seven tanks and at least two hundred infantry in Wallerode so I recommend that in addition to your bazookas you take along any Panzerfausts your men can pick up. Due to the slope I doubt if you'll be able to use your tanks in taking the place except for covering fire, but you'll have them for defense as soon as we can get a road plowed.

"Colonel Griffen, your battalion with one platoon of M4s and one platoon of tank destroyers attached will move from the Bois de Born to In der Eidt, no Colonel Wemple will have your tanks and destroyers waiting for you in In der Eidt. You will attack on this line, Gut Eidt Farm–An der Strasse, and capture Keppelborn. You also should bring along Panzerfausts—they'll shoot through seven inches of armor while your bazookas only penetrate two and one-half inches. You won't be able to use your tanks in the early phases of the attack, but Captain Hochberg's engineers will get them up to you as soon as possible.

"Colonel Seitz, you will move your battalion from In der Eidt through Hervert and this ravine up the north slope of Langterberg and clear the hill. This move will be impossible for armor so your tanks and destroyers will revert to Colonel Wemple until after you and Colonel Griffen have your objectives and a road has been plowed. I see your men frequently lugging Panzerfausts so I don't need to caution you on this point.

"Colonel Wemple, your task force will be in reserve in the southern part of In der Eidt and the eastern edge of Kninelsberg Woods where your tanks and destroyers have the best fields of fire on the objectives. As soon as objectives are cleared you will move to a position at An der Strasse.

"We will be supported by division artillery and a battalion of eight-inch howitzers from corps. Each assault force will have the firepower of at least one battalion on call at any time, more if you need it. Use your forward observers and pour it on.

"I have a chemical mortar company attached. The captain is familiar with our plan and states that he can give us a smoke screen across the two thousand yards of front, providing the wind is favorable. Since this will be primarily an infantry-artillery show we will try to use smoke to protect our riflemen through that slow uphill drag through the snow. I know that tankers don't like smoke, Colonel Wemple, but you'll get your chance if the Krauts move their armor forward to meet us.

"Captain Hochberg, your company will advance with Task Force Griffen. Find and develop crossings of the Born–St. Vith railroad embankment. Thereafter start clearing tank trails from Colonel Wemple's reserve at An der Strasse to all three objectives as shown on your map. I believe you have the equipment from division engineers."

"Four tank-dozers and two plows from division, sir."

"Excellent. As usual your work on the crossings and the trail net is of vital importance. We're hamstrung without them.

"For all of you, your movement orders, times and routes, are shown on the tables attached to your maps.

"Time of attack, 1000.

"Questions?"

There were the anticipated questions and complaints. How impossible the mission was for armored troops, tanks and half-tracks couldn't be used, the men were tired, and the heavy weapons would have to be hand-carried, an infantry division would be better suited for the job, and smoke would hamper precise shooting. Everyone had something to say except Seitz—he wouldn't have complained if Langterberg had been a vertical ice wall.

While making the rounds that evening, I found Colonel Wemple and Captain Britton hashing over the details of the night move and joined them. Britton was using an improvised crutch, the crotch of a tree limb, and was unable to put his broken foot to the ground.

"Don't think I can claim a 'bloody heart' on it," he remarked. "The skin isn't broken and it was a 'billiard.' When the Krauts were moving in on us last night a screaming meemie blasted the top out of a tree and the butt end smashed my foot flat. Damned silly thing but it hinders me a little."

I saw a demonstration of this hindering at that moment; another flight of rockets screamed down and while Wemple and I leaped for the protection of a wall Britton hobbled, fell, and scrambled on his three serviceable limbs. "You can't stay up here in that shape, Britton," I told him as soon as the volley of bursts permitted conversation. "You turn your company over to your exec and get your foot fixed up."

"Maybe I'll have to, sir. If I ever take this boot off I'll never get it on again."

"Who will you leave in command?"

"I'll turn the company over to Lieutenant Perry. Of course he's a college man but I don't hold that against him. He's the senior officer and he's a pretty good fighter too. I'll send him up here."

"And by the way, Britton, this will make your fourth Purple Heart and the odds are heavy against you. Stay in the hospital, don't come back till the war is over. You're too good a man to get yourself killed."

"Oh, I'll be back, sir," and he jeeped back to his company.

I had met Captain Britton in the Twenty-third AIB area a few days before. Tall, thin, slightly stooped, lean, weathered face, dark hair, and intense expression. Two Silver Stars and three Purple Hearts. Seemed to be hyperactive. Stuttered. I inquired about him and looked over his record. Found that he was disliked by Colonel Rhea, was overaggressive, was liked by Colonel Wemple for the same quality, was an old Regular Army sergeant with a battlefield commission, was a fourth-grade dropout, and disliked Reserve officers and college men. Always carried an M-1 rifle instead of the carbine suitable to his rank.

"Reminds me of 'Abdul the Bul-bul Ameer,' " I commented.

"And a third-grade education," remarked Wemple. "Just imagine him with a college degree."

Getting Through

We had had plenty of time for route and area reconnaissance so the units moved into their jump-off positions after dark in good shape and without the usual pre-attack confusion. Most of the men set up light housekeeping for the night by coiling up in the nearly snow-free hollows under the evergreens. The temperature was way down but there was no wind, so the men were able to get some sleep.

There was a flurry of small-arms fire during the early part of the night when one of Griffen's patrols encountered a German combat patrol just south of Gut Eidt Farm, and our patrol returned two men short. That was bad news. The enemy now might have our complete plan of action for the day.

Came 0600, the morning was clear and cold and heavy artillery firing began in CCB's sector on our right. The blasting tapered off shortly to only occasional concentrations, so resistance was probably light.

Shortly after 0600 the two missing members of the Thirty-eighth Infantry patrol came in, somewhat the worse for wear. They had both been wounded during the clash with the enemy patrol and unable to keep up as our men withdrew. They had made their way to Gut Eidt Farm, where they had been hidden by the Belgian family during the German search of the place. Amazing. An exception to the pro-Nazi loyalty of the Belgians I'd seen so far.

At 0800 the 424th jumped off on our left with a thunderous roar of artillery and the rattle of machine-gun fire. The blasting, bickering, and snarling continued in that area for the full allotted two hours.

Just before 1000, I had Tiger Bait and the jeep on the road through In der Eidt where I could observe the 4.2 mortar company. This was the first time I had been able to see these weapons in action. The plump and ruddy captain assured me that with no wind his mission was a sinecure. He had ranged in with single rounds of high-explosive shells on the three objectives and was ready to drop the screen.

At 1000 there was a hurtling, whishing of metal overhead and rolling thunderclaps on the hill-mass ahead announced that the 489th and her sister battalions were on the ball.

A rapid muffled thudding from the mortar positions indicated that the smoke screen was on its way.

Tank exhausts roared as the anxious drivers jazzed their engines to prevent stalling when they moved out. No hurry, this was primarily an infantry-artillery show and the armor would have to wait for crossing points and roads. In the meantime the riflemen emerged from the woods in thin lines and irregular groups and started the long hard climb to the heights.

Following the fall of the mortar shells, I was startled by the ineffectiveness of the smoke screen. It was scattered and thin—by this time I should be unable to see the crest and we should be completely screened. I walked over to the battery. "Pour it on, captain. I want a heavy screen up there."

"We're pouring it on, colonel. I don't know what in hell's the matter. Looks like defective ammunition."

Both the captain and I learned something that day, or rather we finally thought it through. And our solution explained the inability of the 489th Artillery to screen our railroad-swamp crossing from the antitank and artillery fire three days before. Apparently when the phosphorus shells burst in two or three feet of snow an initial puff of smoke shot up from the hole, but most of the phosphorus was driven sideways into the surrounding snow while the other burning granules that had blown clear fell into snow and were extinguished. Then a recurring cycle was set up. The dry phosphorus would start to burn and melt snow, form water, wet the granules, and stop the burning. Latent heat would dry the granules, start more burning, melt snow, and the burning would stop. It was fully ten minutes before we had a thin, fairly effective screen, but due to the slow burn-melt-dry-burn cycle it certainly lasted the rest of the long day.

Griffen's tanks moved out toward the railroad and Tiger Bait followed in their tracks. Passing Gut Eidt Farm, we halted and O'Hare and I waded up the short lane to the house. We knocked, and the door was grudgingly opened by an apprehensive-appearing, lean, stooped man of middle age with his fearful woman peering past him.

"Ich danke Ihnen fuer die Hilfe Sie haben unser Verwundete gegeben," I told him, thanking him for hiding our men the night before. He brightened up and gabbled something that I didn't get at all, seemed to sound like German but not quite.

The woman seemed to be trying to control several children who wanted to get into the act, so I asked him how many people were in the family. And I got the answer clear—one spread hand plus one thumb.

An idea—O'Hare always kept the tire-chain lockers of his jeep full of

D-rations—bars of chocolate of an eighth of a pound each. Wonderful for warming a person on a cold night and an instant restorative, but eat two or three and, oh my.

"O'Hare, get these people six D-rations, will you?"

My wild leprechaun dashed back, rummaged, and returned. I think he exceeded his orders. There must have been at least ten bars in the pillow slip he passed through the door. Beaming, handshakes, and more Franco-Walloon-Deutsch dialect that seemed to mean they wished us lots of luck. In contrast to the neutral, sullen, or even hostile attitude of the Belgians I'd seen to date, this family actually seemed to want us to win.

Beyond Gut Eidt, I halted Tiger Bait and stood on the turret to get a better view over the hedges bordering the road. It looked good, considering. Griffen's platoon of tanks was up under cover of the railroad embankment. The riflemen were slowly, very slowly, floundering through the snow in irregular groups all along the front. That long advance upgrade through the snow was going to be deadly wearying. The haze above was slowly thickening—

While I was standing at gaze an assault gun or destroyer poked its nose out of the haze on the right front and blasted three rounds at Tiger Bait. Fortunately the scared German didn't take the time to aim well; he hit both hedgerows and the road behind us and backed up fast.

I had formerly complained that the M5 light tank turret wasn't big enough for a man of my size, but by the time the second shell cracked in the hedge alongside I had everything inside except my head and helmet, which took a sharp rap from a splinter. The only reason for this exposure was that I could get no lower because I was sitting astride the shoulder-piece of the 37-mm. gun. O'Hare backed out from under his jeep, I fought clear of the gun, and we were making thirty miles per hour when we reached the cover of the railroad ahead.

At the point where the railroad crossed the Amblève–St. Vith highway I found a hell of a mess. The underpass was blocked and heavily mined, so the tanks had moved to a grade crossing at a possibly feasible point two hundred yards to the left and found that it was mined by getting the leading tank's track blown off. The rest had swung wide, managed the embankment at steeper points, and were butting their way through the snow after their riflemen.

Captain Hochberg's heroes were working at the underpass with marrow-chilling indifference to the sudden death they were dealing with. Some were swinging shovels, clearing the snow away from a checkerboard of mines as casually as though they were clearing their front steps or sidewalks back home. Others barehanded were fumbling for hidden triggers and personnel mines with numb and wet fingers. One doesn't feel around for booby traps while wearing mittens. An assault gun annoyed the clearing party now and then with three-gun volleys of 75-mm. shells, but again the unaimed fire by a nervous or scared gunner burst wide of the underpass and remained only an annoyance. The two men hurt to date had been killed by mines. One was blown to unidentifiable bits and the other had lost both legs at mid-shin. The body was still steaming. I went over to where Hochberg was advising one of his men about how to disarm some hellish contrivance. "Captain Hochberg, have your men slow down to a reasonable speed. We aren't in that much of a hurry now. Griffen's mediums are across and the light stuff can't be used up there. We need the crossing this afternoon of course but take your time about clearing it."

"Yes sir, we've been pushing pretty hard. I want to get those plows through here. Hold it, men. Five-minute break. Warm your hands."

Tiger Bait tried to make the crossing in the track of the M4s but just dug herself in and bellied. On the other side of the railroad the German vehicles had beaten down a fair road net, so Hochberg's men gathered around O'Hare's jeep, grabbed handholds, and practically carried it to the highway beyond.

The going was fairly good where the German vehicles had beaten the snow down. I wanted to follow Griffen's force but the trace angled up toward Wallerode. OK, we'd go to Wallerode.

We approached a road junction where a left branch of the east-west road led into the town. "Let's stop behind this hedge, O'Hare. We're in Colonel Rhea's sector now and I don't know just what the situation is."

"Yes sir." A mortar shell slammed down into the road junction and a handful of Schmeisser bullets clipped through the hedge we were cowering behind. Someone had seen our approach and we were about as far forward as a CP Forward should be if it expected to continue functioning.

"Yes sir, I think we ought to name this place 'coffin corner,' " announced O'Hare, brushing away the twigs and bits of bark that another Schmeisser burst had sprinkled over him. "But come to think of it, down there where that tank zeroed in on us was 'coffin corner number one'—this is number two."

"Nothing for you to worry about, O'Hare. Figuring out how many more square inches I have to get hit I'll probably get hit seven times before you win your fifth Purple Heart."

"Hmmm, well, I'd just as soon not get one Purple Heart, sir."

During the ensuing idle moments I followed out this line of thought. Might be a good idea here. In the olden days of big, cold, brawny bastards bashing about the battlefield with broadsword, bill, and battle-ax, the large man had a decided advantage. But in modern war the small man could handle the tools just as well with a lot less chance of getting hurt. In forming my army for World War III, I would select my combat soldiers starting with the Singer midgets and ending with the tallest not over five feet four inches in height. They would take only 70 percent of the casualties we take today. Other advantages—they could be housed, fed, and clothed at much less expense, we could build smaller, lower-silhouetted tanks for them, more of them could be transported in a truck, plane, or ship, they would make easier parachute landings. Keep the big men back in the Services of Supply and the factories.

Radio queries to all task forces, "What's your situation?"

Answers from all task forces, "Moving ahead, no problems."

Mission Accomplished

The nearby shooting had tapered off and Wallerode appeared to have quieted down except for a little bickering east of town, so I walked around the corner and started up the road to see what went on. There was a short squad of the Twenty-third standing or squatting behind the first house on the left with one sad sack peering cautiously now and then around each corner.[1] The support or flank security, I thought, and moped on my way.

"Hey, colonel. I wouldn't walk up there in the middle of the road like that if I was you." The advice came from the droopy-looking rifleman at the near corner. I stopped.

"Why not?" I inquired.

"Well, maybe it's all right for you but the Krauts in that big house up there shoot at us every time we try it and I don't think—"

I had joined him behind his corner by that time, resenting his long-winded warning; found that they'd had two men hurt when they'd previously tried to move forward, and now were just waiting for something to happen.

The big house was a large, stoutly built manor house of two or three stories, with slate roofs and French towers at the corners. I didn't want to see any more men wasted on its capture and told the acting squad leader to hold there until I could get some help for him. I cut across the field to the hedge where my jeep was hidden. I called Rhea's CP and got his executive. Rhea was forward, so I asked the exec to send a tank or destroyer to checkpoint nineteen.

"We don't have any armor up yet, colonel. I'll send something as soon as we get it. Checkpoint nineteen?"

"No, cancel it."

I called Griffen. He had his platoon of tanks and would send a section right away.

Shortly thereafter Colonel Rhea barreled up the road from the south in his mine-proofed jeep, radio operator–bodyguard behind him. "What's it like over here, colonel?" he asked, dismounting.

"You have a squad just around the corner that's been stopped by some Krauts in that big house, first house on the right. I'm borrowing a couple of tanks from Griffen to set it afire."

Rhea went to the corner where he could get a good view. "I wouldn't stand out there if I were you, Rhea—"

"Oh, but that's a nice house," explained Rhea. "Don't shoot it up. If I take it can I have it for my CP?"

"You take it and it's yours, but just remember that Belgian real estate is not as expensive as men. And be careful."

"I'm always careful."

He mounted up and took off around the corner. I presumed he was going to instruct or reinforce his halted squad.

Report from Griffen: "Objective taken, outposted, patrols out." All doubt as to the success of the operation was removed. Even if Rhea couldn't clear the town and stay there, Griffen's men, attacking from Keppelborn, would be able to help him.

Rhea and his jeep crew boiled around the corner again with a scrawny little German bracing himself on the hood. "Here's four Germans, colonel," he grinned, signing this Teutonic runt to dismount. "You don't need those tanks."

"What happened, Rhea?"

"We just drove up there, hammered on the door, and told this maid to take us to the Germans. She said there weren't any Germans anywhere in the house but when I opened a closet door there he was.

"Sure nobody shot at us all the way up the road, so there probably weren't any Germans in there. Nice house, colonel. I'll set up my CP in there." And he mounted up with his pair of fellow daredevils. Looked at his watch and promised he'd have the town cleared by 1630. Then off around the corner again.

Well, my ears were red and I made a mental note to recommend Rhea for a Bronze Star for, no, I just couldn't write up a citation as ridiculous as that.

A section of Griffen's tanks waddled up and I sent them back with my compliments and thanks.

Tried my meager German on the very cooperative prisoner but the only information I understood was that there had been a thousand men in his unit and that all of the Panzers had left this front during the night.

Rhea returned, his jeep trailing a double column of eighteen Germans his boys had winked out of sundry attics, closets, casements, and corners of his CP where they'd been hidden by the pro-Nazi servant of the estate.

"That's a big place, colonel. You ought to set up your CP there too. It's the best place in town and I'm only going to use part of the basement. They've got forty cows stabled next door in the other part." Sounded attractive—I might just do that.

Since Rhea had recommended the manor house as a joint CP, I moved into the parlor and adjacent rooms on the ground floor while Rhea and his headquarters crew occupied the cellar. Rhea had been right—it was a nice house, beautiful, magnificent. It was surrounded by an eight-foot brick wall, loopholed for musketry in the days when muskets were in vogue. Inside, the large hall and wide staircase were lined with suits of armor, helmets, ancient weapons, and game trophies. Although hit several times by our own and the preceding German bombardment, the place was not seriously damaged. Rhea had been wrong on one point, about the cows in the basement stable; there weren't forty cows, the number was thirty-two. The owner of this chateau also owned the village and most of the surrounding land according to the housekeeper and was now residing in Germany. The old man in charge of the stable was in real trouble; a herd of cows and most of the servants had fled with the Germans.

The sight of those medieval helmets gave me an idea. I'd found that riding the turret of Tiger Bait with my head exposed to thirty-mile-an-hour wind chill was most uncomfortable, face and ears freezing and half blinded by tears. If I could just find a helmet with an adjustable face piece. I tried on a dozen but couldn't get one down past my ears. It appeared that a size 6½ was the largest head among the ancient Teutons and mine was 7½, so my dream of splitting the Arctic breeze with a jousting helmet had to be discarded. Too bad, my thirteenth-century headpiece would have certainly been one up on Patton's gold-lacquered star-spangled helmet.

Tiger Bait and the track clanked into the courtyard and CP Wretch Forward was complete. Hochberg had cleared the underpass for all traffic and was plowing the road net, Langterberg-Wallerode. The radio operators ran a line into the house and hooked up the remote control squawk box. We were in business in comparative comfort.

Message to Workshop: "Mission Accomplished."

At 1935 a message from division required that CCA establish contact with CCB by patrol every hour on the half hour at a small house in a patch of woods on the slope a kilometer southeast of Wallerode. Immediately thereafter I got a call in the clear, person to person, from Clarke. I'll omit the call signs and "overs."

"Wretch this is Speedy. Have you received the Big-6 requirement for contact with me?"

"Just got it."

"Can you make contact at 2030?"

"I'll have a post there at that time, a permanent post. I think that contact by patrols is too dangerous, subject to ambush and mistakes in recognition. I suggest you furnish a group on a permanent basis also. That will make a strong weld rather than a contact point between us."

"OK, I'll send out a group for permanent contact also."

Colonel Rhea dispatched a squad to take possession of the small stone house, but there was no contact by CCB until the morning of the twenty-seventh, two days later. "Speedy?"

About 2100, January 25, a patrol brought in five prisoners from the Bosenberg Woods fifteen hundred yards east of Wallerode. I interviewed one of these men. Among other matters, I asked the strength of his company. The open-faced Obergefreite was very cooperative.

"Now they are seven."

"You have me not understood. How many men in your Kompanie?"

"They are seven. This morning we were ninety. Twelve of us have you now prisoners taken. The Kompanie is now seven. There is the Oberleutnant, the Feldwebel, one Koch, and four Mann," counting them off on his fingers.

Confirmed by the others in varying degrees of accuracy, this was good news, and my fears of a night or early morning counterattack were dissipated. The flights of Nebelwerfer rockets we were receiving from time to time were evidently only retaliatory or bluff, so I called King to take over CP Forward and went back to the CP at Born in a relaxed frame of mind.

The Wallerode-Langterberg push was most satisfactory—in decided contrast to the Hunnange show where everything was in hopeless confusion and until the last moment impossible. Our small losses as compared to the bag of eight prisoners proved the effectiveness of detailed planning, strong supporting fires, and double envelopment. The only change I would make in an attack under similar conditions—I would drop the smoke screen fifteen minutes earlier and give it time to thicken before the jump-off. I was amused by the reported statement of the German colonel who had been in charge of the sector. He told the PW interrogation officer, "If you had attacked as we had planned, we would have beaten you."

This skirmish confirmed my belief that battles are best won not necessarily by killing or wounding the enemy but by scaring him so badly with the threat of killing, wounding, or encirclement that he is afraid to fight. Fear is contagious. If the alleged fifteen-hundred-man garrison had dug in and fought like the two-hundred-man garrison of Born they might have thrown us for a loss. But panicked by Rhea's attack from the east and Seitz's surprising them from the west, the devastating effect of the time-on-target concentrations of radio-fused shell, and the smoke screen that hindered their defense, they surrendered or fled to the frosted hills beyond.

Good news at the CP in Born—Major Larsen had just returned from division with the directive for tomorrow's assignments. They were: CCA, hold present positions. CCB, continue to push to the line two kilometers inside the Bois de St. Vith; 424th RCT, complete clearing the Bois de Depertsberg.

Wonderful. We'll sure enjoy holding present positions. And we did. A battery of eight-inch howitzers that had moved up practically into our backyard boomed a cheerful lullaby throughout the night, interdicting the distant roads on which the Wehrmacht was in retreat.

Sixteen.

In and Out

In

O'Hare and I were making the rounds in Wretch Forward over the recently plowed road net toward Langterberg. It was so cold that in order to live I'd told him to put the windshield up and to hell with regulations. I was dreaming about getting back to my billet and a fire when I heard the menacing rush of a large howitzer shell. "Duck."

O'Hare was way ahead of me—he had knocked her out of gear, braked briefly, and was diving for his snow bank when I yelled and dived for mine.

Crash.

Yes, it had been close enough, in the hedge forty yards ahead.

O'Hare stood up out of his burrow, shaking off the snow. "Hah. Missed us a mile—Holee Jeeze. Lookut my windshield."

Checked in at our luxurious CP Forward and found King hollow-eyed but still cheerful. He apparently hadn't slept. "Got a present for you, colonel," he remarked. "Griffen's boys caught them last night. Owens, bring in those prisoners."

The orderly went out into the courtyard and returned escorting two men in light blue uniforms, with army overcoats and field caps.

"Are you under the Luftwaffe?" I asked the fellow with the most impressive collar tabs—too dumbfounded to ask his unit.

"Jawohl, Herr Oberst."

"Why fight you here on the ground in the snow? Why are you not flying in an airplane?"

"While we no benzine have, Herr Oberst."

So, since the Panzers had failed to seize our fuel dumps and Goering's proud Luftwaffe had no gasoline, they were using air crews as replacements for the wavering Wehrmacht.

"How find you the life of the Infanterie in the Schuetzengraben?"

He expressed his opinion of existence as an infantryman in the trenches with a vulgar seven-letter word. Thoroughly disgusted, scared, low morale—there wasn't an ounce of fight in a truckload of them.

"King—you have only two jobs today. First, jeep this pair of Krauts to division and deliver them to POWINT in good condition.[1] I think that Hodges, Montgomery, and Eisenhower will be very interested in what they have to say. Second, CCA hasn't a thing to do today, so you pull a featherbed over your head and get twelve hours sleep."

I made the rounds, partly by jeep, farther by Tiger Bait, more in a borrowed M4, and finally by walking according to the snow and slopes of this rather rugged terrain. On the extreme left I found that the paratroops were still being annoyed by sniping from Depertsberg, where the 424th Regimental Combat Team was still trying to push ahead. The occasional shots were not effective at that range but still annoying. Colonel Seitz commented darkly that if the 424th didn't win the place that day he was going to send a squad over to clear it for them.

Was completely blown by the end of my tour and went to see Hochberg about more and faster road clearing so that our reserve could be rushed to any threatened point (and I could jeep the front in comfort). But when I found him and observed what his men were doing—mine detecting and snow plowing—my only comment was, "Nice going, Hochberg. Keep up the good work."

Gritted my teeth and stayed observing as long as I could in spite of my twitching toes. Can't stand mines. They're so damned sudden.

I was called to division in the cold predawn. General Hasbrouck had been thoughtful enough to have coffee available. "Triplet, you're going to have to release your parachute battalion to the 517th this afternoon. The Eighty-second Airborne Division will attack through the Seventh Armored tomorrow morning. The question is, can you hold your front with what you have left?"

"Yes sir. I'll move Task Force Wemple from An der Strasse to relieve Seitz's battalion and I'll still have a company of the engineers as a reserve."

"I think that may be spreading you too thin. The 424th has their objective cleared—I'll have them send you a reinforced rifle company to relieve Seitz. You can stiffen them up with the armor you've loaned Seitz. That should secure your front and still leave you an effective reserve."

"Since I'm facing Luftwaffe-reinforced infantry, I'm sure it will."

It was a busy day. Trucks to be furnished by G-4 to pick up Seitz's battalion. A rendezvous for the pickup at An der Strasse. The reinforced rifle company was hand-led into position by the paratroopers, taking over Seitz's attached tanks and destroyers in place. The Eighty-second Airborne Division reconnaissance parties were met, briefed, and set up in their advanced CPs. Speedy informed me that he was sending a squad to the contact point agreed upon two days before.

Colonel Seitz came in to report that his lads were relieved, loaded up, and on their way, and expressed his satisfaction in working with us. His men were delighted with the teamwork and cooperation given them by the tankers of the Seventeenth and the destroyer crews of the 814th, as well as the comparative speed and safety of working with armored troops.

From my point of view I was impressed by the courage and the capable, uncomplaining performance of these men of the 517th Parachute Regiment. The spirit of Seitz's battalion was well described by a tank commander whom I talked to the day after their relief. "I sure like the way them parachutes work. We're outposting this crossroads, see, and my squad (of parachutes) is digging in around the tank, and this guy comes up to me and says, 'Say, chum, I've got me a German bazooka, see? Now if you hear a Kraut tank coming up that road tonight don't you shoot it—you call me, I'm digging in just this side of that clump of bushes. And make sure you don't call that sonofabitch on the other side, he's got him five already and I ain't got me but one.' Yes, I sure like the way them parachutes work."

So did I. With infantry-tank teams like that the worries of the commander are limited to logistics and to the tactical planning required to ensure the economical use of his men. Their performance is never in doubt.

Late that afternoon I went to Langterberg to visit my new unit from the 424th and unfortunately decided to leave O'Hare and take a short cut. Tracked vehicles could make the road, but it was still impracticable for a jeep. The shortcut involved plowing through a kilometer of heavy snow and forward slope. I had to keep moving in order to discourage Jerry observers, so I arrived at the CP thoroughly blown. The company was evidently widespread in large clumps, since I saw no one en route.

At the CP, I came around a fir tree face to face with a sentry who gaped, exclaimed, "My God, a chicken colonel," and disappeared into the former German dugout to give warning of this visitation. The resulting flurry indicated that this outfit wasn't accustomed to visits by chicken colonels or other brass.

I found the unit widely deployed, of course, but in platoon or section groups, leaving wide gaps that should be covered by squad-tank teams. I discussed the deployment with the embarrassed captain of the 424th. No, I gave him a well-deserved working over.

"Your platoons are placed in the critical points, I see, but a brigade could be moved between them with no warning. You are to place squad-tank teams out on the flanks of each section or platoon group until your front is visually covered.

"See that every tank and destroyer has its infantry protection with it at all times. (I was really angry to find tanks unprotected.) Run patrols from your support throughout the night between your outposts. Your opposition is of very poor quality but you can't afford to take chances—they might hit you tonight with a Waffen SS battalion. Last, post double sentries at your CP. If I had been a Landsturm veteran of the Franco-Prussian War, I could have taken that drop-jawed yokel out with my crutch and rolled a grenade down in your hidey-hole. A Hitler Jugend could have eliminated your command post, so look to your security. I'll be back to see you."

During my return by the same route I was hurried along by a few mortar rounds that were evidently fired from a considerable distance as shown by their inaccuracy. But they did force me below the ridge line, so my shortcut became a very roundabout route before I rejoined O'Hare on the beaten road.

About January 31 at a division conference Hasbrouck announced that General Clarke had departed for treatment at a hospital in England, something to do with a gall bladder. "Bruce is a very sick man."

Colonel Joseph F. Haskell commanded CCB for the rest of the war.

Some time in September 1945 all combat commanders were called to division headquarters to a farewell party for General Clarke. We didn't even know he'd rejoined, and a stickier affair I've never attended. What with Hasbrouck's cold reserve, Clarke's broodiness, Ryan's silence, and no drinks or edibles, Colonels Tompkins, Raske, and I were left wondering what the hell we'd been invited for. The one sentence I remember just before Clarke started for his limousine was Hasbrouck's caution, "You should wear your general's belt, Bruce." So Clarke buckled on the brass-gold belt with a .32 caliber pistol.

In 1951 while I was chief of development in the Pentagon, I went to personnel and looked over my 201 file. I was astounded to find that Hasbrouck had in February 1945 recommended my promotion to brigadier general and noted the favorable endorsements by Generals Ridgway, Hodges, and Bradley. The last endorsement was, however, an informal scribble in ink, "We don't need any more generals. DDE." OK, Ike, I don't like you either.

In 1954 while chief adviser to the First Korean Division, I was at General Kim Dong Bin's headquarters to meet the corps commander. And there, pushing through the dust of the chopper landing, was Bruce Clarke, sulkier than ever, and with three stars welded on the front of his helmet. Time for me to retire. Note: God and promotion boards move in mysterious ways their wonders to perform.

In 1984 a historical writer, Clay Blair, asked me by letter on what date Brigadier General Clarke had been relieved in the Hunnange–St. Vith skirmish. Hell, I hadn't known that he had been relieved. Oh well.

Conference at division. "The Seventh Armored Division will move to XVIII Corps reserve in the vicinity of Eupen."

I directed the reinforced company of the 424th Regimental Combat Team to revert to their regimental control. Didn't have time to check the security measures I'd ordered and was glad of it.

CCA bade a mutually delighted farewell to the pro-Nazi inhabitants of the St. Vith area, moved to Welkenraedt, and settled down to a well-deserved period of rest, relaxation, rehabilitation, and fraternization.

As soon as we had settled in our winter quarters I took Tiger Bait to the ordnance shop and outlined to the shop officer some changes I needed. "Major, there are a number of alterations I'd like to have made on this crate. She's a damned nice tank, fast and reliable, but damned inconvenient as a command tank. Are you familiar with that armored car of Colonel Tompkins?"

"Colonel Tompkins? Oh sure. We worked on that one. Turned out to be a nice job."

"It sure is plush. I've been using it. Now I'd like the same thing done on this tank, and a little bit more."

"Such as?" and he got his notebook and pencil poised at "ready."

"First thing let's take the 37-mm. and coaxial gun out, just weld pipes of the right size to the gun shield so she looks dangerous."

"Take the gun out?"

"Yes. I don't ever plan on shooting it and it's in the way. My job is to tell the other tankers where to go and what to shoot, and I can do that a lot better if I have room in the turret to unfold a map and reach the radio."

"OK, guns out and pipes welded on, you'll keep the bow gun?"

"Yes, we'll keep the bow gun and the AA gun. Those are all I'll ever need.

"Second I'd like to have a map table with fifteen-watt red lights over it run off the battery like Tompkins's car."

"That's easy, map table, map drawer, and lights."

"And anything else you can think of to make her a rolling OP."

"OK, ammunition racks out, gunner's seat out, commander's seat in front of table or vice versa rather. That's about it, isn't it?"

"Yes, that's it. When can—"

"Should be able to work it in during the week. I'll give you a call."

Tiger Bait was returned with a very realistic piece of Belgian plumbing welded to the gun shield and cocked at an aggressive ten-degree angle, plus all the required interior alterations. Plush.

The R-R&R period of the Twenty-third Armored Infantry Battalion came to an end when Rhea was required to take over a sector in the Huertgen Forest in the area of Schmidt.[2] I jeeped up to the line to look over their situation in a purely infantry role. On entering the erstwhile battle zone I was impressed. Trees shredded by artillery fire, earth thoroughly pulverized with overlapping shell holes, the village reduced to the foundations—reminded me of the Verdun landscape of 1918. Must have been quite a fight.

The road of course was also in sad condition, almost impassable in places. It gave me an idea. I cautioned my carefree companion. "Look, O'Hare, let's slow down to a crawl. Stay out of those potholes. It'll take some doing but keep your wheels on the unbroken asphalt."

So at a crawl with considerable to-ing and fro-ing, O'Hare sneering with commendable restraint at my timidity, we finally reached the CP. From there we walked.

I found the living conditions on the outpost line exactly as grim, unbearable, and impossible as they had been on the front line ever since trenches had been invented. The big melt of the snow was well started and the principal occupation of the outposts was bailing the ice water out of their holes. Horrendous.

On a subsequent visit to the line I noted stacks of two to five metallic antitank mines at intervals along the road. When we drove up to the former German dugout that was the command post, Captain Paulhamus walked out to greet us. He had good news. "Well, colonel, we don't have to worry about that road any more. Engineers came up a couple of days ago and pulled out all the mines."

"Holee Mother of Gawd," remarked O'Hare with deep feeling as he devoutly dabbed at his chest.

My young men of the junior mess organized a party, inviting the wit and beauty of Welkenraedt and surrounding villages to a dance at the Rathaus. A bevy of beauties attended, liquor and wines were provided, and hors d'oeuvres were contrived with the contents of K-rations and the chocolate D-rations. Task Force Coombs had rigged an electrified phonograph with loudspeakers and squawk boxes and assembled a number of records from the natives.[3]

The party was not a total success. We had assumed that in Belgium the natives liberated from the oppression of the Hunnite hordes would be friendly, even grateful, and respond to the passes of their liberators in kind. Not so. The ladies surrounded the table of hors d'oeuvres, finished an amazing amount of K- and D-rations, and fought over the six-pack Camels. They then took their places at the tables in close-knit groups of four, gossiped, made snide remarks about the Americans, libeled each other, and griped about the music.

"But vare ees the orkaystra?" "You 'ave no orkaystra?" "When the Gairmans were here they always had an orkaystra." "Do not talk to that (those) woman (women)—she is (they are) Gairman."

I finally found one young lady sitting by herself at a corner table. Having heard several of the other harpies warn our men that "She is Gairman" and feeling for any women having to be alone at a party, I joined her.

"May I join you?"

"You should not sit here. My husband ees een the Gairman Wehrmacht and my two brothers areen the Belgian Schuetzstaffel."

My God, I'd found the only honest woman in Welkenraedt. So I stayed.

Found that the records contributed by the locals included "Lili Marlene" and the "Horst Wessel Lied." "Lili Marlene" is a nice tune to dance to—the "Horst Wessel Lied" had barely started before Lieutenant Kirschbaum snatched it off the platter and stamped it to splinters.

It was not a successful party.

Seventeen.

Remagen–Rolandseck–Bad Godesberg

Nidiggen and III Corps

Aachen had been taken, the Roer River had been crossed by the First Army, and the Seventh Armored Division was soon to leave the Eupen area to join the fight for the Rhineland. The tentative plan for the division was to march via Aachen to Brandenburg, pass through the current front line, cross the Roer River near Niddigen, and attack in the direction of Eschweiler-Euskirchen. CCA was to lead the column, capture Niddigen, and leave a small force to secure the place. The town must have been considered of paramount importance because I was given an air photo of the place with the air force intelligence interpretation attached, one of the two photos I saw during the war. The photograph showed a medieval, walled and moated town, with a solid-looking castle (Burg) and keep integrated with the wall on the west side of town. Five roads (the reason the place was important) crossed the moat on solid-looking bridges and met in a traffic-jamming Platz in the north center of town. Streets were narrow and winding.

The interpretation stated that the castle was occupied. The walls of the town were ten to fifteen feet high and fifteen feet thick, built of squared stone with a probable filling of earth and rubble. The moat was filled with silt up to five feet below the base of the wall and while no standing water was visible the silt was doubtless saturated. Bridges were stone or masonry and would probably support heavy traffic. The gates had probably been removed, but modern obstacles and mines could be expected.

I spent the evening studying the photograph and interpretation, using a magnifying glass until my eyes felt sunburned. Finally gave it up and turned in to enjoy a colorful night of nightmares concerning the attack of medieval fortifications with modern weaponry. Ghastly.

I just can't say with historical accuracy how the Seventh Armored Division moved from Eupen to the Rhine. Everything was confused, with orders, counterorders, disorders, attachments, detachments, changes in boundaries, excited military police, arrogant staff officers of First Army and III Corps, collisions between columns, and rumors.

The general called me to division one night with the general staff and other combat commanders. "The First Army has crossed the Roer and is moving down into the Rhine plain. We are to get going. Plan 4 with CCA leading. Are there any questions?"

"Yes sir. What about Niddigen?" I was still worried about those walls.

"The situation there is not clear as yet. We only know that the Roer is crossed and being bridged somewhere south of Niddigen. You will have to take it as planned."

"Yes sir."

"Get your outfit going."

I was reminded of General Harmon's order, "Boil down the road with everything you've got and grab Ciney," but not quite as explicit.

We got going toward Aachen in the black night and reached the city at daybreak. We drove through the ruins on the partially cleared Eupen-Eschweiler road and the view was beautiful. The place was totally destroyed to partial fire-scarred standing walls and caved-in cellars, a monument to American artillery, phosphorus shell, and incendiary bombs. I got on the radio to Wemple, Rhea, Griffen, and Milner. "Have your men take a good look as they go through Aachen. We are in Germany now. Aachen is what I want every town where you meet resistance to look like. By burning the enemy out you save the lives of your men. Pass this on to every man in your command."

We pushed on toward Niddigen, were shunted off the main road on a mucky detour, and crossed the Roer River on a brand-new bridge with the engineers still twisting the nuts on the restraining bolts. Down a steep approach and up a steeper departure.

And as we topped the bank, there were the grim walls of Niddigen, with the town burning briskly at all points. Even the castle on the high ground to the west was satisfactorily aflame. The town had been abandoned by the enemy and occupied by infantry of the III Corps. Bridges were intact, so we boiled on through.

A squadron of the Eighth Air Force loaded with incendiary bombs had been unable to find their designated target in the Ruhr due to heavy cloud cover and had commendably unloaded on the first German town they could find—Niddigen. We considered that hitting a German target was pretty damned good for the Eighth Air Force, even if it was already abandoned by the enemy and was occupied by our own troops.

And let that be a lesson to me—don't worry yourself into an ulcer about things that probably won't happen. But no, situations usually are bad and get worse—and worrying about them in advance and expecting the worst is a good way to stay alive. And when one expects the worst he is never disappointed and is happy when the danger evaporates.

Eight scruffy members of the Wehrmacht were ranked in front of a burning Bäckerei in the Platz, a forlorn lot, hopefully placing their hands on their heads on the approach of every American vehicle or tank, inviting someone for God's sake to stop and take charge of them. They had probably hidden out and deserted when their unit had abandoned the defense of the town.

Slidex radio message: "Workshop-6 to Wretch-6. Wretch attached III Corps Zuelpich. Wretch-6 report CG III Corps soonest. Wretch column follow."

Person to person: "Say, King, just got word we're attached to III Corps at Zuelpich. I'm going ahead to report to the CP. You bring the column up at the best reasonable speed. We don't want a lot of barefooted tanks."

"OK, I'll hold them at fifteen. That'll keep the treads and bogies plenty cool."

And to Wretch Forward driver: "O'Hare, III Corps in Zuelpich and don't spare the horses."

It took some driving on O'Hare's part, what with the rough, potholed road and heavy traffic that we had to pass, but we made it just before sunset. Found the headquarters in a rather scrungy office building that neither Colonel Wemple nor I would have considered as a CP—very unsuitable for a corps commander.

Well, it was just like old times in Fort Ord and Monterey—there was grandfatherly old Colonel Phillips who used to usher me in to get chewed out by General Millikin for my methods of training amphibians in Monterey Bay—especially the size of my TNT charges.

"Colonel Triplet, commanding CCA, Seventh Armored Division, sir. My command will be here—"

"God help us all," Phillips rudely interrupted. "The Terror of Monterey. Come in here, the general wants to have words with you." He escorted me to the adjoining door and continued. "General, the Window Smasher is with us again, only now he's destroyed bridges."

Yes, my luck was running true to form, it was Millikin.

"Hell of a note" were the general's welcoming words. "I'm really getting paranoid about you, colonel. You kept me in trouble with California politicians and the Monterey Chamber of Commerce. Hoped I was rid of you and your destructive ways. And now you follow me to Germany and collapse the only bridge I have."

"I don't understand, general. I'm unaware of—"

"This bridge, here. Barely strong enough to support one tank and you run three tanks out on it at once. Naturally it caves in."

"I can't believe that my men would run three tanks on any bridge at once, general. Not on any engineer bridge or on any span of a civilian bridge, unless they were ordered. It must have been your engineer guides that pushed them. How many tanks did I lose?"

"All three went into the drink but that's not important." (I thought that fifteen good men and three tanks were very important. But maybe corps commanders are different.)

Millikin continued. "This is. I'm attaching you and your vandals to the ?? division. You take off and report to General Blank at his headquarters—

here, immediately. We'll send your troops up if or when we can get a bridge that they can't wreck."

I took notes on the division, name of the general, and the map location, and took off into the night again. Odd, forty-eight hours later I had forgotten both division and name, and just haven't been interested enough to look them up. So I'll continue to call him General Blank. Found him at a miserable place called Gemuend.

General Blank, a square, midsized, gray-haired type who obviously had no idea of the limitations of armored troops, had it all laid out on his situation map. He gave me a quick briefing. "The Ninth Armored Division has grabbed the railroad bridge here, just south of Remagen. We are putting troops across to clear a bridgehead the enemy is holding along these lines north of Remagen with centers of resistance here, here, and here. Our front-line units are pinned down by enemy fire. Our present line is stopped, generally along the eastern edge of this forest. You will move through the forest on these roads, pass through our lines, eliminate these centers of resistance, and take the Rhine bank from Remagen to Bad Godesberg, both inclusive, by noon tomorrow."

"Yes, general, I understand the situation and the requirement. But just now we're having a little difficulty with a—"

"So General Millikin informs me. But some of your troops had crossed before the bridge failed. If the rest cannot find a crossing take what you have and proceed on your mission."

"A question, sir. What is the condition of these forest roads and trails, this low area may be a bit marshy?"

"The infantry has reported that they have difficulty with their wheeled transport but the roads and trails are easily passable by foot troops and shouldn't give your tracked vehicles or tanks any trouble. In any case they are the only roads available to you. These roads on either flank of the forested area are strictly off limits to you. Any other questions?"

"No sir."

"All right. The chief of staff will arrange anything further you may need. You're to have your objectives by noon tomorrow."

"Yes sir."

And having handed me this can of worms, General Blank toddled off to bed. His staff stayed with me briefly.

Corduroy

I went over the map, made a few measurements, and did some basic arithmetic. Good God. What sized army did the general think I had? Remagen was a small town and Rolandseck was just a village, but Bad Godesberg looked to be a small city, all to be taken and cleared by one combat command of four thousand men by noon tomorrow? And the distances, ten miles of front. With all three task forces on the line they'd be operating five miles apart, out of supporting range.

And the artillery with a range of ten thousand meters, they'd have to choose their firing positions well forward to be able to hit both Remagen and Bad Godesberg. Probably have to detach batteries.

But most of all, that approach through three miles of wooded area crossed by a couple of marshy streams, to quote the general: "The roads and trails are easily passable by foot troops and shouldn't give your tracked vehicles and tanks any trouble."

Little did he know, the ignorant old sonofabitch. The average foot soldier has a ground pressure of seven pounds per square inch, a tank puts twelve or thirteen pounds on a square inch. But General Blank had probably seen propaganda or training movies and seen a demonstration at Fort Knox and believed that a tank could go anywhere and do everything but make beer.

The Germans probably wouldn't cause us much trouble; what information I could get from the G-2 and G-3 was to the effect that most of the Krauts on this side of the Rhine were only interested in getting across the river. Exceptions were the hard-nosed rear-guard machine-gun crews that were holding up the advance of this division.

Oh well, we'd have a go at it.

The chief of staff was a competent, understanding, cooperative type for a desk soldier. He showed me to a small room with a table and a number of folding chairs, managed a couple of folding cots with blankets, a pot of coffee with assorted cups, and provided the two dozen maps, crayons, and writing materials I needed.

Radio contact with Colonel King was impossible due to static and the German jamming of our channels, but I could rely on him to do everything that was humanly possible, so I went to work on the assumption that he'd bring our little army up in time. If General Blank thought that I was going to tackle the Krauts on this front with one battalion (less one company) and fifteen tanks, not when they had his two regiments stopped, I wouldn't. "O'Hare, take a look at this map. I'd like to have you go take an educated look at these roads through this wooded area. See if they are passable for tanks and tracks. They look like they're just firebreak trails to me. Anyway, let me know what are the best bets."

O'Hare gulped down the last of his coffee and took off into the night. He probably knew more about the driveability of roads than most engineers.

I went to work marking the positions of enemy and friendly troops, boundaries, objectives, checkpoints, and probable artillery concentrations on the many maps required. As soon as I got O'Hare's report I could indicate the recommended routes through the forest.

Then several sets of handwritten orders, they would save time when the troops showed up.

Shortly after midnight O'Hare staggered in, mud-plastered to the knees. "They're all mighty bad, colonel. Reminds me of what we got into at Hunnange. But I've marked them in both sectors—bad, worse, and worst. They can probably get through on the bad ones with a lot of work."

"OK, nice going O'Hare. Now turn in and get some shut-eye. Tomorrow's going to be a hard day."

I went over the maps again, using red, blue, and black crayon to correspond with O'Hare's bad, worse, and worst routes.

Reviewed the written orders. Seemed all right except that no times could be stated. King might bring the tail of the column up by dawn, or never.

O'Hare had it good—sleeping audibly. I envied him.

About 0300 came the news, corps to division by telephone, the attached combat command was reunited and should arrive within the hour. About two hours later Colonel King stomped into my cubicle, muddy, worn, red-faced, and mean as a snake. He looked like I felt except he was brimming over with anger and adrenalin while I was just feeling flaccid. I sure was glad to see him.

"Goddamned engineers claim we broke down their bridge," he exclaimed. "That's a lie. Their engineer guides directing traffic got excited and signaled our tanks across too fast. Cost us three tanks."

"How many men?"

"They all got out, shook some of them up and that ice water didn't do any of them much good. Bernardi sent four or five back, breaks and bruises."[1]

"Artillery all up?"

"Yes sir, everything is up, and a harder fight to get here I've never seen. Every idiot that has a truck or tank is on the road claiming priority. Had to go ten miles north to find another bridge. And then got them across only by outranking a quartermaster column of ration trucks. I'll probably get my buttons pulled off tomorrow. Any coffee in that pot?"

"Cold and poison. O'Hare, see if you can manage for a pot of coffee. If anybody tries to pull your buttons off for this night's work you'll have me and a couple of major generals as defense witnesses. Damned nice going, King."

The unit commanders looked in worse shape than King, thoroughly beat. The coffee seemed to help. I issued the handwritten orders and marked maps. "Read through these, gentlemen, it's all there except the times, which cannot be predicted."

The task forces had been formed in almost equal strength for this move and were all suited for the maneuver that I'd laid out. About eight minutes of profound silence, broken by the occasional rustle of paper, ensued. Then they began to look up, their expressions ranging from eager through calm and puzzled to apprehensive. I thought I'd better tell them a bit more. "Gentlemen, the Ninth Armored Division has taken the bridge just south of Remagen. That was the hoped-for escape route for the Germans west of the Rhine—who now realize that they are cut off. You will note that we are going to take over a ten-mile front and that your task forces will be operating five miles apart. I would normally not consider deploying at such a distance—now I believe that the enemy is so demoralized that it will be safe. We will move abreast of the Gelsdorf-Meckenheim road. When we reach this road Colonel Rhea will move to Remagen, Wemple to take Bad Godesberg, and Colonel Griffen will move toward Rolandseck.

"Colonel Griffen, I said toward Rolandseck because you have three missions. You are the reserve and until both our other forces are on their objectives you are not to become heavily engaged—you are to hold your force in readiness to assist either Rhea or Wemple. Your second mission is to clear areas that Colonel Milner may require for his batteries supporting the other task forces. Your third mission is the capture of Rolandseck and clearing your sector to your boundaries.

"Colonel Milner, your support of both task forces as far apart as Remagen and Bad Godesberg will be difficult. They are sixteen thousand meters apart. But you have an extreme range of ten thousand meters so from a midpoint you should be able to do it. Call on Colonel Griffen to clear any areas you may need, particularly if you have to detach batteries. Questions?"

"What are these trails like through the woods, sir?" Rhea asked.

"At the best they're bad. I've marked the best two that you are to use in red, you followed by the 489th on the right, Wemple followed by Griffen on the left. We'll spend less sweat working on two roads than on four. Getting through this wooded area will be the major part of our day's work. Further questions?"

A glum silence.

"All right, let's go."

This was the first time I'd used the modified Tiger Bait in the field. Sheer luxury. White lights illuminated the interior for map study during daytime use, another switch turned the red bulbs on for night work. And the map table was placed and angled just right for an occasional nap during quiet moments.

Radio reports: "We can't possibly get our tanks through here." "The tracks are bogging down to the axles." "I've got the three guns in the lead bellied down." Radio replies: "That's all right. All hands abandon your vehicles, take individual weapons, and move out on foot."

That did it. Instead of obeying my order, tankers, infantrymen, and artillery soldiers pulled the axes out of their brackets and spelling each other cut a two-hundred-yard, three-mile swath through the woods to corduroy those woodland lanes. The engineers largely supervising never had it so good.

Aha. Wemple reports that he is through and deploying in front of the forest with no opposition. Tiger Bait surges out on the relatively dry open field and joins him. No machine-gun fire, no snipers, no Germans. The infantrymen of the —th Division emerging from their holes along the edge of the woods are amazed. So are we.

Surrender

Wemple moves his tank out to a slight knoll and stands up on his turret, waves "cease firing" and "for God's sake come here." I join him again. "Take a look at that, colonel."

I stood up and took a look. A battalion of motorized infantry in two-and-one-half-ton six-by-six trucks was moving north across our front on the Gelsdorf-Essig road. Jammed with American trucks, at least the white stars on the sides announced that they were American. And it wasn't just a battalion, the column was endless.

At that point our plan of action went into the discard. Radio message: "Cease firing. Friendly troops on the front. Task forces proceed individually to objectives. Artillery to positions east of Meckenheim."

I thought that our troubles were over, but two of our hardest battles were ahead of us: breaking through the American columns and the column commanders, military police, and senior staff officers, who were not much friendlier than the Germans we'd expected. The American army also had gone temporarily insane; the static plus the effect of all the chatter on the crowded network kept me in total ignorance of the status of any of my far-flung command, and my attempt to make the rounds was found to be impossible.

Gave up my attempt to reach Bad Godesberg when darkness and the blackout reduced our progress to a half-mile-an-hour crawl and asked the sergeant to find the CP in Meckenheim. By a good deal of daring cross-country driving and a hell of a lot of waiting at bottlenecks we pulled into the command post shortly after midnight.

By some miracle of radio communication Lieutenant Coombs had gotten through the interference and Colonel King was able to report that all forces were settled down on their objectives without German opposition. Every town, village, and house had had the laundry hung out.

I should have stayed up and jittered all night like every other American commander west of the Rhine but didn't. I went to bed.

At the staff meeting next morning immediately after breakfast all of the news was unqualifiedly good. The Seventh Armored Division had moved into Bonn during the night. We were to be relieved from attachment to III Corps and revert to the Seventh AD at 1200 today. Praise God. I wanted no more to do with Generals Millikin and Blank. All three task forces were in their assigned positions and in control of their sectors. German resistance west of the Rhine was nil. The mob scenes of yesterday had been sorted out and intruder units had cleared our assigned sector. The only casualties during the shambles of the past forty-eight hours were the bruises and chilling incurred in the broken bridge incident. Several hundred prisoners had been captured in this bloodless travesty of a battle and more deserters, evaders, and suspicious civilians were being picked up hourly. The POWINT teams were very busy. Reports on the pertinent parts of the above had been made by the radio to the ?? Division (God bless 'em).

The sector that CCA occupied was an equilateral triangle, Remagen on the right corner, connected with a good road along the bank of the Rhine to Bad Godesberg. The command post at Meckenheim was at the apex of the triangle center-rear. The sides of this triangle were ten to twelve miles of good road. Several small villages in the interior of the sector were connected by a web of fair to very poor lanes by which it was difficult to navigate from any place to anywhere else. Most inconvenient, and the situation caused a revival of the ancient joke, "You can't get there from here."

We found Rhea's task force comfortably occupying the best Gasthauses and homes in Remagen. Rhea had a complaint—which neither of us could do anything about. "This damned antiaircraft fire, it doesn't hurt the Germans but it sure worries us. The Krauts are putting everything that can fly in the air trying to knock out that bridge. That's OK, of course they can't hit it, they drop their bombs close enough so they don't worry us. But every time a plane comes over, every antiaircraft gun we've got opens up—75s, 40s, 20s, and those damned .50 calibers. Shooting in every direction, looks like the Fourth of July. We don't stay outside to watch it. It all comes back down again, splinters and .50 caliber pattering on the roofs like a Montana hailstorm. They have some artillery pecking away at the bridge too. They're accurate enough to hit it now and then. But the bridge is so important that they don't bother shooting at us."

Rhea took me on a tour of his infantry-tank team outposts, which were well sited and guarded by double-sentry posts. "The Germans are still holding across the river so we don't patrol the bank or suicide trail except at night," Rhea explained. "We just have observers check to see that there's no attempt to cross the river in the daytime." The rattle of machine-gun fire not far downstream emphasized his statement.

We took Rhea's advice and went inland over a maze of unmapped farm lanes to reach Task Force Griffen. It wasn't easy and took forever. It was also nervous work; these patches of woods and the small farms made perfect hideouts for holdouts.

On the way I noticed a large patch of something white on the ground in a grove of trees. "Let's have a look over there, O'Hare. Cover me."

"Looks like it might have been one of Colonel Skorzeny's boys," I speculated. "Dropping him in here to raise hell in our rear areas."

"But why would he leave his uniform?" wondered O'Hare.

"May have landed in the German outfit so he wouldn't be shot as a spy in case he landed in a group of Americans. Probably had an American uniform under it, or a civilian outfit."

That was my best guess. O'Hare improved on it.

"Or maybe he just landed, saw what he was up against, said 'To hell with the war,' and took off in his long johns. I've felt like that myself sometimes."

I suspect that my leprechaun was right. We certainly had no trouble with any Germans in this sector. And the mystery of the parachuted stripper remained unsolved.

We found Griffen's force in Rolandseck by encountering one of his well-sited infantry-tank outposts. "Just backtrack your tank down this road, colonel. One left, one right, and four hundred yards ahead to the river."

Griffen and his men were well settled in their little Dorf. They had searched the place and pried out a couple of dozen hideouts who had been hoping to raft across the Rhine after dark. The natives, while not friendly, were coldly courteous and cooperative.

"You were lucky to get in without getting shot at, colonel. We're right under the gun here. We haven't lost a man yet but we've learned to move fast between houses and we don't stand in the open. We've outposted and patrol the rear areas in the daytime all right, but we're going to have to wait till dark to patrol the riverbank."

We found a totally different situation in Bad Godesberg, a small, neat, prosperous residential city. Wemple's small force had a very low and unimpressive visibility among the numerous inhabitants, who seemed just to ignore the invaders. Not many children in sight, but a great many women and old gaffers were standing in shopping lines and milling about the streets with baskets and bags. Unarmed German soldiers were marching in small unguarded groups, hands on heads, toward the center of town. Several civilians moving in the same direction were gingerly carrying weapons ranging from halberds of the twelfth century to the latest Schmeisser Maschinepistolen. Enough to make my hands sweat all over the M-3 I was gripping. Aha. There was an M4 and a squad of my lads of the Twenty-third. We pulled up. "Where is the command post, sergeant?" I asked the squad leader.

"Take a right at the next corner and six blocks to the big hotel on the right, sir. First hotel beyond the Platz. Turn in the alley and use the back door—the front door might not be safe."

"What about all these Krauts and these people with weapons? What are you doing about them?"

"They're surrendering, sir. We're here just to sorta keep an eye on 'em."

"Oh, I see." But I didn't, and was still nervous about them.

We turned the corner and jeeped on toward the Platz and the hotel. A very old, bareheaded, white-haired, tall, well-dressed civilian stepped off the sidewalk in front of us and held up his hand, the international signal. "Halt." Must have been ninety-five or one hundred, tottering, wavering, carrying a scabbarded saber. O'Hare braked just short of him.

I recalled my limited German vocabulary and put on my grimmest expression, only way to deal with Germans. "Was wollen Sie?" I inquired in my nastiest tone.

"The police say that I must to the Polizei Prasaedium go to capitulate. But the way is too long and the sun is too warm. I will to you capitulate." And he presented his ancient saber, hilt first.

But you've got to be hard with them. Never give them a break. "No—I will your sword not take. Go you to the police."

"Then will I not capitulate. I will to house go and sleep," and he turned away and tottered toward the sidewalk. Well, I guess I'm just not psychologically equipped to deal with Krauts. I gave in. Softy. "No, it will give trouble. You can capitulate to me."

The old gentleman handed me his saber with all the dignity of General Lee at Appomattox, and turned away to go home and have his nap.

"O'Hare, do you want a souvenir of the Franco-Prussian War of 1870?"

"Yes sir, it's a nice-looking sword. I'll ship it home."

Eighteen.

The Autobahn War

Surprise

On the morning of March 24, I visited Remagen and was handed a message that had been forwarded by King. "Wretch-6 report to Workshop soonest."

When used in a military message the word *soonest* means emergency, I want to see you ten minutes ago. So there was no time for that twenty-five-mile detour.

"How's the footing down the west bank road, Rhea?" I inquired.

"It's a little rough in spots, colonel, but no mines in our sector. We patrol it regularly with jeeps, after dark."

I climbed aboard O'Hare's chariot. "We're needed at division, O'Hare, let's take the river road."

"You mean Suicide Lane, sir?"

"Yes. I think it's safe enough now. Nothing but long-range stuff to bother us, two thousand yards or more."

"But sir, if we go by way of Meckenheim, I think we'll probably live fifty years longer."

"The message said *soonest,* so we'll go the short way."

We started on the short way, but I could tell from O'Hare's grim expression that he had lost his normally childlike faith in my judgment and our luck. I tried to cheer him a bit. "Look at it this way, O'Hare, suppose they do have a machine gun way over there laid on this road."

"Yes sir, that's what I am supposing."

"Well, their guns fire at a cyclic rate of six hundred rounds a minute. That's ten rounds a second. The muzzle velocity is twenty-seven hundred feet per second, that's nine hundred yards. So those ten bullets are spaced out ninety yards apart. You sure ought to be able to drive this buggy through a ninety-yard gate."

"Yes sir, I should, but it gets chancy when those gate posts are moving sideways at a couple of thousand miles an hour."

We were still driving behind a nice screen of bushes and trees, well masked from the enemy side of the river, but O'Hare was obviously not comforted. I tried again. "All right, let's say you're driving at sixty. That figures out to thirty yards a second. You're nine inches thick through the body, that's a quarter of a yard. Suppose a bullet hits that thirty-yard space and you take up only a quarter-yard of it. That means you have only 1/120 chance of getting hit. That's less than 1 percent."

"I guess you're right, colonel, but didn't you say that gun fires ten rounds a second? Ten rounds while I'm driving that thirty yards? That brings my chance of getting hit up to damned near 10 percent."

"I'm afraid you're right about that, O'Hare. I forgot about the ten bullets per second."

"And that Kraut gunner is probably going to be leading me and let me run into the stream of tracers. Then he's not going to be shooting at that thirty yards of space—he's going to be shooting at me. And you say I have a 1 percent chance of getting hit by any one bullet. But he's shooting six hundred a minute. So the way I see it if I'm in his sights for one minute I get hit six times. Or if I'm right about that 10 percent I'll get hit sixty times."

"Maybe you're right again, O'Hare. I'll have to refigure the whole thing when I use a pencil. By the way, there's a long open stretch coming up ahead of us. See if you can get this crate up to sixty."

"Holy Mother of God," said my leprechaun, dabbing reverently at his chest while flooring his throttle.

It was the first time I realized that a loaded jeep could make seventy-three miles an hour over a shell-pocked road.

We didn't hit the holes, we sailed over them. First time I was ever air-sick in a jeep.

I was the last one to show. Naturally. Everybody else was cushily quartered in the suburbs of Bonn and had plenty of time for coffee. I didn't get any.

Colonel Ryan went to notify the general that all were present. The G-3 and his henchmen distributed maps of the Remagen area, marked with bivouac goose eggs along the winding road running northeast from Linz to the main north-south road that the Krauts call an autobahn. I found the oval marked CCA, damned near touching the autobahn. Order of march: A, B, H, HQ, artillery, and trains.[1]

Hasbrouck appeared from his inner sanctum and took his place at the head of the conference table. The rustling of map folding ceased. "Give me your attention, gentlemen. We will make a tactical march tonight in the assembly area as shown on your maps. Details are given in the attached movement order.

"I called you here to stress the secrecy of this move. You will inform no one in your commands of the march, time, or destination until 1800. At that time you will inform your commanders and staffs, emphasizing that the details be passed on only on a need-to-know basis.

"In the meantime certain preparations will be made.

"Immediately on returning to your units you will have all unit designations painted out on all vehicles and equipment.

"Your men will all stitch handkerchiefs over the Seventh Armored patches on their uniforms—like this," and the general half turned to show his left shoulder with a crudely sewn OD handkerchief concealing the patch.[2]

"At 1730 a division radio team will report to each of your headquarters.

"At 1800 radio silence will be observed by your units. At that time the division teams will take up the normal radio traffic, using your call signs.

"Now read your orders."

The rustling of paper and the crackling of folding maps resumed. I studied the movement order. "Tactical march"—I'd have to get going on that one. I had been impressed by Colonel King's aggressive attitude, and intended to use him as a task force commander in our next brawl. Major Larsen could run the command post. But I'd have to start the formation of three balanced task forces right away.

No additional units attached.

My leading unit to arrive at pontoon bridge approach at 2000, OK.

Understood. I looked up. Everyone had finished studying their orders and were waiting on me.

"Do you have any questions, gentlemen?"

There were none.

Since Wemple's CP was directly on my way back I stopped there to give him what he needed to know, send one medium tank company and a light tank platoon to the reserve at Meckenheim to arrive at 1400. Paint out unit markings. Sew handkerchiefs over the Seventh Armored patch. Report to Meckenheim for a commanders' meeting at 1800.

At Meckenheim, I dispatched Lieutenant Irwin to Remagen with a directive to Rhea about the handkerchiefs, unit markings, and commanders' meeting. Finally a staff meeting in which I informed Colonel King that at 1400 he would have that task force that he'd been honing for, while the obviously apprehensive Major Larsen would take the job as executive. Pending that time, King would see to the painting and handkerchiefs and Larsen would mark a hell of a lot of maps for distribution at the 1800 meeting.

The move went off perfectly. At 1800 CCA's radio traffic ceased and the division communications teams took it up, by 1815 all commanders were off to their units, by 1915 it was black dark and Wemple and King were rumbling their task forces into column on the Remagen-Meckenheim road, and at 2000 Rhea's first tank trundled onto the first pontoon. A very good, reliable lot.

King's column, the last in line, had started coiling in their bivouac area so I went forward to find the CP and my trailer. I found both. That stupid sonofabitch Powell, the headquarters commandant, had parked my trailer on the German side of the house. And the Krauts were dropping all the artillery they had into the bivouac areas this side of the Rhine. Was he just careless? Or did he want to get rid of me? I started around the house to where the CP track was safely parked, in a flaming rage, but stopped and took thought. What would it do to my image if I demanded that he move my quarters to a safe place for the night? I'd be ruined. So I went back vowing that I'd have another man as HQ commandant as soon as one was available.

Went into the trailer and turned on my high-powered radio, tuned to the Berlin propaganda channel, they always had the best music. I was just in time to hear the nostalgic strains of "Lili Marlene," and why the propaganda people play that is a psychological mystery. Hearing that song should induce the German army to mass desertion. "This evening we extend a hearty welcome to the boys of the Seventh U.S. Armored Division who are now crossing the Rhine at Remagen. Our men are preparing a warm reception for them and very few of the poor fellows will ever cross the Rhine again. Why don't you men of the Seventh throw down your arms and return to your—" I turned it off. Sally's dulcet tones this evening were not entertaining.

So much for paint, handkerchiefs, and radio silence. No wonder the Krauts were shelling our bivouac.

Found my new bunk was much better than that soft, sway-backed featherbed I'd been using in Meckenheim.

Dour comment by our communications officer at evening mess: "paint 'em out, sew 'em on, and radio silence—nobody knows who or where we are except Lili Marlene, Axis Sally, and the German army."

Limburg

Orders: "Order of march, CCA, CCB, division artillery, division head-quarters, CCR, trains.

"CCA will move southeast on the autobahn and capture Limburg. The 489th Armored Field Artillery will be in direct support of CCA."

I suppose CCB was to extend our flank or leapfrog us if we ran into serious trouble. But we didn't have that much trouble and I never heard anything of the rest of the division during the battle of the autobahn.

At 0400 on March 26, Rhea's vanguard infantry-tank platoon team moved up a steep approach road and lunged out on the concrete-paved autobahn we'd heard about. Order of march—Rhea, CCA headquarters, Wemple, King, Milner's artillery. The first twenty minutes were peaceful until we passed through the front line outposts of the bridgehead troops. The movement slowed to a walking pace.

It was still black dark and tanks just won't move in the dark unless their infantry friends lead the way and cover their flanks on foot. We'd made two miles by the crack of dawn with frequent flurries of small-arms fire and the occasional crack of a tank 75. The only mines encountered were merely laid on the pavement, no booby traps, and were easily removed.

Came the dawn and we saw the autobahn in all its glory for the first time. It was a concrete highway, a double concrete highway, and what a double concrete highway it was. This was the first time I'd ever seen a road on which a platoon of tanks could be deployed abreast.[3]

The autobahn led me to the treasonable thought that Hitler was a great man, a genius. Anyone who could take over a country as thoroughly broken down as Germany was, revise the currency, force 100 percent employment, and build roads like these had a lot going for him. If he'd only kept his sticky fingers out of Poland—

The riflemen remounted and the point section of tanks began leapfrogging. We began to make better time.

On reaching a crest both tanks paused while the commanders studied the terrain beyond with binoculars. In the low ground four hundred yards ahead both roads crossed a long bridge with a secondary road running under the bridge.

Three hundred yards beyond the bridge the autobahn took an up-grade curve to the left through low wooded hills.

As the point leader directed his driver to move out, a small German automobile came boiling around the curve toward us at high speed, evidently with no idea of our presence. The car was a Volkswagen, a civilian type, painted in the sand-colored shade of the army. I wanted the occupants of the car as prisoners and yelled "Don't shoot," but since the tank commanders had their earphones in place my preferences were not considered. *Crack,* and the section leader's tank sat back gently on her haunches. The shell burst directly under the front axle. Just a hair too much lead but a good fault and damned good shooting. The car slithered, fish-tailed, and skidded a good fifty yards before it stopped, still upright. "Damned good driver, or lucky," remarked Colonel Rhea.

The moment the wreck ground to a halt both doors sprang open and two lanky Krauts jumped out and dashed for the woods, each to his own side. Considering their agility and speed, I expect that this pair never saw each other again. A good laugh was enjoyed by all and the section leader took off for the bridge with speed, overwatched by his partner.

Karummmpf.

The center span of the bridge (really two bridges side-by-side) jumped five feet in the air in five-foot chunks and dropped through a thirty-foot chasm. Damn them, had it wired for demolition.

A frenzy of machine-gun and cannon fire from the advance guard sprayed the woods ahead. And now the second platoon in column lined the crest while the vanguard tried to find a way around the bridge by the network of concrete circles that we now call a cloverleaf. The use of this confusing maze was necessary since the small stream that ran under the bridge was running full and the ground probably too boggy to risk with tanks. So they used the cloverleaf.

Remember this ingenious method of using circles to divert vehicles in totally different directions was totally unknown to these men who were using it for the first time while under considerable stress. The results were most amusing, five olive-drab mechanical mice in a concrete maze. No, it wasn't at all amusing.

For ten minutes we had lost tanks rumbling away in three wrong directions, one exasperated tanker even returning via a second curve to his starting point. Aha. One tank finally made it and halted near the wreck of the Volkswagen. Then a little radio guidance from the leader got the others into the right curve combinations and the advance guard was on its way again.

O'Hare and I paused to look over the wrecked car. All tires were blown and one torn off, and the trunk was riddled by splinters. No bodies, no blood, no abandoned briefcases, a miracle of survival. As O'Hare remarked, "Damned good man on that wheel."

Our men became rather expert about cloverleafs by the time they were relieved by the next platoon, because every bridge that we approached with hopeful speed was either blown before we came in sight or went up with a *karummmpf* just before our vanguard reached it, which is proof of the stupidity of some Kraut engineers. I should think they'd try to blow the bridge with a tank on it.

We were going through a spottily wooded area when one of the 489th artillery planes buzzed out ahead of the column in that high-nosed way of observation planes (they're scared to shoot at me—anybody shoots at me and I drop a battalion of artillery on 'em). Five minutes later he came back at treetop level, swooping wildly from side to side at full power, urged on by 88-mm. antiaircraft shells bursting in a halo immediately behind his tail. The Krauts must have had a full battery on high ground to be able to follow him at that hedge-clipping level. As he passed the head of the column he dropped an aluminum tube with a yellow streamer that due to the violent evasive action landed fifty yards distant. O'Hare who was trailing Tiger Bait dashed out and retrieved it.

I pulled out and unfolded the message. My God, the observer not only couldn't write or print, he must have been scared. I finally figured it out. "F A Btry unlimbering 300 yds from you."

It would have been real nice to know in what direction the enemy was readying his guns; motorized, armored, or horse artillery, and caliber.

But the lad had been in a hurry and we were thankful for the warning. I passed it to Colonel Rhea and in five minutes sections of infantry-guarded tanks were butting through and around the clumps of timber in all directions.

A heavy burst of firing of all calibers broke out up the lane leading eastward; all tanks began crashing toward the sound of the gunfire, can't go far wrong doing that.

A smallish, tawny, blocky horse with black mane and tail of a palomino came at full gallop out of the woods, white-eyed with fright. I was walking toward Tiger Bait and when the horse saw me afoot he selected me as his friend, cantered up and settled his muzzle firmly on my shoulder, panting, slobbering, and eyes rolling with fear. Nice horse, fifteen hands, fully harnessed, not a scratch on him. I'd sure like to keep him.

The massacre of the German battery was simmering down so I pulled off bridle and harness and slapped him on the rump meaning "take off, you're free." But he was having no part of freedom—he wanted human company, to wit, me, and kept his chin on my shoulder.

Rhea jeeped back from the scene of the brawl, complaining about the message. "For an artilleryman that flyboy doesn't know much about artillery. That battery wasn't unlimbering to fire. They were trying to harness up and get to hell away from here."

The vanguard platoon reformed and we moved on, leaving a clump of fifty prisoners, several of them wounded, to be picked up by someone else who had the time and transportation to do it.

Over a hill and down the slope toward a bridge that crossed a rivulet. The bridge, which was really only a large culvert, had been blown, of course, so the vanguard waded the stream to the right, climbed to the pavement again, and started up the next slope.

I was in Tiger Bait and had dropped back behind the first tank destroyer. Since he couldn't have his head on my shoulder my new-found friend was trotting close behind the tank, muzzle at the left track shelf.

The leading destroyer was just crossing the stream when there was a hellish *clank,* a simultaneous *crack* from the woods to our right rear, the destroyer shuddered to a halt, and the crew piled out for cover, all except one man. He, I think it was the destroyer commander, stood up to his full height, clasped both hands over his chest, and toppled slowly sideways. Shoulder on the track shelf, he pinwheeled and fell flat on his belly, arms outflung.

"Damn. Another good man gone," I thought, as I clambered out of Tiger Bait's turret.

Smart German, taking cover in the woods, with a field of fire to cover the crossing. The destroyer commanders in rear were starting to scout through the woods on foot to locate the gun. Might be a tank, a Jagd Panzer, assault gun, or an antitank horse-drawn gun. I'd get a tank in the advance guard looking for him from the front.

Couldn't take Tiger Bait across that field of fire so I started across the stream afoot. But as I passed the dead hero he raised his head slightly, rolling his eyes from side to side. He then scuttled most capably for cover under the abutment of the culvert. That lad had missed his calling. Paramount or Goldwyn-Mayer would make a star of him. I've never seen a man killed more convincingly in a John Wayne epic. And he'd had the sense to stay that way until he was sure the German wasn't machine-gunning the survivors.

I overtook the last tank in the advance guard. The commander was intent on a small-arms brawl ahead but I got his attention by standing in front of his machine and waving. He removed an ear phone and leaned over the turret. "A Kraut tank back there (pointing) just shot that destroyer from the rear. He's close, not more than three to four hundred yards."

"Yes sir." A moment of radio-intercom talk and the tank swung around to face the threat in rear. The sergeant raised his binoculars to search the woods behind the crippled destroyer, moving his tank forward a few feet at a time. He had a serious problem: the German gun had a line of sight through the trees, through which he could see and shoot any of our vehicles that lingered in that opening. The sergeant was trying to find another line of sight through which he could see the German without being seen himself. It would be most unfortunate if his first sight of the German were the muzzle of the gun. He kept idling his tank a few feet forward, halting, and searching. Finally he found what he was looking for. "Gunner, tank. Traverse left, steady, on. See that patch of brown paint between them two big pine trunks? Fire."

Crack.

The tank curtsied with the recoil, there was a rumble of heavy explosions in the target area, and a plume of pyrotechnics shot up above the treetops, as though a torch had been dropped in a barrel of skyrockets. He'd hit the ammunition.

"Nice shooting, sergeant," I yelled, giving him the "OK" sign.

The tank commander nodded and grinned, clearly meaning, "OK, sir, now that I've taken care of that little chore for you I'd better get on with my main job." The driver jazzed the engine as he spun the tank to follow the advance guard.

Damned good lot of men I had in this outfit.

Tiger Bait was coming ahead. I looked for my horse, but the racket had been too much for him. I'd sure have liked to keep him. Use him for making the rounds where jeeps couldn't make it.

Ninth Armored

We were making good progress. Someone else was evidently doing well near the Rhine on our right. There were occasional heavy explosions in that direction, followed by the sight of tall, mushrooming clouds of black smoke. I'd seen such clouds before, during the Argonne drive when the retreating Germans were blowing up their ammunition dumps. So somebody over there must be crowding them.

We were at a halt for a few minutes while the point tankers looked over the next valley and set a couple of haystacks afire. Colonel Wemple had indoctrinated his young men well and they never passed a haystack unfired. They'd seen too many such stacks built over a tank or gun.

A handkerchief was waving over a clump of bushes a hundred yards on the right flank.

"Kommen Sie heraus," yelled a rifleman from the next tank.

A trio of Germans stood up, hands overhead, and came trotting over to halt in front of the German-speaking infantryman. They were young but mature, capable-looking Krauts, regular army who logically should be giving us a very hard time.

"What make you here?" asked our linguist.

"We will capitulate, Herr Feldwebel," promoting our man two grades.

"Under what unit are you?"

"We are antitank-cannon crewmen."

"Where is your gun?"

"There over (pointing to the right front) one and a half kilometers." That was within easy range of our column.

"Where are your group comrades?"

"They remain with the gun." That was bad; persistent Germans and a Panzerantikanone within eighteen hundred yards of us could cost us some casualties. I had an idea—called our interrogator aside, and sold him on it. "That man, the corporal with the Iron Cross, says that gun is still manned. It might cost us a tank or a few men if they get their nerve up. Let's send him back to talk the crew into deserting. We throw one seed back and we might get a crop. Tell them to put their hands down, give them a cigarette apiece, and try it."

"Might be a good idea, sir. Never heard of it before but it sounds worth trying." The soldier put the prisoners at ease and resumed. "You are a courageous man, the Iron Cross," fingering the decoration on the German's chest.

"Will you it have?" queried the Kraut, anxious to please.

"No. I mean that you brave enough are, your comrades to rescue."

"I understand you not."

"Will you again to your group return? Say to them they should come back with you."

The German was horrified at the idea. His eyes bulged. He turned pale. "Nein. That will I not," he declared emphatically, and I wondered about this sudden resurgence of patriotism.

"Why will you not?"

"They would me shoot."

And so it was. They cheerfully pointed out the site of their gun as we passed but their comrades must have moved. Combing the area with .50 calibers drew no response.

Oh well, it was a good idea. It just didn't work out.

At 1200, Rhea halted and Wemple brought his crew up to furnish the advance guard. Rhea took the center position and refilled his ammunition racks. I was saving Task Force King for the main effort in taking Limburg.

About 1300 we were still making good time. I was at my desk in Tiger Bait beginning to do some worrying in depth about how to capture Limburg. All I really knew about the town was that they invented a very smelly cheese. The Lahn River looked on the map to be one hell of an obstacle. They would blow the bridge, of course. I could take the section north of the river with Wemple's force, then send Rhea and King out on the right and left to find a bridge so we could do our principal work south of the Lahn. And if they made it hard for us at any point, back up and burn them out. No river crossing or house-to-house fighting for—

The sergeant interrupted my unhappy contemplation of the impossible situation. "Colonel—Colonel Wemple wants to see you."

I popped my head out of the turret. "Look at that, colonel. They're lucky we recognized them in time." He was pointing to the forest wall five hundred yards to the right rear. A thinly spaced column of American tanks, half-tracks, and jeeps was emerging from the woods on a country lane that ran under the next blasted overpass. It looked like someone was lost.

A couple of jeeps worked to the front of the column and buzzed up to where we were working to bypass the wrecked span. A sharp-looking young officer was directed to Tiger Bait and I dismounted to meet the intruder. I don't like to be crowded in combat. I prefer plenty of elbow room so we can shoot anything that moves without inquiring friend or foe.

Hmmm, a spread eagle welded on the front of his helmet. He saluted. "Brockman, CCB, Ninth Armored," he introduced himself.

"Triplet, CCA, Seventh Armored. What are you people doing in this area? You're supposed to be over there on the Rhine."

"Change in orders, colonel. I've just been ordered to attack down the autobahn and take Limburg."

"Your people are confused at division or corps level. Limburg is our meat. My orders are to attack down the autobahn and take Limburg. You'd better recheck with your division."

"According to my information you are supposed to halt here and turn the job over to me," he persisted.

"No way. Not until I get the word, Brockman. But until the big brass gets the mess unsnarled I'll be glad to have you people along. Here's a compromise, the autobahn has two highways. I'll take the left side and you take the right and if the gilded staff doesn't tell us different we'll split Limburg between us."

"A pleasure, colonel. We'll do it."

And so it was for the next fast half hour. Two combat commands from two different divisions from two different corps, dashing down a superhighway abreast. Due to the natural rivalry between the advance guards, we really moved.

But all good things come to an end, usually too soon. I had called Larsen, told him the situation, and directed him to find out where the mistake lay. Within half an hour he relayed the order to halt—we had a new mission.

"Have commanders assembled, Larsen. Tell Gruen we'll have time for fuel and ammunition refill." I bade farewell to Colonel Brockman, "It's all yours, colonel—have a good time," and moved back to the headquarters group.

Nineteen.

On the Way to Giessen

Cross-Country

The new mission was a dilly. CCA was to move northeast and capture bridgeheads over the Dill River at Ehringshausen, Wordorf, and Asslar, by dawn tomorrow, March 27.

Three bridges—three task forces. I decided to give each task force part of the action for a couple of reasons. First, the road net was atrocious. All of the improved roads ran across our front and the secondary roads just didn't go in the right direction. We couldn't get there from here. We'd be forced to use what roads, farm lanes, and trails existed, possibly move cross-country at times, and many of the lanes were not even shown on the reprinted German maps we were using. Such lanes and trails would not stand much traffic before they became impassable. Second, if we made our approach in a column of task forces surprise would be lost and the bridges we needed would be blown in succession.

Therefore I decided to give each task force a zone of action and move with forces abreast on a necessarily broad front. We would pause overlooking the objectives until if possible we could attack simultaneously for the surprise effect. Maps were marked with zones of action, entry points, the pause line in the Closterwald, and the check points for use in clear radio conversation. After the maps were distributed I gave the commanders the bad news. "Gentlemen, this is going to be a most difficult job. You see your zones of action start at your present positions and end at the village and bridge that you are to capture at dawn tomorrow. You may move anywhere in your zone to find passable roads. If you have to move into another zone to find a road notify the force concerned."

Considering the impossible conditions, the approach march went off very well. There was a misty moonlight from a full moon from 2000 until 0400. Both King and Rhea encountered German truck and infantry columns on the main roads crossing their fronts, but since the enemy fell back in both directions in every case they butted their way through with tank-rifle sections securing the crossings until the trains and artillery had passed. Wemple had a skirmish with five or six tanks that retired after losing one Mark IV.

I could see no method, pattern, or reason in the German troop dispositions. Every other village or town would yield a small group of prisoners, now and then a squad or platoon manning a log roadblock. But there was no massing of troops or weapons, no line or center of resistance, and practically no resistance. The reason might be surprise. It simply didn't occur to the Germans that anyone would be stupid enough to move through the hinterlands at night, and being awakened by the menacing rumble of enemy tanks at point-blank range simply took the fight out of them.

It was a long, hard, cold, and miserable night. The column would pull ahead, making good progress in the fair visibility of the misty light of the full moon, idling along in second gear at five to six miles an hour. The next village sighted, the speed might drop or the advance guard might rush the place, depending on what their guide had told them.

Riflemen dropped off their tanks and piled out of half-tracks, covering the town in two-man or three-man teams, smashing at doors and windows.

"Heraus."

The next guide hauled out of his warm bed protesting and trying to get his trousers and shoes on as he is rushed to the column commander.[1] The interpreter asks a few leading questions and gets honest answers. "What is called this village?"

"Misthaufen, Herr General."

"Where are the German soldiers?"

"It gives no soldiers in Misthaufen" or "in the third house left and the town council hall." More "Heraus" and gathering of prisoners.

"Where is the telephone office?"

"Over the street from the council hall."

"Show me." Forcible entry and destruction of switchboard. As our vandals gained experience this became the first question asked, to obviate any report of our progress by telephone. "Now take us on the best road to Holzenhof."

"But it gives a road block and soldiers at Holzenhof."

A study of the map by pen-light. If there is a way around Holzenhof take it. If not approach quietly, go in with all guns blazing, round up prisoners, and grab another guide.

It was a long, miserable night.

By daylight, Task Force Wemple was on a fair secondary road following the Lahn River west of Leun. Not much of a town, but it had a large railroad marshaling yard. The parallel tracks were packed with flat cars and gondolas that were loaded with heavy weaponry. There were enough tanks, 88-mm. guns on their triple-threat carriages, assault guns, AA quadruple mounts, everything necessary to equip a German Panzer division. There were a few locomotives here and there but no movement, no weapons, crewmen, no railroad workers, nothing—weird.

As a precaution I asked Captain Donovan, the artillery liaison officer, to register on the railroad yard for possible firing if anything developed. He called the fire direction center. The mission could not be fired.

I learned that the Germans, if any were over there, were protected by something more effective than the Lahn River—the Lahn was the boundary between corps. "The corps boundary? But there's none of the other corps in sight, they're in no danger. But if there's a dozen gutsy Krauts over there we are." I was being quite unreasonable about it. "The only way we can get artillery on those targets is for our request to go through channels to III Corps, asking that they fire on the targets. And III Corps artillery will reply that they're not in range."

"That is a brass-bound, bureaucratic, impossible situation, and—"

"But colonel, if we're really threatened from over there, believe me, Colonel Milner will shoot—and we'll apologize to III Corps later."

The main road from Oberbiel to the objective bridge at Asslar went through Wetzlar. But Major Sorenson, the S-2, had been advised that there was a Schuetzstaffel officer candidate school and a Panzerfaust factory in Wetzlar, and I can think of no combination of men and weapons more poisonous than that. So when Wemple clashed with a determined outpost south of Neustadt he backed off and took a farm lane that led to his attack position in the Closterwald above Asslar.

Rhea and Wemple were in position by 0900. Due to distance or terrain I had to relay messages through Rhea to King, but he assured me that he could jump off by 1000, so 1000 was set as the time for a simultaneous move.

The attack, or rather the occupation of the objectives, was made with quiet speed and without resistance. I suppose the enemy was expecting and prepared for us at Wetzlar. The bridges at Asslar and Ehringshausen were intact; Rhea's bridge had been damaged but the foot troops could still cross and a prefabricated span dropped into position by the engineers made it passable for his armor.

I chickened a bit while making the rounds. I was beginning to feel somewhat lonesome out there twenty to thirty miles ahead of friendly troops. Wouldn't admit it, but I was beginning to feel like O'Hare about the situation. We'd just discussed the matter while following Wemple into Asslar.

"Colonel, seems to me we're getting a long way into Germany all by ourselves. Do you think it's safe?"

"Oh sure. We've got over a hundred cannon, four thousand men, and enough ammunition for a three-day fight. We can whip anything they can send against us."

"Yes sir, but we're strung out pretty thin on these break-through maneuvers and I know there's Germans out there in the woods on both sides."

"That's right. But the Germans are afraid of being surrounded, like they cut into and surrounded the French and British during the Blitzkrieg, and like the Russians grabbed off General Paulus and half a million Germans at Stalingrad. When they see us pushing ahead on a one-tank front they don't realize that they could cut our column at any point, they could ambush our gasoline trucks or blow up our ammunition trucks, and we wouldn't have a chance. But when we pass [illegible] of them take off for the woods and some come out with their hands up. I don't understand it either but that's the way it is."

"I see, sir, you mean they are scared we've got them surrounded?"

"That's right."

Major Larsen reported that a lieutenant with a squad of engineers in a half-track on the way to Rhea's force at Wordorf missed Colonel Wemple's turnoff on the farm lane. They were seen to have been halted by the German outpost. A trio of German guards swung aboard and the track was last seen headed for Wetzlar. In order to avoid losing any more men at that point I asked Wemple to place a light tank and a Cossack post at the junction.[2]

On my return to Oberbiel at 1800 a message was being decoded. It read: "CCA, 489 Arty atchd, attack at 2100, capture Giessen by 0600." Goddamn. No rest for the wicked.

The command had not suffered heavily during the breakout but was practically exhausted. Since the morning of March 24 all hands, particularly the officers, had been on the move, dozing in snatches as we maneuvered for position, reconnoitered routes, or fought down the autobahn and across country for sixty miles, clearing Germans "to hedgerows only." This gain in itself affected morale since the men were beginning to feel our exposed position out on the point. I had repeated the explanation I had given O'Hare to several wondering NCOs as I made the rounds—we weren't surrounded or in a dangerous position when knifing into Germany on a single-tank front. We were throwing a steel loop around a large potful of Germans who would probably surrender without fighting.

I studied the map. Giessen lay ten miles east of Asslar, a nice-sized town on the southeast bank of the Lahn with one bridge available to us. Only one road was of use for an Asslar-Giessen attack; all other roads in the area ran across our front connecting the wooded, rugged country to the north with the Wetzlar-Giessen road via bridges over the Lahn.

I wanted to bypass Wetzlar; that Schuetzstaffel OCS with their unlimited supply of Panzerfausts would be vicious.[3]

OK, we could do it, but it would have to be done fast and we needed more planning time. I called Workshop and talked to Hasbrouck in the clear, stating my position about the timing of the operation. "Received your message and will do the job but I want a three-hour delay. My people have to come quite a distance for briefing and they have to have time to get the word down to the last man."

"Are you sure you can make it with a three-hour starting delay?"

"It has to be well planned, well briefed, and done fast. Without the delay it's chancy. With the delay we can do it."

"You have the delay you want. The objective time is unchanged."

Nearly Killed

The night was cold and clear, lit by a bright, silvery full moon directly overhead in a cloudless sky. It was a perfect moon for a night attack, light enough for use of small arms but dim enough to render enemy antitank guns useless. Tiger Bait, following at fifty yards, was clearly visible, as was the white ribbon of the highway ahead. On the left high banks led up to the wooded hills. On the right the road was bordered by tall poplars, beyond which lay cultivated fields sloping down to the Lahn River.

We passed two or three lanes that led to the high ground on the left and were moving at an easy twenty miles an hour in the bright moonlight. Should be nearing the outpost at the turnoff. I was watching the shrub-covered high bank on the left when things began to happen, some instantaneously, several simultaneously, and all fast.

A sudden reddish glow from the bank on the left, an instantaneous white glare, total blackness, a wave of heat on the left cheek, a hefty blow on the left ear, and a harsh swish like a locomotive letting off steam.

Odd, there was the jeep, completely aflame, running down the road with O'Hare still hunched behind the wheel. The jeep and the road were upside down, or I was.

Then I was turning cartwheels and rolling down the roadside ditch at twenty miles an hour. Finally came to rest spread-eagled face down on the low bank. The road was aflame with spilled gasoline and O'Hare's jeep had sagged over into the ditch on my side thirty yards ahead and was burning briskly. The light made my position very unhealthy so I scrambled up the bank, stumbled a few yards into the field, and dropped.

Tiger Bait was barreling ahead at full speed through and over the burning trail of gasoline, another flash and whish but she kept on coming. Just beyond the wrecked jeep she wheeled sharp right across the ditch and into the field.

By a miracle I still had my pistol so I used a two-handed grip, glanced along the barrel, and threw a shot where I thought I could see movement of the men in ambush. The answer was another flash, whish, and a shower of molten debris a yard to my left front. I didn't know what kind of a weapon the Krauts were using but it sure outgunned an M-1911

.45 caliber pistol, so I took off again toward the river. Something was decidedly wrong with my legs, felt like I was on stilts.

Tiger Bait was completing a wide sweep through the field, heading up toward the ambush. I waved and yelled, unnoticed. A white flash on her front plate and she shuddered to a halt. From the waist up I was outrunning my legs and slid to a stop in the soft plowed soil.

The situation looked bad. O'Hare was dead and I had no illusions about the effect of that last hit on Tiger Bait. That left me, and I was certainly in no condition to battle this pack of werewolves. Felt like I'd been kicked in the tail by a trip hammer, my legs wouldn't work reliably, and I couldn't hear a thing except the ringing in my ears.

Another flash against the turret settled Tiger Bait for good and she started to burn.

I heard the mumble of talking, seemed to be somewhere to the rear. Swiveled my head around by millimeters and cocked an eye on Tiger Bait but though I was sure a Kraut patrol was looking it over I could see nothing. A look over the other shoulder, nothing. A bit later I again heard talking and the crunch of gravel. Certainly not one of our patrols, they wouldn't talk and they'd be more careful with their feet. Aha. I saw them, a couple of characters coming back from looking over O'Hare's ruined jeep. Finding no survivors they were getting careless, which was perfectly all right by me.

As the Krauts came closer I saw that the taller one on my right had his submachine gun in his hand. He was the one to watch, number one. The other, number two, had his gun slung behind his back, sling across the chest, a most unhandy way to carry a weapon. They were both gabbling, careless, sure of my watch, rings, and pistol as souvenirs.

At fifteen feet I heaved up on my uncertain legs and swung my pistol on number one. "Hoch mit die Haende."

They were undoubtedly the two worst-scared Krauts on the western front but they still weren't going to put die Haende hoch. "Aiee." That was number two, clawing at his sling. "Ach Gott," number one yelled and swung his gun up, so I shot him amidships and he spread-eagled on his back. Too bad, but I still had number two, who had dashed off a few steps to his right trying to unsling his gun. I swung toward him. He gave another despairing wordless yell, gave up the gun, and came in low on my left, tackling me around the waist. I'd tried to stiff-arm him but the left arm was dead as a two-by-four. Thank God the fellow was small—I barely held my feet.

Turned back to make sure of number one and found him on his knees, gun in both hands. "Kommen Sie hier," which was a silly thing to say and I started toward him, which was even sillier. He swept the Schmeisser across, a tiny blue flame flickering at the muzzle, and I felt a blow on the right thigh that threw me off glance. I steadied and shot him again as near center as possible, and he went over backward.

That had torn it! I was really crippled now, with one or more holes in my leg. But I still had one prisoner, and turned to get him on his feet.

Worse and more of it! Number two was up, fifteen or twenty yards away, and emptying his gun in my direction. How he could miss I'll never understand, but he just cut out my silhouette with the full thirty rounds in one burst. I pointed and carefully squeezed at his middle (you can't aim in moonlight) and he sat down. Very effective gun, the .45.

"Ahgottahgottahgott!" Number one again. I was getting mighty tired of these characters—they were so durable.

I turned back to number one, fearing another resurrection, but he was scrabbling away like a broken-backed rattler, trying to hold himself together, so I turned back to number two.

He, God help me, was up again, jamming a new magazine into his squirt gun while backing away.

"Komm hier, du stinkende Schwein!" I yelled and started to run him down. Distance was in his favor. If he gained on me he could cut me to pieces, while I couldn't touch him. But with a leg in bad shape I was losing ground—he could back up faster than I could move forward.

He was firing again, short bursts this time. I was pointing and squeezing, but missing. Thirty yards was just too damned far for moonlight shooting. I was very careful with the next shot—and the damned pistol was empty.

"Hahrrr!" I stumbled a few steps toward him, waving the gun—if I could only get close enough. "Schurke!"

"Aaaiiee!" he howled, turned, and ran back twice as far. At fifty yards he started firing again. Noisiest fight you ever heard—sounded like a couple of squads bickering around there.

Great God. What the hell was I doing out there, chasing a fighting Kraut with an empty pistol? I swiveled back and hobbled off at a rapid dot-and-carry-one pace toward the tank. He blirped a last handful of bullets overhead. I glanced back, but he was staggering toward the Lahn.

A hell of a funny battle with all the participants wobbling away from the field in all directions.

Short of the tank, I recalled the possibility of more Germans in that direction, and changed course parallel to the river. There was some shouting between the road and Jerry number two, and several pints of bullets crackled by—but after surviving a couple of quarts of them within twenty yards I couldn't be bothered much by burp-guns a city block away.

The leg caved in and I hit the ground again. About time. I needed a breather and figure things out. Pulse and respiration rate way up again. Badly scared. Right leg bleeding badly—artery possibly nicked. If so, it was just too bad unless I could get help quick. I felt the holes in the trousers. Too high for a tourniquet, even if I had time for first aid. An inch left would have been serious.

Another spray of bullets in my general area. Time to be on my way.

Right away a big farmhouse and a couple of outbuildings loomed up near the road. That was damned odd. I flattened out and reviewed my mental map and the skirmish of that morning. There was no house between the road and the river between Oberbiel and the turnoff.

I plastered moist earth over hands, face, and hair, and started to move toward Oberbiel, keeping halfway between the road where I knew there had been a Jerry outpost and the river where there would probably be one.

Then I had it. I'd be a liberated slave laborer, out on a spree. The areas we'd gone through had been full of them, Russians, Belgians, Hollanders, and Frenchmen, all popping out and waving and yelling after the advance guard had passed. I'd been thoroughly kissed a couple of days ago by some bewhiskered foreigners who swarmed out while the bullets were still flying. Granted that this area hadn't been liberated yet, I would be a slave who had defied curfew and gotten drunk in anticipation of liberation. The olive-drab of sweater and trousers could be any color in moonlight.

I'd just finished the "Marseillaise" again when there was a stir in the bushes just off the road and I heard a Schmeisser bolt click to a full cock. This was it. I gave my audience the works—"Vive la France," a fist-shake at the moon, and a gay rendition of "Madelon." It worked. I believed that I was past the last German post but kept up the act loud and clear. If there were no Germans ahead there would probably be Americans and they'd be just as dangerous to approach at night. I'd hate to emulate Stonewall Jackson and get shot by one of my own men.

A quarter mile farther on I saw the tail of a jeep headed into a side lane up the hill and froze when someone in the brush at my elbow said "Halt." He followed up with the garrison challenge, "Who's there?"

"Colonel Triplet."

"For God's sake. Is that you, colonel? Your tank crew said you and O'Hare were both killed." It was Captain Butler of military government.

It was quite a reunion. Butler and three men of his team had been on the way to the PW collection point at Altenberg when they'd heard odd noises and singing down the road and fanned out to see what it was. They stowed me in the jeep and drove up to the 489th Artillery CP where Milner took charge and guided us to his dressing station. "What happened to the attack?" I asked him.

"It was called off, sir. You were reported killed and Major Larsen refused to take responsibility for the move as planned."

"Did Workshop give permission for the cancellation?"

"No, radio to Workshop had failed due to static."

Milner's communications officer had the remote control rigged and I called the command post. Got Sorenson. No time for code. "Orders: The move will be made at the scheduled time plus 4. CP will move at once to follow Wemple. Do you understand? If so, repeat the orders."

I called division and due to distance, terrain, static, and signal strength had a hell of a time getting through. Finally got the idea across that we had been delayed and would move four hours late.

I borrowed a jeep from Milner, a helmet and pistol ammunition from one of his men, a trench coat from a POWINT officer, and a quart of whiskey from Captain Butler. Off once again through the wooded lanes in the bright moonlight—had a feeling of here we go again or dèja vu. But this time there were two medium tanks instead of little Tiger Bait with her 37-mm. drain pipe welded to the gun shield and there were five mean-looking riflemen on each tank. I felt much better with them aboard.

Back on the Way

When O'Hare returned from the hospital we talked over his rather miraculous escape.

"After that hellish white flash I looked over and wondered where you'd gone. Then I saw I was sitting in a gas fire so I twisted the wheel right and fell out to the left. Rolled into the ditch right near that log barricade. Felt like there must be a dozen Krauts watching me. Remember that Kraut .25 I got in Bad Godesberg? Well, I finally couldn't stand it so I pulled that .25 and eased over into the brush. Wiggled ahead till I could see behind the barricade and there wasn't a damn soul in sight. So I went across behind the logs, down in the field, and headed back for Oberbiel. Crossed the road again and pushed up through the woods till I ran into the 489th. Told them that you and the tank crew were dead. We sure were lucky."

A moment of thoughtful silence. "Colonel, remember that day at Bad Godesberg when I ran up on the sidewalk on account of that shell busting alongside? Remember you said, 'O'Hare, keep your mind on your driving. I'll tell you when it's time to duck.' Remember that?"

"Yes, I do, now that you mention it."

"Well, sir, this last time you didn't give me much warning."

We arrived at Wemple's advance guard just as they started to roll, 0400. A very reliable lot, Colonel Wemple and his men. As the point disappeared into the light ground haze that had risen along the Dill, the thought occurred to me that the Regulars never fight a war in modern times. Wemple an expert in the oil business, King a high school teacher, Gruen in the watch business, those lads shooting out all the windows in Hermannstein had just graduated from the twelfth grade, and that gunner who had just slammed a phosphorus shell through the wall in answer to a burp gun was probably an Eagle Scout when the draft board called. I was the only Regular in the whole outfit, but they were doing awfully well for amateurs. They settled Hermannstein in short order, only a platoon outpost there, and the platoon was coming cautiously out now, waving white.

At Niedergirms there was a brisk exchange of fire and several houses were blazing before we could get through. Again the policy of shooting a burst through every door and window paid off and pacified Jerries were popping out all over.

At first glance it looked foolhardy to leave only a squad and a couple of tanks to outpost the road against the Krauts in Wetzlar, but actually it was quite safe. The miles of heavy stuff in the column rumbling toward Nauheim would keep them cautious, I hoped.

The dawn broke as we started toward Nauheim, then daylight, and I was sorry to see it. We could see distant figures trotting toward us from the northern outskirts of Wetzlar, but when Wemple's main body sprinkled a few belts of .50 caliber among them they dropped out of sight. In the light haze we couldn't tell whether they were attacking or trying to surrender. An afterthought—they might have been slaves trying to welcome their liberators. Anyway, at that extreme range we probably didn't hurt them much.

The Leica camera factory was a massive brick building inside a high board fence on the left side of the road. Apparently it was totally deserted and we didn't search the place, just a little shooting by bored riflemen as the column passed was sufficient. If there were any Germans in the place they went out the back way. But I was glad we didn't learn that it was a camera factory until later. If my young men had known that, our attack might have bogged down until they had thoroughly looted the place.

At Nauheim, Waldgirms, and Arzbach we had flurries. There were some sheets hanging out the windows but not enough. The streets were completely deserted and the reconnoitering small-arms fire of the advance guard was always answered by a few diehards who caved in and waved white when our guns started tearing the houses to pieces. I urged the force commanders to answer every rifle shot with a platoon of tank guns, every machine gun with a battalion of artillery, and never do any house-to-house fighting. Burn it. The policy of destroying real estate paid off.

Along the road we were harassed by occasional mortar fire from somewhere north of us. The shells were dropping nearly straight down, so the mortars couldn't be pinpointed and we just had to disregard them. Another anti-shock dose of medicinal alcohol helped.

Time was passing fast. It was noon by the time we settled Arzbach. I had called for the CP Forward to send up a jeep and T-5 Sauer arrived with Captain Powell's well-padded job so I sent the artillery mount back to Milner. I was glad to see Sauer. He was a good driver, a very solid citizen who normally piloted the command half-track and seemed to enjoy the war—Hunnange. I asked him to manage for a stout cane so I could get around on foot. He hammered on the door of the nearest house until it was cautiously opened. He reappeared a few minutes later with a cane and two cups of ersatz Kaffee. "Pretty sure it isn't poisoned, colonel—she drank a cup too, right out of the same pot."

"What d'you mean she?"

"The old lady that gave me the cane, sir. Offered me the coffee too."

Arzbach was settled; only Heuchelheim remained before Giessen. Rhea came up to look over the situation and I got him and Wemple together. "Wemple, I don't think it will be necessary to outpost this place. I'd like to have you push ahead with everything you've got and clear Heuchelheim fast. Rhea, you push in right on his heels and take off for the Giessen bridge at full speed."

Wemple's men went into Heuchelheim with speed and Rhea provided the recklessness by leading his force toward the bridge in his jeep until a machine gun shot it from under him. He, his driver, and radio man abandoned ship and flattened until his leading section of tanks caught up and swung into position to shield and pick them up. He went on with marching fire from all guns but found the bridge damaged and passable only by foot troops. He called for engineer help.

As King's column turned off and started across the plain, a column of men was seen crossing the Lahn bridge from Deutenhofen and moving toward Arzbach. Captain Donovan gave the data for an artillery concentration but held his fire—it looked more like a mass surrender than an attack. King's advance guard, holding fire, found that it was a column of American and British prisoners, complete with their erstwhile guards carrying white flags. When they arrived at the eastern outskirts of Arzbach they fell out in a meadow. A quartet of senior American NCOs reported to me with the guard detail.

"This is Captain Bieler, colonel. He's a damned good fellow, gave us every break he could. We'd like to see him treated right." It was an interesting story. Bieler had been ordered to march his column of twelve hundred Allied prisoners from Wetzlar to Giessen. When he had seen us moving through Heuchelheim and starting toward Giessen he had seen the futility of further flight and turned the column to join us. I scribbled a note to POWINT. "Captain Bieler is recommended as a nice guy by his former POWs. Treat him accordingly." Didn't know if it would have much effect on his treatment by my Hebraic POWINTs but I could do no less.

Six former members of the Seventeenth or the Twenty-third who had been captured at St. Vith in December came to see me. I admired their spirit. "All I want is a chance to kill the sonsabitches," said one. "Just gimme a rifle and I'll show the bastards," announced another.

"Glad to have you," I said. "You can rejoin your units right now. They'll be glad to see you and there won't be any shortage of rifles—they've been having casualties."

My announcement didn't have the expected effect. There were no rousing cheers, no rush to rejoin. In fact there was a rather heavy silence. The flashing eyes became shifty and I was almost as embarrassed as they were. "Well, sir, maybe we'd better go back and get processed through the hospital with the rest of the gang," decided the one spokesman. "Yes sir, we can come up and join the outfit later, maybe," added the other Hun-hating type.

And bang went another of my illusions, an unwarranted belief in the pugnacity of the American soldier. I have since noticed that men who have been captured are generally seriously affected by having been prisoners. They may have been unreliable or neurotic before they were captured. That may have been the reason they surrendered. Or the blow to their pride may have changed their outlook. Their life under the weapons of their guards may have given them an unreasoning fear of the enemy. The hardships of their life as prisoners may have affected them mentally. But the fact remains that given a choice between untried recruits and veteran former prisoners, I would choose the recruits to form a fighting unit.

It has been alleged that I knew of the prison camp at Wetzlar and had planned my attack to rescue them. That is totally false. I would never risk the life of one Georgia rifleman to rescue any number of prisoners regardless of nationality or identity—including "Ike."

While I was talking to Rhea, General Hasbrouck and Colonel Ryan jeeped up. Both shook hands enthusiastically, especially Hasbrouck. "Congratulations, Triplet," he said. "I'm sure glad to see you," and that was quite a speech for anyone as painfully reserved as he.

"Hello, soldier," said Ryan, grinning. "You look good, considering."

"I feel pretty good," which was a damned lie. "The boys are doing all right. Rhea will be in Giessen by 1500 and King is going to be through with Kleine Linden before that. Then he'll move into south Giessen. We'll have the place cleared by sunset."

"That's fine—very fine." First time I'd ever seen Hasbrouck smile.

Days later I had an inkling as to why Hasbrouck had been so pleased to see us going into Giessen. First and Third Armies had been ordered to drive northeast and northwest respectively and meet at Giessen on March 30, surrounding a German army between Giessen and the Rhine. Patton had bet a new hat that the Third would get there first. Hodges took him up on it. Patton lost the bet by two days.

Price of hat: fifty dollars and ninety-three men.

No, that's not quite right. For ninety-three casualties we won a fifty-dollar hat and nearly two hundred thousand prisoners.

Twenty.

To Hemer

Cleanup

The penicillin shots at three-hour intervals were a damned nuisance, particularly at night, and the cheery attitude of the nurse or orderly who gave them didn't deceive me—it was merely the mask over the fiendish glee of a sadist.

The Germans nearest my bunk were spared the misery of these shots. They'd both been hit in the abdomen and were being fed via a quart glass container, rubber tube, and needle arrangements taped to the arms. At mealtimes the orderly would pour glucose into the container; now and then the nurse would add a pint of blood serum, and after gouging me with my dose of penicillin she'd just slip the needle into the Germans' rubber tubes. Neat.

One more day to go. I caught Pillroller and Hackencutt together in the office and reminded them that I was due to return to my unit. To prove my excellent condition I did a full fingers-to-floor waist bend that almost killed me. I'd intended to do a full knee bend as the encore but abandoned the idea as foolhardy. "I'd like to call the Seventh Armored and have them send a jeep or plane tomorrow." I was pushing just a bit, but I could get the rest of my shots from my own surgeon.

"All right, colonel. I'll write a note to your surgeon about advisable further treatment. Use this phone."

It took a bit of doing, but by dint of field telephones and radios through First Army and VII Corps the transport was arranged.

Damned good to be back. The outfit was in reserve in and about Winterberg, a nice mountain town. All hands were busily cleaning weapons, bathing and shaving in ice water, lubricating, changing spark plugs, spot painting, bore sighting, achieving amiable intoxication on looted wine, and sleeping.

The rest that Hasbrouck had promised them had started badly. When Task Force Wemple reached the reserve area they were immediately engaged in a brisk brawl with a Wehrmacht mixed force that was already in possession. After that situation was cleared up, CCA had barely caught up on lost sleep when the drive to take the Ederstausee dam had begun. CCB took the brunt of the Edersee show, A traveling in reserve, but King finally won the Purple Heart he'd been working for on April 4 and Wemple lost several men when CCA went into action on April 6 at Assinghausen.

After fighting through Kirchain, Eustelberg, Oberkirchen, Wiemeringhausen, and Assinghausen, the vital dam was captured intact and the "ghost division" was resting and refurbishing in the Langenberg-Kahler-Asten area.

General Hasbrouck dropped in, solicitously inquired about my well-being (forcing me to lie outrageously), and outlined our probable chores for the immediate future. Making broad sweeps worthy of an army commander across the situation map, he sketched out a mission that would probably keep us happily busy for a week. "I want you to move north, clean up and occupy this area contained by Berghausen-Ramscheid-Eslohe-Bremke."

"Is anything known about the enemy strength or dispositions, sir?"

"No, corps intelligence states that you'll probably find nothing more than a few deserters. The operation is principally to clean up our backyard in preparation for our attack on Hemer. By the way, I'm attaching a platoon of armored cavalry to you for personal escort and security duty. Use them."

OK, I'd use them, but I'd be going some places where an armored car just couldn't make it.

I studied the troop list and decided to make no changes in the task forces. The division into three forces commanded by Rhea, Wemple, and Dailey gave me well-balanced units that worked well together and were able to meet any normal situation and win.

The road net in this rugged, mountainous, wooded terrain was inadequate and atrocious, so we started the cleanup job in one column, prepared to deploy as or if resistance developed.

The cleanup campaign really wasn't worth the effort and fuel spent in combing out the villages and woods. Only twice did we find resistance.

Rhea ran into a roadblock defending a defile during our approach to Berghausen. Reducing it would have been practical but might be costly, so Rhea put up a show to contain the enemy force while Wemple looked for a way to bypass. Wemple's men found a forest trail that appeared promising, a woodcutter's or charcoal burner's lane, leading up to the left. His force was easily able to reach the crest and found that below the wide sweep of meadow they were looking directly down on Berghausen.

It was a picture-book, tank-school demonstration type of attack. Ten medium tanks loaded with riflemen formed the first wave on a quarter-mile front, each tank followed by an infantry track. A medium tank platoon and a light tank platoon followed as the second wave. The tank destroyer platoon followed to the military crest, halted, and sniped off the German heavy stuff and vehicles as they tried to leave. The engineer platoon and I enjoyed the show.

Surprise was complete. Wemple's tanks topped the crest and moved down the slope at a reckless speed, an infantryman on each tank swinging the .50 caliber AA gun, the other rifleman holding on for dear life. Sixteen tanks and four destroyers were blasting the bass notes, while the .50s and .30s were singing the contralto and soprano parts. An assault gun and four trucks burning at the far exit, individual figures in gray, green, or black green running for the woods, sheets flung to hang out windows, beautiful. "Ride of the Valkyries."

I followed the attack, enjoying the show, but grunting and cursing with every bump. Sauer was driving well, carefully avoiding irregularities but even at that—on getting into town I was surprised to find that I was being closely followed by my action-craving headquarters commandant, Captain Donaldson, and shortly after Colonel King pulled in with the staff.[1]

Headquarters CCA assembled at the town hall (too modest a building to be called a Rathaus) where Captain Donaldson found tables with thirty place settings laid out, Wienerschnitzels and fried Kartoffeln sizzling on the ovens, and a number of girls huddling in the cellar. Apparently a banquet had been laid on by the citizens for their Germanic heroes, who by this time were dead, PWs, or fugitives.

It was dusk, getting dark, and no time to chase Germans, so we took our places at the festive board, Donaldson organized the scared females as a serving force, and we enjoyed one of the tastiest dinners I can remember—sure beat the K-ration.

Wemple deployed to the northwest, capturing Langenholthausen, Balve, and Helle. The flow of beat-down men in feld gruen led by their haughty officers in leather overcoats and escorted by riflemen of the Twenty-third continued.

The command post was settling for the night in Langenholthausen. While the staff was setting up the war room, I walked across the square to where the prisoners were assembled for truck transport to the cages. My suspicious young riflemen kept them standing with their hands on their heads. Rightly so—five sentries versus five hundred prisoners who still hadn't been thoroughly searched.

One of the guards approached. "Colonel, one of these Krauts says he's a Dutchman and wants to see you."

"Show me." I was a bit curious. I knew about Belgians in the Nazi army, but a Dutchman? A Hollander? The lad led me over to a large, leather-overcoated officer standing in the front rank, hands properly on head. "Was wollen Sie?" I asked in a nasty tone.

"Colonel, I introduce myself. I am Generalmajor Van Au (I'm not certain about the name). I am sick and very tired. I request your permission to rest in a house until your transport arrives. I give you my word as an officer that I will not try to escape." He spoke English more understandably than most Englishmen. I took an interested look at him. Yes, he was gray in the face with just a touch of blue in the hollows—about sixty-five years old, shaking with fatigue or fever, and my diagnosis was a serious heart condition. And why the hell should I care if the treasonable Dutch SS bastard dropped dead? He probably would, looked worse than I felt. And then, to my surprise, I found myself giving him permission to lower his hands, take one of his officers with him, and get a bed in the nearest house.

I still wonder if he kept his word.

We were pleasantly surprised when a Twenty-third Infantry half-track halted in front of the CP with a full standing load of German officers who proved to be the rear echelon staff of the XXXI Corps. Nice going, Wemple.

Lieutenant Kirschbaum donned a pair of eagles and had a couple of the general staff officers brought in for questioning. I was amazed at the immediate success of his interrogation. He promptly learned that we were engaged with elements of the XXXI Corps, that we were hitting them from the rear, and that the corps commander, Generalleutnant Koechling, and his forward command post people and general staff, were hiding out close by.

I asked if it was likely that the general would try to escape posing as a civilian. The officer being questioned was quite indignant. "Unheard of. The general is an old soldier. It would never occur to him to do anything so dishonorable."

OK, if he prefers to get captured in uniform in consonance with German honor—

Ventured forward to follow Wemple's advance guard and witnessed an outstanding case of heroism on the part of a company aid man.

A rifle squad had moved out to the right front across a long-grassed meadow to investigate a suspicious clump of woods where the Germans might have an ambush waiting for us. They did, have an ambush, that is. Two machine guns crackled into action, one driving the rifle squad to ground while the other swept the length of the advance guard column. All hands not protected by armor dived for cover. Sauer hit the left ditch while I hugged the low stone wall on my side. The tank gunners began searching the edge of the woods for the well-hidden guns. A faint call was heard from the field. "Aid man. Aid man."

The lad who was hugging the wall just in front of me—he had jumped out of the half-track ahead of my jeep—was wearing a Red Cross armband and red crosses on his helmet. He took a couple of deep breaths, jumped to the top of the wall, and waved both arms above his head. He then walked upright, still waving now and then, until he reached the wounded man. The machine-gun fire had stuttered uncertainly to a halt, then resumed, with the bursts carefully placed on each side of the medic, who was still in view while he padded and tourniqueted the wounds. Finally he appeared again, standing, carrying the casualty with a fireman's lift, and deposited the man behind the wall with the enemy gunners still carefully missing him.

I admit that I know of no case where Germans have fired knowingly on ambulances, aid men, or dressing stations. But I will also state that I do not have the cold nerve required to stand up among a cloud of bullets and wave like that young man did, hoping that the enemy had heard of the Geneva Convention or had a spark of chivalry in his soul.

Sauer made a cogent comment after the tanks had eliminated the guns and progress was resumed. "I know that guy—conscientious objector. I just can't understand those people."

Neither can I.

Held Up

During the night of April 12–13, Wemple kept pushing, making re-peated attacks to gain the road intersection at Sanssouci, without success. He was up against a new unit, the 116th Panzer Regiment and their attached panzer grenadiers, who were putting up a stubborn fight. His front simmered down to an Indian-fighting type of patrols and unsuc-cessful shots at Tiger tanks with our pitifully inadequate 2.5-inch rocket launchers. It passeth understanding why our geniuses invented the bazooka, which penetrates 2.5 inches, for use against 4-inch armor, while the Germans developed the Panzerfaust capable of shooting through 7.5 inches for use against our 2.5 inches of armor.

Why didn't we use captured Panzerfausts? Because I had had that idea during our occupation of the west bank of the Rhine. It was a good idea, it just didn't turn out well.

I had asked Captain Hochberg to have one of his explosives experts put on a demonstration for the assembled NCOs. He furnished a ca-pable lieutenant and hauled the carcass of a Panther tank to serve as a target. The lieutenant put on a good show, explaining the makeup of the Panzerfaust head, fuse, shaped charge, folding fins, tube, pro-pelling charge, sights, and ignition system. He then selected a Pan-zerfaust from the dozen stacked for the demonstration, raised the sight-trigger, and took the firing position, tube under arm. "You people back there, stand farther back, over to the sides. This thing has a hell of a back-blast."

He aimed carefully at the Panther front plate, pressed the trigger, and the Panzerfaust exploded and blew most of his head off. Since that sad day no man in CCA would even approach a Panzerfaust.

Good idea, it just didn't turn out right.

The accident was generally blamed on a booby-trapped weapon, until Lieutenant Kirschbaum came in one day waving a captured order: "The Panzerfaust 65 fuse number XZ312 has proven repeatedly unreliable and subject to premature detonation. These fuses will . . ."

While having a cup of coffee in the cold, gray, miserable dawn, I received a message from Lieutenant Carraway of the Eighty-seventh Armored Cavalry Squadron. "Have just captured six officers, including a general. On my way to the CP."

So instead of seeing to the security of the command post as his mission required, young Carraway was out beating the bushes for stray Krauts. Dereliction of duty. Leaving us exposed to the hordes of werewolves. I'd have to have a word with that young man.

But could he have caught General Koechling and his general staff? They were alleged to have been hiding out in this area. If so, all was forgiven.

Aha. Here they were, another Twenty-third Infantry half-track sandwiched between two armored cars. Krauts unloading, polished boots, red tabs, lapels, shoulder boards and striped breeches, genuine staff corps.

How does one receive a general, a captured Nazi general? I had read a few days before how General Bob Stack, an old friend of the Tank School days, had captured Goering and since it was lunch time he had had the prisoner take a chair at the table where fried chicken was the pièce de résistance. Some carrion-loving buzzard of the press, trying for a Pulitzer prize, wrote it up under the headline: "General feeds Goering chicken while his troops starve on K-rations."

Since our number-one politician, Eisenhower, catered to the press, it was a moot question whether Stack would be busted to permanent colonel or court-martialed for giving aid and comfort to the enemy. Quite a problem for a temporary colonel with the permanent grade of major—I couldn't make it on a major's pay. So I donned my most arrogant sneer, swung Betty Boop forward at a threatening angle, and swaggered out to meet the party.[2]

But as they came up the walk the old gentleman in the lead, erect, medium build, pink complexion, gray mustache—well. He was the living image of my father.

I dropped my swagger and sneer, pushed the "grease gun" muzzle down behind the waistline, and limped out to greet him. Saluted and offered my hand. "General Koechling, I'm very glad to see you."

The hard-faced former police provost marshal stomped in and reported. "Major Hurlbut reporting to take charge of the prisoners, sir."

Another handshake and they were gone. Nice fellow, Koechling.

A report from G-2. Generalleutnant Koechling stated that his reception and treatment by the American commander was very korrekt.

Still sorry I didn't serve coffee—after all, the poor devils hadn't had breakfast and probably no supper.

That night while worrying myself to sleep with the plans for tomorrow and reviewing the events of the day, it suddenly occurred to me, what in hell was General Koechling complaining about when he said my men would fight and his wouldn't? He and his general and special staff veteran professionals had surrendered to my comparative recruits without a harsh word or a shot being fired.

About 0800, General Hasbrouck arrived at the CP in a good mood. "Congratulations on your catch this morning, Triplet. Corps intelligence is very happy about the opportunity to talk with General Koechling."

"Glad to hear that, sir."

"When are you going to grab Hemer?"

"We'll get in there all right, general, but it's impossible to guess when right now. We're up against a new outfit, the 116th Panzers and a good grenadier outfit, and they aren't giving an inch without a fight. Rhea is having a hard time on the right at Beckum, Wemple is still stopped at Sanssouci, and I'm deploying Dailey to the left through Balverwald to take Deilinghofen. If he can—"

"I'm sending you two more battalions, Chappuis with the Forty-eighth Armored Infantry Battalion and the third battalion of the 359th Infantry. They look like a good outfit."

"Glad to hear I'm getting more infantry—I'll need them in Hemer."

"By the way, Triplet, I haven't seen anything of your cavalry platoon. Where are they?"

"Carraway has them out around the area trying to scare some more generals out of the woods I expect."

"Listen carefully, colonel. I attached an armored cavalry platoon to CCA for your personal security. In the future when I visit your command post I expect to find it surrounded by armored cars. And if I meet you on the road, your jeep is to be preceded by at least one car and followed by another. Is that clear?"

"Very clear, sir. But I'm careful about ambushes and feel so silly with a procession like that. And even if I do get clobbered, Colonel King can take over. You don't have to worry about me."

"I don't care about you. I'm just afraid that if you get hit your men will quit." (Aw gee, Bob, and I thought you really cared.) You be damned sure you keep your security with you."

"Yes sir."

Chappuis of the Forty-eighth AIB was a tall, dark, and handsome New Orleans Creole type. Having roomed with a tall, dark, and handsome Creole type for three years at West Point, I was initially skeptical about his usefulness in combat. The handsome lads are frequently loathe to risk burring up their Adonis-like faces and physiques. But after scanning the row of ribbons on his bulging chest, starting with three Silver Stars, I was reassured. He must be a roaring lion in combat. "Glad to see you, Chappuis. Here's the situation." And I gave him a rundown on the enemy as we saw them and on locations and missions of CCA and the three task forces. "I want you to pick up a platoon of tanks from Rhea and extend our envelopment of the German rear on the right flank. You are to push through Hoevel-Wettmarsen-Albringen-Eisborn-Horst-Raustadt, swinging in on the rear of this hard resistance and folding it up. Rhea on your left will move through Beckum and drive in on the rear of Sanssouci to help Wemple."

"I understand, sir."

As he left I felt vastly relieved. The right flank was in good hands. I could now concentrate on the left.

Damned imposing row of ribbons.

Chappuis was a great disappointment. He moved through Hoevel and Wettmarsen without meeting resistance, but ran into a hard knot of fanatics at Albringen and was stopped. My urging him on via the radio had no effect in moving him and a visit by Colonel King was little more stimulating. The situation reminded me strongly of the fiasco at Rochefort with the Second Armored Division. I could now understand why, with Chappuis commanding the Forty-eighth AIB, General Clarke was unable to capture Born. At the end of the fight Chappuis was still nibbling halfheartedly at Albringen.

I dimly recall that while Colonel King and I were doodling solutions to the Chappuis-Albringen problem with the map spread on the hood of Wretch Forward, Captain Butler and Lieutenant Kirschbaum came up quite agitated. "President Roosevelt is dead," blurted Butler without ceremony. "He died yesterday," added Kirschbaum.

"Is he?" I commented with polite intonation (an officer should be courteous to subordinates). "I still believe that Chappuis should bypass and envelope the north flank. But you'll be able to see it better on the ground. Good luck, King."

Some three days later I recalled the above incident and figured out why my two young men were looking at me quizzically, expectantly, nonplussed, as I turned back to the S-3 track.

Good God, the president was dead.

There must be a serious fault in my nature when I am more concerned with the well-being of riflemen, tankers, and engineers than I am with that of the president of the United States.

Good news. By sunrise it looked like we might win this show. Dailey and "Danube Blue" had gotten their hard stuff up during a long and laborious night, had jumped off at dawn with a fast attack that got them both on their objectives with little opposition, a fair bag of prisoners, and few casualties.[3] Wemple had taken Volksringhausen and Binolen during the night and was shoving on to Honnethal. Rhea was trailing Wemple in reserve.

Only one difficulty—Chappuis was still at Albringen. Every time he was urged to shove ahead into Eisborn his men would lean aggressively forward in their foxholes, look fierce, and probably yell "boo." But nobody moved on that front.

We moved the command post to Beckum.

A gratifying flow of prisoners marching to the rear continued. The Germans of today don't resemble their fathers. The old-timers of 1918 could not only dish it out, they could take it too. Their sons can't.

Moving the command post to Beckum was a mistake. On the map it was ideal, but the hilly terrain interfered with radio transmission and I completely lost contact with all forces on the line. We could reach division, but that was little help in fighting the war.

Lieutenant Task Force Coombs took off with the half-track to find a better location and returned shortly with good news. "Just over this hill, colonel. We can't reach division clearly but we got everybody on the line five by five. Nice house for the CP too."

That was ideal—I didn't want to talk to Hasbrouck anyway, so we moved. It was a nice place, a large, two-story manor sitting in the middle of acres of mostly mowed lawn with a wonderful view of the valley and hills beyond. The owner, a proud Prussian type of military age and physique, was in residence, and made no objection when informed that we were moving in. He appeared much the country gentleman in his gray costume coat with seams bound in green leather, his plus-fours, and golf stockings. Probably a member of the minor nobility that the Germans still retain in spite of Bismarck and the democratic government forced on them after World War I.[4]

This young man took a great deal of interest in our activities as we set up the command post, placing the CP Rear track behind the house and dispersing the other four tracks on the lawn to each side. I went into the house expecting to set up the war room in the main hall, but gave up on that idea when I found that the front gave a magnificent view of hostile Germany through one of the largest plate glass windows I've ever seen. I visualized what a shell burst would do to that window and what the glass shards would do to Wretch CP Rear, shuddered, and explored the other ground floor rooms further. Interesting, found a good many photographs of our aristocratic host in uniform. Home on leave? Recuperating from wounds? Discharged? I still don't know.

But when I decided to leave the CP outside under cover of the house I found the German hovering interestedly over the situation map and coldly disregarding the protests of Captain Kennedy, the S-3 (opns), who was being too damned polite about it.

"Why is this Kraut allowed here, captain?" I asked.

"He just keeps coming around, colonel. We can't keep him away."

OK, I'd have to try to give him the word. Lieutenant Kirschbaum wasn't in sight so I reviewed my high school German II. "Mein Herr, es ist verboten fuer Zivile hier zu umschauen. Bitte gehen Sie weg. Bitte gehen Sie ins Haus." (Forbidden for civilians to look around here. Please go away. Please go in the house.)

It must have been the bitte (please) that threw him out of line. Since I had said bitte I must be inferior—he had the upper hand. He drew up a couple of inches, got red in the face, bulged his eyes, and shouted. Kept it simple enough for me to understand. "This is my house. This is my land. I am the master here. I have the right to—"

With no intention on my part my pistol jumped out of that Abercrombie & Fitch spring holster and slapped him right, left, and down before he dropped. Must not have hit him hard because he was scrambling away on all fours, bleating "no—no—no" like a lost lamb. Sounded like "nay"—probably meant "no—no" in the local dialect.

Colonel King, who had just been up with Rhea, had returned in time to see the incident. "How did you do that?" he asked, ever eager to learn new methods of dealing with Nazis. I showed him. "You don't want to kill them unnecessarily so you leave the safety on," I explained. "Draw straight out for the right ear, flex the wrist and forearm over for the left, and if you're fast enough you can catch him on top of the head on the way down."

"By gimminy, I'm going to try that. It would be better than shooting them in some cases."

Pushover

The German defense of Hemer began to collapse rapidly. Wemple's task force drove on into Honnethal, Task Force Rhea following closely for possible envelopment. Wemple went on to take Brockhausen, and Rhea moved over to the right to take Riemke. The two task forces then charged rapidly across the landing field east of Hemer and took positions overlooking the town. I had hoped to have Chappuis threatening Hemer from the north, but he was still stalled at Albringen. By 1000, however, we were in position for the final push to be made by Danube Blue supported by Dailey and overwatched by Rhea and Wemple.

Since Hemer was the hard knot and we had plenty of time, I set the time of attack tentatively at 1200 and in the meantime requested and received the support of all the division and some corps artillery in demolishing the place. They covered the town like a blanket, a magnificent show.

Major Dailey was the outstanding individual of the operation for the rest of the day. I consider him responsible for the liberation of 23,200 PWs and the surrender of the remnants of the XXXI Corps plus additional units on both flanks of the German defense, a total of 40,000 men. Dailey, at Deilinghofen, called me about 1015. "Colonel, I've got something down here that's too big for me to handle. There's a German major here, came in under a flag, that says he's the commandant of a PW camp. He's raising hell about our artillery bombardment, says we're shelling hospitals and churches, killing civilians, and claims we're shelling his prisoners. The prisoners are rioting and escaping and he has only three hundred guards to keep 24,000 prisoners under control. He wants help from us. Says 'You don't want the battlefield all cluttered up with prisoners, do you?' He says that if we will loan him one company he and his three hundred guards would surrender to the company commander and then save many lives by keeping the prisoners in during the rest of the fight.

"I asked him about the rest of the Germans in Hemer surrendering. He says that they're line troops in a different command. He can't guarantee it but believes that General Waldenburg would like to surrender providing that we cease fire and send in a representative to discuss the matter. What action do you want to take?"

Dailey had said it was too big for him. Hell, it was too big for me. This was corps stuff.

"Dailey, have your FO call the fire off the area where this fellow claims his camp is located.[5] You can't spare your medium tanks or rifle company but if you believe the fellow is honest loan him your light tank platoon. I'll send you the rest of the company right away. Send it in to take charge of the camp. I'll consult General Hasbrouck on further action."

I passed the information to Hasbrouck, who consulted the corps commander and came back with a directive for me to follow. I passed a cease-fire order to the artillery battalions and all task forces and called Major Dailey. "Dailey, I have the artillery and all our units on a cease-fire status that we will keep providing the enemy stops all movement and fire. The rest of the light tank company will report in shortly for prison camp duty. You are to go in with a flag, contact General Waldenburg, and direct him to march his command into our lines."

I should have been the one to go but just wasn't in shape for the trip and my battle garb, cane, overshoe on one foot, and air of obvious misery, wouldn't have impressed the German commander. The next obvious choice would have been Colonel King, but he was far away to the rear trying to encourage Chappuis. Major Dailey on the other hand was on the ground in contact and was a neat, soldierly, impressive young man and an intelligent, coherent, persuasive talker. So he was it.

The cease-fire (Waffenstillstand) was meticulously obeyed on both sides. An amusing picture, German and American tanks, destroyers, and self-propelled guns cautiously poking their noses around corners at each other. And it was certainly an unusual international picture around the PW camp, where German guards and American tankers were trying to persuade 24,000 PWs of six different nationalities to stay behind the wire and stop looting the kitchen storerooms.

General Hasbrouck jeeped up to the CP in an understandably good humor. "What's the situation, Triplet?" I took him over to the situation map posted by the G-3 half-track. "The third battalion of the 359th, a platoon of tanks attached, is deployed here on the outskirts of Hemer ready to move in and clear the town. Task Force Dailey is in Deilinghofen prepared to support or reinforce the 359th. Task Forces Rhea and Wemple are deployed abreast east of the town prepared to enfilade the enemy in front of the attack. Good visibility on the cross streets. Waldenburg wants to declare Hemer an open city and retire. He's sending a delegation here under a flag to talk over the details. They should be here shortly. In the meantime everybody is holding the cease-fire—peaceful as Easter Sunday."

"Where is Chappuis?" asked Hasbrouck.

"Oh yes, I'd forgotten Chappuis. I'd planned on him swinging around to threaten Hemer from the north but he's still at Albringen and not moving. And general, I don't ever want Chappuis attached to CCA again. Griffen is excellent and Brown is superior but Chappuis is a deadweight. King is over there now trying to move him without success. After this show I don't ever want to see him again."

Hasbrouck disagreed. "But Chappuis is an excellent battalion commander. He has three Silver Stars."

"Yes sir, I read his ribbons and he has a very imposing spread on his chest. I'll go so far as to admit that he probably was a good commander but now I think he figures the war is almost over and he wants to be sure he wears those ribbons in the victory parade. If this was a regiment I would have relieved him yesterday."

"Hmmm, well, we'll see—" The general was not convinced.

Hemer was a pushover. The peaceful interlude had evidently had a softening effect on the German garrison and the fifteen-minute storm of steel by the 489th and her sister battalions had really cowed them. Danube Blue moved into the town overwatched by Dailey's armor while the tanks and destroyers of Wemple and Rhea on the right flank sniped at anything that moved in the streets in front of his advance. While there was no mass surrender, there was also no resistance. Individuals and small units simply waved white as soon as our men got within surrendering range. By 2000, Hemer was cleared to the cellars and attics and Danube Blue (a damned good outfit) was detached and reverted to the Ninetieth Division that was now in neighboring Westig. Dailey took over Hemer.

We moved CCA CP into modest quarters in Brockhausen, an eastern suburb of Hemer. Colonel Wemple, who had captured the place, occupied the comparative palace across the street—he always got better quarters than I did. He got there first.

Twenty-One

The Baltic Front

Prisoners and Other Confusions

The most important problem at the moment was the PW camp, but I couldn't hack it. I asked Colonel King to see the place and report on conditions and the situation. He grabbed the surgeon, supply, intelligence, military government, POWINT, and the headquarters commandant and took off down the road in a cloud of jeep-flung mud. King was back in an hour, loaded with information that his staff had obtained from the PW camp commandant, the senior Polish PW, the captain commanding Company D of the Seventeenth Tank Battalion, and the Buergermeister. It was probably not completely accurate, but on observing the situation he had realized the need for speed. We composed a message to division that contained the following information and requests: "PW camp SE Hemer contained 24,000 prisoners of seven nationalities, principally Russian and Polish. Camp was an elimination facility for undesirables who are all starvation cases. Normal death rate 300 per day, from starvation and sickness. Prisoners broke out of control during attack. Several hundred escaped. Kitchen storerooms looted. Eight hundred now dead from overeating.[1] Hundreds seriously ill. No more food in prison stocks. Buergermeister complains escaped prisoners murdering, raping, and looting, and cannot be controlled by police. Note that observed condition of prisoners probably precludes above activities. Request PW camp be taken over by higher authority with appropriate force of military police, military government, medical corps, and supply services to provide control, medical care, and food."

The PW camp problem was too big for division too and it was naturally passed on to corps, who passed the buck to army. That takes time, and while we left the place to military government types and military police, I don't know if the poor devils ever got fed. I personally saw only two of the PWs. One man in a ragged Russian uniform was lying down beside the carcass of a horse that had been dismembered by a shell burst. He was crawling around the body, pulling off fragments of meat and eating them. He probably survived—he was chewing well and eating slowly. Another in the remnants of a uniform that we could not identify had crawled up on the front steps of Wemple's CP, wrapped a ragged gray blanket around him, and died during the night.

It had been a delightful night, lulled to sleep by the thunder of the 155-mm. Long Toms and 8-inch howitzers that had moved up to throw their shells into road junctions in the enemy rear areas.

It was a beautiful morning, foggy and cool. CCR (Task Force Chappuis attached, praise God) moved through our outpost lines toward Menden, Wickede, and Wert. CCB was moving on parallel secondary roads on CCR's left rear.

A horde of administrative troops arrived in midmorning to take charge of the PW camp and D/Seventeenth was released to rejoin us.

I had a brief verbal skirmish with a light colonel of military government in charge of the camp when he dropped in during the afternoon. He had the supreme gall to ask me why I had done nothing about giving the prisoners food and medical attention. I pointed out that I had four thousand men, most of whom were in contact with superior forces of the enemy, and four thousand rations to feed them. As for medical attention, my five surgeons were completely occupied in saving the lives of our combat casualties. I then reminded him that I had reported the existence of the camp and the condition of the inmates at noon the day before and had urgently requested assistance at 2000. I then asked him where he and his people had been for the last twenty-two hours.

His excuse was that army intelligence hadn't known about the camp and it took time to organize the relief force. It was a petty affair, but I enjoyed bickering with staff officers.[2]

Columns of prisoners were moving back to the pens in organized units commanded by their own officers and accompanied by only a token guard here and there.

It was a very good day. CCB's tail hadn't cleared Hemer yet so it was likely that we wouldn't move tonight. A day to bathe, shave, and sleep.

At mess that evening my euphoria was shot right out from under me. Lieutenant Kirschbaum was talking about his conversation with Captain Greenberg of division POWINT. "We've taken in over forty thousand so far today, twenty thousand apiece for B and R. CCR took in a whole division plus spare parts. Captain Greenberg says the division commander told him that he wanted to surrender yesterday but that his emissary was received with great discourtesy. He was told to go back to his troops and fight."

That rang a bell. I recalled my unfortunate words to Dailey the evening before when Dailey had reported his second emissary. "We ceased-fire for him once and the sonofabitch wasted four hours for us. The answer is no."

"But this is a different colonel—"

"Just another stall. Tell the bastard to go back and fight his outfit."

Goddamn. I could have spat blue flame. Again I'd made the mistake of talking when I should have been listening. If I had talked to the emissary—if I had ceased fire so the Germans could reach our lines—

then CCA would be credited with forty thousand more prisoners, a total of fifty-eight thousand instead of the beggarly ten thousand we'd taken since crossing the Rhine. Including the remnants of the 116th Panzer and grenadier outfit.

Further information from division POWINT. There was a general collapse of the Germans encircled in the Ruhr pocket. Army intelligence had estimated that eighty thousand Germans were in the pocket. The prisoner bag was three hundred thousand. The prisoner units surrendering to CCB and CCR included some that had sideslipped from the flanks, funneling into our front. The reason—they preferred the honor (or less dishonor) of capitulating to a panzer division.

Captain Hochberg received a report that the pump at the water point some miles back had failed. He called for a mechanic, "Kubchec, remember that water point you put in at Frankenberg? The pump has quit. Go back and get it going."

Kubchec jeeped back to the water point, dismounted, and started working on the pump. Someone tapped him on the shoulder. Kubchec in a foul mood snarled, "Can't you see I'm busy?" Another tap. That was too much. Kubchec turned with wrench poised and was facing a German officer with forty men behind him. The German handed the fainting soldier the carbine that he had left in the jeep. "You vill us to your prisoner of war lager take."

The Seventh Armored Division has practically never been mentioned in the newspapers. There is a good reason for it. The Seventh is a traveling circus, what we used to call mobile or shock troops in the last war, shifting from front to front where the going is particularly soft or hard. Each corps or army generally has an armored division permanently attached. When the Germans capture an infantryman from the X Corps they know that the Y Armored Division is on that front. Also, the public relations officer of the Third Army takes every opportunity to see the exploits of the Fourth Armored Division in print.

But the Seventh Armored, an orphan that has fought for four armies and five corps, is never mentioned, beyond the possible line, "Today First Army armor advanced from here to there and captured the vital communications center at Misthaufen."

Since we're never mentioned, we're generally a surprise to the enemy when we show up on the front and they do us the honor of naming us Panzer Division Geist (the Ghost Armored Division).

In spite of our anonymous status, we have receipts from several corps and army cages for 61,386 supermen whom we've put on ice to date. That's four times our weight in live Krauts. Not bad.

The division marched east to billets in Goettingen and environs, where for two delightful weeks we did nothing but repair, refit, bathe, rest, sleep, and eat. It may seem odd to mention eating, but the cooked C-ration was vastly superior to the cold K-ration or the chocolate bar D-ration that we'd been getting during the campaign. Yes, the C-ration served hot on plates or trays and supplemented by liberated wine was a pleasant experience.

I spent a good deal of the first day writing and tearing up drafts of a memorandum I wanted to put out to the troops, something cheering and stimulating, a morale-raising report on their accomplishments during the Rhine-crossing Hemer campaign. But being cheerful and stimulating when reminding the men that 269 of their friends were killed or wounded is difficult. If I left out the cost I'd be descending to the level of Goebbels or Axis Sally, so to hell with it. I polished the grammar and checked the figures of my last effort and had the staff put out one copy per man to include Lieutenant Carraway's armored cavalry platoon 3/359th and the Forty-eighth Armored Infantry Battalion as well as our regulars. I thought that the lads would like to have such a précis of their work to send home—the Ghost Division never appeared in the newspapers.

A trio of the headquarters staff, out for a walk through the picturesque countryside, flushed a couple of the Wehrmacht out of the woods this morning. Brought them in, fed them, and the mess sergeant put them to work. They are delighted with the job. "Das Essen ist herrlich." The mess sergeant is highly pleased with the shining pots and pans they work on. The company enjoys less kitchen police duty so we aren't going to turn them in to the cages. Our young men are going out for walks in all directions, planning to catch a dozen more, bringing them back alive.

On the move again, attached to the XVIII Airborne Corps that has been loaned to Montgomery's Second British Army.

A night march in the British zone is a horrifying experience. We of course drive with blackout lights that give the same visibility as a pair of glowworms. The British have found that they lose fewer trucks and men by accidents and enemy action if they run with lights full on and to hell with the German Luftwaffe and artillery. They also drive on the wrong side of the road. By the time we reached the Elbe we had compromised, half of the Americans and half of the British had changed to the other side, which made survival a very sporting proposition.

Sauer coped well with the blinding headlights–complete blackness by closing one eye while dodging the approaching vehicle, then opening it as soon as the menace had passed.

Actually, there were very few British vehicles, engaged in administrative chores, and they were driving cautiously, probably more frightened than we were.

I have the feeling that the men are high-spirited and enthusiastic about being on the move again. It's not for pay, patriotism, or promotion—the rumor is going strong that we're going to drive east and they want to meet those Russian women tankers they've been hearing so much about.

The Elbe and the Russians

Had a terrible experience on the second day of May, had the whole damned war shot right out from under me. Blew right up in my face. Hasbrouck had given us the situation the evening before. The German armies occupying Denmark were moving east to reinforce the garrison of Berlin. The Seventh Armored was to cross the Elbe into the bridgehead established by the XVIII Airborne Corps, drive north, and cut the enemy off from Berlin. Order of march, CCA, CCB, division headquarters, CCR. CCA, 489th Armored Artillery attached, would capture and occupy the peninsula and area bounded by Wohlenberg-Boltenhagen-Neuenhagen-Dassow-Grevesmuehlen-Gressow-Wismar (exclusive).

I decided to go back to the two-task-force organization and make the advance in two columns in order to have as much force as possible immediately at hand. The principal problem was finding a net of parallel roads that would keep the two forces within mutual supporting distance. Since the principal enemy pressure was expected from the west, Rhea with the bulk of the infantry and CCA headquarters would move in the right (eastern) column while Wemple with his tank-heavy force and the artillery would move up the left (western) roads. Rhea would take Grevesmuehlen-Klutz-Boltenhagen and everything east thereof, Wemple would take everything west to Travemuende.

We crossed the Elbe in the cold, misty dawn on the longest pontoon bridge—it went on and on and on, a monument to the engineers who built it and to the airborne who had won the bridgehead that made the building possible.[3]

Deployed on the two parallel roads and started forward. Passed through the paratroop outposts and surprise, surprise. Encountered small columns of Germans in organizations led by their own officers, unarmed with a white flag at the head of each unit. The columns thickened, but there was no interference—they kept to the right of the two-lane road as we did, paying no attention to the scurrilous remarks made by our tank-mounted riflemen. Came the deluge, charcoal-burning trucks, horse-drawn wagons, bicycles, Kubelwagens, Volkswagens, sedans, buses—all loaded to the fenders.

It was a long and very confused day. The German columns broadened from four to eight abreast to a confused mob. We progressed for a while by dint of the leading tank commanders waving and shouting and the

Germans crowding over. But when the charcoal-fueled trucks broke down, as they frequently did, they had to be shoved clear off the road. We finally called on Captain Hochberg and he spearheaded the advance with a section of tankdozers that are more adapted to shoving vehicles into the ditch than are the tanks. Tanks generally just squash and climb over anything they try to shove.

I left young Carraway and his crews beating the bushes around the modest chateau where the staff were setting up the command post and jeeped west to see how Wemple was getting his PW camp organized. It had certainly been a good day—we'd made the fifty-five miles from the Elbe to the Baltic in five hours instead of the three days of hell and high water that I had pessimistically estimated. The country road was well graveled with the usual villages now bedecked with sheets hung out the windows. The local farming appeared to be principally grazing and orchards, no grain crops. The road apparently made a right-angled bend to the north in the next Dorf. Fifty yards this side of the bend, hell's afire, we'd done it again. Four Germans in field green stood up in the bushes on the left of the road, rifles held at an uncertain "ready." One held up a hand in the halt signal, tentatively.

It was the uncertainty that gave me hope that we might not end the war in a Gefaengenenslager. Would another bluff work out well?

Sauer had automatically started to slow down, but if we could just make that corner. "Go on, Sauer." I looked at the indecisive outpost, waved cheerily, and we passed them at a reasonable twenty, slowing down for the corner, chills and hot flashes chasing each other around between our shoulder blades. "Pour it on." Sauer tromped on the accelerator and promptly took his foot off, worse and more of it. The village street was lined on both sides by what appeared to be a short infantry battalion. The well in the center of the street was surrounded by a group of men filling canteens. Beyond the well was a traffic jam of wagons and ambulances.

"Pull up to the well, Sauer." We had to continue the bluff.

He stopped just short of the Germans, who were obviously as baffled as we were scared. I dismounted with Betty Boop pointed down and used my hog-calling voice. "Wo ist der Kommandant?"

"Der Kommandant" was repeated several times by the audience. "Ich bin der Kommandant." The speaker was a major who had come up from the right rear, capable-looking light-heavyweight.

"What make you here?" I asked in an outraged tone. "Know you not that the war to end is?"

"No that knew I not. But I wish to find someone to whom I capitulate can."

Praise be. We might live after all.

"You can to me capitulate."

"Are you officer?" They just don't understand American insignia.

"I am colonel," indicating the eagle soldered on my helmet.

"Already good, I capitulate my battalion to you."

"Made. Leave you your weapons here. March you your battalion with a white flag to—" and I showed him on his map the route to Rhea's lakeside resort.

"Understood."

I mounted Wretch Forward II and muttered, "Let's go, slowly," and Sauer put her in gear.

"But Herr Oberst—" It was the major again.

"Yes?"

"Will you not my pistol take?"

I remembered the ancient warrior in Bad Godesberg, they seem to want a capitulation to be a ceremony. OK. I dismounted again. The major drew his pistol from the holster and presented it, butt first. It was a beautiful gun, a Walther .32. Gave me an idea.

"Good. Now have all men who have pistols lay them in my wagon."

He gave the order and an amazing number of men came forward and placed their pistols in the back of the jeep, half a bushel of handguns of all sizes and types, Lugers, Mausers, Walthers, and a number of those little Kamerad guns in .25 caliber. When the lineup came to an end we left, slowly. They still had rifles, and I didn't want to excite anybody by any sudden moves.

I kept the major's Walther and Sauer selected a 9-mm. Luger as his memento. The rest I distributed to the headquarters and headquarters company people by the drawing of names from a hat. There were almost enough to go around.

Message from Rhea. "Have captured company of ninety German WAACs. What shall I do with them?"

"I compliment your men on their courage in capturing a company of Blitzmaedels. I'm on my way." I grabbed Lieutenant Kirschbaum and we took off for Rhea's resort. It was quite a problem. We had really no facilities for keeping male prisoners, nothing but guarded meadows and lots of water. Major Gruen had requisitioned twelve thousand rations and received nothing but a hollow laugh from division. We certainly had nothing suitable for females.

On reaching the camp, Rhea took me over to the east side of the meadow where he had parked the German trucks, trailers, and wagons. He had done very well, considering what he had to work with. He had installed the women in four large buses, giving them a full double seat apiece. Rough living and uncomfortable sleeping, but a lot better than the open ground. GI cans of lake water and a canvas screen completed the installation. I didn't ask Colonel Rhea if they'd been fed. I knew his men had extra rations squirreled away in their vehicles and sure enough, there was part of a K-ration wrapping dropped by the canvas screen, and when we entered one of the buses several of the girls were smoking issue Camel cigarettes.

Our entry caused mixed reactions—I noted expressions of curiosity, interest, contempt, extreme dislike, disgust, and studied disinterest. In contrast to the conduct of the men, who would have Achtung-ed and saluted, deadpan, these Lili Marlenes just lounged, stared, and to hell with us. Giggling and whispering in rear.

Except one. The tall brunette with the tabs of a lieutenant clicked up from the right front seat, saluted, and gabbled a report that was too fast for me to get. Salute acknowledged, she went into a further tirade, pointing at a rather pretty brilliant blonde, also wearing officers tabs, who occupied the rear seat of the bus. When she ran down I turned to Lieutenant Kirschbaum. "And what was that all about, Kirschbaum?"

"Sir, she is protesting that she and the other Helferinnen must occupy the same quarters as the woman on the back seat. She says that the other woman is from the Konzentrationslager and is a very bad woman. She requests that we remove that woman from this camp."

"From the concentration camp? Hmmm. Have to think this over. Tell her that nothing can be done about it at this time, too damned late, but we will arrange separate quarters tomorrow morning."

"May I make a suggestion, sir?"

"Please do."

"I suggest that if Colonel Rhea will let me have a jeep and an extra man as a guard I should take this woman to division headquarters."

"I'll furnish the jeep," said Rhea, "but what are we going to do about the rest of these girls? Can't we send them all back to division? They ought to be—" Rhea was really wanting to get rid of this lot.

"Another suggestion, sir?" Kirschbaum having another idea.

"Certainly." I'd be glad to hear any solution.

"I can order the Buergermeister of Grevesmuehlen to take in these women, fit them with civilian clothes, and give them food to start them home."

"Damned good idea, Kirschbaum, but it won't do. They're PWs and if I turn them loose I'll get my buttons pulled off for aid and comfort to the enemy."

Think of what the public press could do with that. A moment of heavy thought.

"But if they have discharges, sir, they will be civilians. I can get a German officer to write discharges for—"

"By God you've got it, Kirschbaum. Make it so. Date the discharge April 1 so I'll stand a chance at my court-martial and get going on it tonight. Tell the lieutenant what you're going to do with the witch and about the discharges and get this lot off our backs."

He did, a very competent young man.

When he reported on the completion of the job next day, I remarked on the attitude of the Helferinnen. "Odd, they didn't seem to be afraid of the brutal American soldiery, not worried about rape or murder that Goebbels has been screaming about."

"Worried about rape, sir? No, they were anticipating it."

Silence for a moment while he reviewed his Webster's Unabridged. "Yes sir, that is the correct word, anticipate, to look forward to an event with pleasure, to enjoy in advance."

And he tells that a day too late.

A Sordid End

A train had been halted by a detachment of Wemple's force on the railway line at Rottensdorf just south of Dassow and a large number of Germans were being herded into a field where they could be controlled. A black-uniformed, English-speaking major burst through Wemple's guard and said he wanted to go back to the train and retrieve something that he had forgotten. "Please return to the field," I said. I shouldn't have done that. Please or bitte brings out the worst in a German. He bugged his eyes, reddened, and shouted. "According to the provisions of the Geneva Convention, I demand—," and my pistol jumped out of that slick shoulder holster and slapped him twice before I could control it.

I wish they wouldn't shout or demand. Maybe I'd better stop wearing that pistol. No, if Betty Boop took action it would be serious.

It was certainly a polyglot crew of prisoners that we'd rounded up on this drive, with some uniforms that we had never seen before. There was the feldgruen of the army, the feldgrau of senior officers, navy blue from the seaplane base, the light green of the marines, and one battalion in camouflage-splotched gear. Oh yes, some of the feldgruen lot wore skirts. And there was one tightly disciplined company neatly uniformed in police green.

As I approached this last lot the commander called them to attention, saluted, and conducted me along the ranks. As each man was approached he snapped his head to "eyes right" and followed me with eyes staring until I reached a point forty-five degrees to his left, then came to "front" with a vertebra-straining snap. Impressive, and disconcerting, so different from our practice of staring past and through the inspecting officer into space.

I was thinking that these men were policemen who should be in their home localities carrying on with police work and should be immediately released to return to their duties. I was quite prepared to do so. I wanted to find out where some of the men were from. "Where here come you?" I asked one of the men.

"Schweig" shouted the commander at my elbow, demanding silence.

"Oh, now makes it nothings out," I told him. "The war to end is."

He just clamped his jaws and looked grim. OK, if that's the way he wanted it, name, rank, and serial number only.

I found Kirschbaum. "That company of police, Kirschbaum, I'm thinking of sending them to their hometowns to keep order. Find out if they're from this area."

"Yes sir, they're from this area all right. They were the guards at the local concentration camp."

"Oh—"

The senior German officer in Rhea's camp was a colonel, a slight, bucktoothed, goggle-eyed type wearing a fur-collared overcoat and a monocle. Rhea had set him up with a large trailer as his office and quarters where he had a cot and typewriter plus field desk. But he wasn't satisfied with these arrangements.

When I first met him, he informed me that I was violating the provisions of the Hague Conference and the Geneva Convention (they seem to be very familiar with the terms of both). He demanded that his men be billeted in the houses and barns of the neighboring villages, that they be issued our rations, and that his sedan be returned to him.

While his adjutant was translating, I couldn't help thinking about the Seventh Armored artillerymen massacred at Malmédy and the twenty-four thousand starving PWs that we'd liberated at Hemer and the sonofabitch will never know how near he came to—but that time I kept my hands firmly gripped behind me and just said no.

Generals Hasbrouck and Ridgway had taken much more interest than I had in the concentration camp that we had passed on our way to the Baltic. I made a trip to division to present my need personally for twelve thousand rations for my hungry Germans. Near Grevesmuehlen, I noted considerable American activity about the wire-enclosed barracks area to the east of the main road. Trucks, ambulances, military police, and soldiers were boiling around the place.

On my return the scene had changed drastically. German civilians driving carts and wagons, others pushing wheelbarrows or pulling Handwagens, were moving loads of naked bodies toward Grevesmuehlen. The bodies were evidently light, twenty or thirty pounds of skeleton loosely covered by waxy-yellow skin. A well-fed Burger or his stout wife could and did trundle four or five cadavers in a wheelbarrow or Handwagen while a farm cart or wagon probably handled twenty or more tossed in like unstacked cordwood.

Not being morbidly curious, I didn't stop or inquire. Civilian bodies weren't of much interest. But at the noon mess Kirschbaum told me that there had been a general roundup of all civilians in the neighborhood and that they were required to remove the bodies and bury them in their local cemeteries. Since none of the local civilians had known the camp existed, it seemed to me that requiring them to bury the bodies was unjust. But it was none of my business, and after all they were just Germans.

The Lazarett (German army field hospital) had been set up in the large manor or chateau in the north edge of camp. The German surgeons were quite proud of their installation and (I believe) bragged about it throughout my guided tour. Too fast and technical for me to follow.

The place was full of patients to include the halls and corridors— reminded me of some of the scenes in *Gone with the Wind*. These Krauts hadn't fought us but they had been badly hurt by somebody before they surrendered. They showed me their operating room, where a surgeon was removing a gangrenous arm while another patient with a badly broken leg awaited his turn. Since the Germans did not have sulfa drugs or penicillin, they always amputated compound fractures at once. The reason: when compound fractures were set they always became infected and had to be amputated later so to save time and useless effort they reached for the knife and saw.

The place swarmed with flies. I'd never noticed flies before in Germany. Farms, villages, and even manors always have delicious manure piles nearby and the flies prefer to live, feed, and breed in those cozy heaps, much preferable to living in a house. There isn't a window screen in all Deutschland.

But the pus, blood, old bandages, discarded limbs, and the bodies of those patients who hadn't made it were much more attractive than the comparatively bland odor of any manure pile. Consequently, the Lazarett was swarming with the accumulated fly population of all the farms and villages within flying distance downwind.

I swatted a couple of flies with my glove and the surgeon took the hint. By the time I left all of the patients who could sit up were swatting flies. The orderlies couldn't kill flies, they were too busy carrying out fly-attracting debris.

The Russians occupied Wismar on our right flank. No great hand-shaking or trouble since my orders were to keep my men half a mile west of the town. Immediately on their arrival the Iron Curtain began to drop. All refugee movement was ordered stopped and Rhea deployed a line of outposts to match the outposts that the Russians had posted two hundred yards distant. I was delighted to receive the "stop refugee movement" order because Captain Butler estimated we had seventeen thousand refugees already, superimposed on the original population of eleven thousand plus two thousand slave laborers.

While making the rounds that evening, I stopped to inspect one of Colonel Rhea's Cossack posts. Found a young lady eighteen or twenty years old holding the hand of a sister of ten years. She was plead-ing with the sergeant to let them pass and when I showed up trans-ferred her plaint to me. "We must to grandmother go, she is alone, it is only eight kilometers, etc. etc." I had to tell her "Verboten, Russen, Gefaengenenslager," and they burst into tears and turned back to the refugee camp.

The two of them so closely resembled my two older daughters that I had the wild idea of going after them with wild advice: "Come back after dark and go around the guard in that direction. Then go around the Russian post—" But that would be a violation of my orders and code—and with the Russians rioting over there it would not have been a kindness. The whole damned continent seemed to be displaced and on the move.

It had been a fast and full three days, and I mean twelve-hour days for the men and sixteen for the officers. But at last we were beginning to commence to feel that we were fairly well on top of the situation. Twelve thousand PWs are well dug in and have improved shelter. PW wounded and sick are in Wemple's chateau-hospital, with German medi-cos, nurses, and a few Blitzmaedels caring for them. Plenty of potatoes and pea soup to keep all hands alive. Hochberg's engineers are pumping and chlorinating water. German camp commanders see to boiling water to wash mess gear. Abandoned weapons are being collected from back roads, woods, and towns, Panzerfausts and bombs defused or blown up. German motor transport and wagons assembled in parks. Horses herded in pastures (won't have to eat them after all), to be redistributed by mili-tary government. German refugees allotted to towns, farms, and villages. Kreisleiter and Buergermeisters responsible for German refugees. Slave laborers sent back to farms to slave a little longer. Released Allied PWs collected and put in barracks by nationality. Tons of DDT powder for sprinkling everybody against typhus.

So everybody is mad at the Americans, insisting on their rights, and at this point I did not consider that any of them had any rights. We had ensured that no one would starve or freeze, and for a small combat unit I felt that my young men had done very well.

Message from Colonel Wemple: "There's a German battleship coming into Travemuende, colonel. What do you want to do about it?"

"What kind of a ship, how big is it? How many guns?"

"I think it's got just one gun on the foredeck. Can't see the rear on account of the bridge." Probably a frigate or cutter.

"Do you have any tanks that can cover it?"

"I've got a platoon right there at the wharf, looking right at it."

"How about dropping a shell in front of him? Better idea, do you have a boat?"

"Yes sir, we have a motor boat and a Kraut to run it at the seaplane base."

"OK, send an officer with a flag out to order him to drop anchor and surrender."

"Wilco."

One of Wemple's officers boiled out in the motor boat with a white flag and boarded the ship, which was slowly feeling its way through the Travemuende sound. He pointed out to the captain that his ship was covered by five tank guns, whereupon the captain obligingly ordered his crew away from their 4.2-inch deck gun, dropped anchor, and lowered his swastika flag.

Too bad, a duel between a German cutter with a 4.2 and a tank platoon using 75-mm. guns would have been interesting. But I doubt if his 3/8-inch armor would have stood up well against us.

Wemple had the ship brought in and tied up at the seaplane base wharf. He left the crew aboard to run the ship and started a daily recreational sightseeing cruise for members of CCA after the official surrender on May 8.

Lieutenant Kirschbaum was quite excited. A German officer had just told him that a Nazi official named Himmler was hiding out in Greves-muehlen. He had passed the information on to Captain Greenberg and all of division and corps CIC, CID, and POWINT were boiling into the place to smoke him out.[4] Kirschbaum wanted to join them. OK, I didn't know who Himmler was, but if everybody else was getting so worked up over him—"Go ahead, Kirschbaum, have a good time."

So Kirschbaum took his team and his two tame Gestapo agents and joined the violent harassment of the citizens of Grevesmuehlen, start-ing with the Buergermeister.[5] Drawing a blank, they worked through the refugee camp. There our Gestapo recruits proved their loyalty to our cause by recognizing and reporting the identity of several of their old comrades who were endeavoring to pass as refugees. Germans are odd people.

Himmler was captured by a British outpost in Luebeck on our left flank on May 7, so our search of Grevesmuehlen was probably responsible for forcing him to break cover. The British interrogators failed to search him thoroughly and he beat the gallows by biting down on his cyanide pill.

As in World War I, the line troops won't celebrate. We're too busy guarding and supplying prisoners, maintaining law and order in the crowded peninsula that is swarming with slave laborers and German refugees superimposed on the original population. We're also assembling and destroying weapons, blowing up ammunition, mines, and explosives, and burning wreckage. And on the eastern border of our sector we have to maintain an outpost line.

I spent the evening composing a letter to the chief of staff, War Department (attention personnel), Washington, D.C., requesting immediate reassignment to the Pacific theater of operations.

Notes

One. The Infantry Board

1. To a later generation the Molotov cocktail, as the bomb was known, might seem of little or no moment, but this apparently fearsome weapon was a staple of the time.

2. In the group photograph, Captain I. R. Clark is next to Triplet.

3. The Infantry School at Fort Benning was near Columbus, Georgia.

4. Here is the first of several references to boots and spurs. Tankers such as Triplet had contempt for some of the former cavalrymen who in the mid-1930s, with their service arm eliminated and cavalry horses put out to grass, came into the tank corps. Well into World War II the émigrés seemed a special group for which the tank was another horse. Whether members of the thinking group of the board were horsed up, as Triplet relates, is questionable, given his respect for the board.

5. Robert G. Le Tourneau (1888–1969) was in the garage business until 1929 when he organized a land-leveling company, of which he was president until his death. He designed heavy-duty earth-moving equipment, huge offshore drilling platforms, and the electric-drive wheel. A benefactor of religious enterprises and founder of Le Tourneau University in his home city of Longview, Texas, he often said that he was "just a mechanic that the Lord has blessed." It is impossible to know if the subject of religion arose during Triplet's discussion with Le Tourneau. If it did, it might have had something to do with the inability to have a meeting of minds, as Triplet was an avowed ("card-carrying" were his words) atheist.

6. A grouser is a large, pointed timber that can be raised or lowered vertically, used as an anchor for dredging.

7. The huge ships of the post–World War II era doubtless could have handled the Le Tourneau behemoths, but the reader must bear in mind that the Liberty ships, the marine workhorses of the forthcoming war, had a gross tonnage of 7,170 and the inventor's machines, lashed to their decks, would have capsized such vessels—if they could have been hoisted to the decks in the first place.

8. Years later the Minuteman missile was designed so that it could pass over the interstate highways—there was no other reason for its design size.

9. In the mid–nineteenth century the change from round shot to rifled guns inaugurated a race between guns and armor, and as fast as armor increased the guns appeared to penetrate it. Sixteen-inch naval guns were the largest at this time, 1941–1945, save for the Japanese 17.9-inch rifles, and Le Tourneau desired the largest, to no avail as mentioned.

10. In the first of five major offensives in 1918 the German army broke through the British Fifth Army's sector of the front, making a huge bulge between British and French forces. For a short time the Thirty-fifth (Missouri-Kansas) Division was designated as a reserve. *A Youth in the Meuse-Argonne: A Memoir of World War I, 1917–1918,* 159–60. In the Spanish-American War soldiers carried blankets slung over their shoulders; in World War I blankets formed an inverted "U" over a man's seventy-pound pack. In 1898 and in 1917–1918 carrying blankets was back-breaking.

11. Invented by a Confederate general, the Sibley tent was standard issue in World War I. A Sibley was conical, erected on a tripod, sometimes with a perpendicular drop at the bottom, and had a hole at the top to allow escape of smoke from stoves.

12. A short-lived automobile, the Bantam enjoyed a vogue in the late 1930s.

Two. Lucky Thirteenth: I

1. As the reader will see, Triplet came to dislike Wogan perhaps more than any general officer he ever encountered, and the fact that Wogan was a member of the class of 1915, that of Dwight D. Eisenhower, constituted one of his measurements. That class, to be sure, provided more general officers—other West Pointers felt unfairly—than any other.

2. The Bren gun carrier was a British vehicle.

3. In World War I, Triplet served on a relatively quiet front in Alsace; then his division was in reserve for St.-Mihiel, fought in close contact with the German army in the Meuse-Argonne from September 26 to September 29, and ended the war in the Verdun sector.

4. Major General Adna R. Chaffee was the champion of armor in the years before World War II. He was commanding the First U.S. Armored Corps when he died in 1941.

5. Jacob L. Devers was commander of armored forces at Fort Knox. Triplet was forty-two.

6. During World War I, as a platoon sergeant supervising a move from one post to another, Triplet unnecessarily aggravated a fellow soldier and found himself in a brutal fistfight that almost was more than he could handle, for which he received this advice from a supporter. *Youth in the Meuse-Argonne,* 23–24.

7. The school was at Leavenworth.

8. The German medium tank, the Mark IV, was battle-tested in May 1940. It had the same road speed as the American M4, the Sherman, weighed twenty-seven tons against the Sherman's thirty, and possessed somewhat less armor, but its principal advantage was in its long-barreled, high-velocity gun, as Triplet related. A new Sherman model, the M4A3, would be equipped with a 76-mm. with comparable barrel and velocity. A very few Shermans were equipped with heavier armor, the so-called Junbo tank. General George S. Patton, Jr., made them his lead tanks in relief of Bastogne during the Battle of the Bulge in 1944–1945. Hugh M. Cole, *The Ardennes: Battle of the Bulge,* 651–52.

9. Triplet met Wogan at Fort Leavenworth, Kansas, and the division then was mustered at Camp Beale, California, north of Sacramento between Marysville and Grass Valley.

10. Major Edwards, like Latta, was what Triplet wanted in an officer assistant. Full of initiative and drive, he had a way of anticipating Triplet that delighted the colonel. These very qualities had gotten Edwards in trouble with earlier seniors, and when Triplet took him he was in danger of reassignment at lower rank.

11. The Forty-fifth was a tank regiment.

12. At Kasserine Pass in North Africa the American tankers fought in riveted tanks, deadly if hit, for the loose rivets chewed up anyone inside.

13. After Triplet left the Thirteenth Armored, with Edwards in charge of trains, General Wogan transferred an Indian-fighting cavalry colonel to the command, and Edwards wrote Triplet, then in command of the Eighteenth Armored Group (Amph) at Fort Ord, California, asking a transfer. Triplet arranged it. "I didn't have Edwards very long. When the 777th Tank Battalion got their port call and made their graduation landing, they hit the wrong beach. This was the climax of a number of errors made by the battalion commander. After six weeks of working in the training area, if he couldn't navigate his outfit to the objective shown on the map furnished with his written orders, what might he do in landing against opposition on an island that he'd never seen before? I relieved him immediately and called for Edwards to take command. He did very well in commanding the 777th through 1944 and 1945 in the Pacific and received the navy Medal for Valor. Added a Bronze Star, a Joint Service Commendation Medal, and the Legion of Merit to his collection before retiring in 1966. I've never bet on a loser."

14. An instructor named Kelly presumably arranged this turnabout system at Benning. George R. ("Machine Gun") Kelly flourished in the 1920s and 1930s as a bank robber, bootlegger, gangster, and kidnapper.

Three. Lucky Thirteenth: II

1. A playful choice of name—Triplet's wife was Fiona.

2. General Lesley J. McNair, a World War I retread and indeed an officer from that war, was head of army ground forces, and a zealot on the need for fitness by way of grueling marches.

3. Letterman was in San Francisco.

4. The designation of "headquarters and headquarters company" might seem tautological but made sense if one saw it as offices (headquarters) together with a headquarters company.

5. Field-grade officers were majors or above.

6. G-3 and G-4 were operations and inspector general.

7. Fiona and three children were living in Grass Valley.

8. Bolo Pasha was an adventurer convicted in France of defeatism and shot in 1918.

9. The Thirteenth had been a square division—four regiments, two brigades—and was to change into a light organization with battalions instead of regiments, combat commands instead of brigades. Square armored divisions had fourteen thousand men, light had 10,666. In the European theater only the Second Armored and Third Armored were square divisions. Most German panzer divisions had the same manpower configuration as the two U.S. square armored divisions. Armored weight strongly favored the Americans, for German panzers averaged ninety to one hundred medium tanks whereas American light divisions possessed 186 and the two square divisions 232. German divisions could compensate with attached battalions of forty to fifty heavy tanks, Panthers or Tigers (for the latter see below, chap. 9, note 1). Cole, *Ardennes*, 651.

Four. Eighteenth Armored Group (Amphibious)

1. It is amusing that Triplet's resentment of the opportunities of the class of 1915, Eisenhower's class ("the class that the stars fell upon"), did not extend to the advantages of the class of 1924.

2. William H. Simpson (1888–1980), West Point 1909, served in the Philippines in 1909–1912, took part in the punitive expedition to Mexico in 1916, fought in World War I, and in World War II commanded the Thirtieth Division, XII Corps, and Ninth Army.

3. Ord was near Monterey Bay, to the east of Seaside and Del Rey, with Monterey to the south, Pacific Grove to the west and south.

4. Pendleton was southeast of Los Angeles, north of Oceanside and Vista.

5. The Food Machinery Corporation in San Jose had obtained a contract for construction of tanks and troop carriers, and would give Triplet

trouble because corporation officials found production more profitable than design.

6. Already the line between tanks and destroyers was blurring, and when Triplet reached Europe and the Second and Seventh Armored he came to see that if anything the tank destroyers held more promise than tanks. Both required accompanying infantry; they were vulnerable without infantry guidance. But their usefulness in combat was moving away from protecting infantrymen and toward tank battles, and in the latter role the destroyers made more sense than tank versus tank.

7. Hull armor was three-quarters of an inch in front and a quarter-inch on sides, bottom, and rear.

8. Triplet was rightfully proud of his safety record in training the battalions of the Eighteenth Armored Group (Amph). As he wrote in his account of the unit, "It cannot be proven that these measures saved lives. But it is a fact that the five marine battalions at Camp Pendleton drowned thirteen men in a year; the Eighteenth Armored Group of eighteen battalions drowned two during the same period. At the marine rate of casualties we would have drowned forty-six. We lost a third man with a crushed skull, but he floated when we pulled the tractor off him."

9. Army Forces in the Western Pacific.

10. A technician-5 was equivalent to corporal.

11. *Sergeant Terry Bull: His Ideas on War and Fighting in General* appeared in 1943 under the imprint of the Infantry Journal Press.

12. Major General John Millikin, commanding general of III Corps, with headquarters in the presidio of Monterey. Triplet would encounter him in Europe, an unfortunate meeting because the colonel's favorite assistant at Ord, Lieutenant Robert (Bob) Spillman, class of 1942, an ebullient officer, had set off mock explosions with such force that they shattered plate glass windows in Monterey and brought a complaint to General Millikin from the Chamber of Commerce and the president of the First National Bank. In Europe, momentarily under Millikin's jurisdiction but unaware of the fact, Triplet's tanks—without being at fault—broke down an important bridge. See chap. 17.

13. An LVT was a Landing Vehicle Tracked (Armored). After nearly two years with the Eighteenth Armored Group, Triplet received orders to Europe. "I had a third talk with General Hardy. 'I've just gotten my orders to Europe, general, and will be leaving your command the last of November.' 'Yes, I saw the orders. I'm very sorry to lose you, colonel. I like your style—I sure like your style.' ????!!!!? Maybe it was the effect of seeing me for the first time in class A dress uniform instead of a rubberized jump suit? 'Sorry to leave your command, general.' And since

God didn't strike me with lightning for that bald-faced falsehood I've been a fearless liar ever since."

Five. Waves

1. Monterey's Fisherman's Wharf was halfway down the east side of the peninsula.

2. A DUKH was a two-and-one-half-ton amphibious truck used for short runs from ship to shore.

Six. The LST

1. An LST was a Landing Ship Tank.

2. Triplet is saying that if there were any good commands, everything else being equal, Annapolis graduates would get them.

3. OD is officer of the deck.

Seven. Guns and Bays

1. The Stuart was an M5 light tank.

2. As all students of the Spanish-American War know, Captain Gridley was commander of the USS *Olympia,* Commodore George Dewey's flagship, and when at Manila Bay the time came to fire Dewey spoke to Gridley just like Triplet spoke to Benz.

3. James M. Hait was mechanical engineer at the corporation and designer of the amphibious tank and carrrier.

4. Thirty-five miles was the wartime top speed, to save gasoline, also tires.

5. To the amusement of all drafted men and enlistees in World War II, everything physical or otherwise provided them was known under the acronym "GI," meaning government issue.

6. The battleship HMS *Dreadnought,* launched in 1905, established a new standard for battleships with its armament of all big guns, caliber over ten inches.

7. Brown shoes for officers of the navy who did not use the top of the water, black shoes for the others.

8. German Stuka dive-bombers.

9. Major General Alvan C. Gillem, Jr., commanded XIII Corps, Ninth Army.

Eight. To the Second Armored

1. The Pentagon had opened the year before.

2. Triplet was referring to the old State, War, and Navy Building next to the White House, erected during the Grant administration, a Victorian edifice of windows and pillars and mansard roofs that sufficed for the War

Department during the Spanish-American War and World War I. The first of the colonel's four wars might have been the last engagements with the Indians, for which the building served. As for the fourth, World War II, by that time the War Department had moved to the Munitions Building on Constitution Avenue.

3. Dinner likely was at Hogate's.

4. Some readers may not remember the light opera singer–movie star who with her tenor-star Nelson Eddy thrilled cinema audiences of the 1930s and 1940s.

5. This was Louis Napoleon, Napoleon III.

6. A repple-depple was a replacement depot.

7. Triplet's World War I experience with French soldiery had not been encouraging.

8. In the male world of World War II, and for half a century afterward, even after women were admitted to West Point, the billeting of officers was in the bachelor officers quarters.

9. In *A Youth in the Meuse-Argonne,* Triplet states that during the war of 1917–1918 with all its combat shortages, he rarely found shoes or boots that would fit.

10. Simon Bolivar Buckner, Jr. (1886–1945), was a lieutenant general at the time he was killed by a shell on Okinawa. Edwin Butcher (1879–1950) became a brigadier general in 1943. Charles H. Bonesteel (1885–1964) was inspector general of the European Theater of Operations in 1944–1945 and a major general. Walter C. Baker (1877–1957) was a specialist in chemical warfare and a major general.

11. Buzz bombs were pilotless aircraft, known also as V-1s; they of course could be heard. The V-2s were missiles, not heard.

Nine. Taking Command

1. Of the three German battle tanks, the Mark IV was the medium; the Mark V a heavy, the Panther; and the Mark VI a heavy, the Tiger. The Panther weighed fifty tons, had a superiority in base armor of one-half to one inch over the Sherman, greater speed, and a high-velocity gun superior to the American 76-mm. It was prone to mechanical failure. The Tiger weighed fifty-four tons, possessed thicker armor than the Panther, speed comparable to the Sherman, and a high-velocity 88-mm. cannon. Like the Panther it was subject to mechanical failure, in some measure because of having twenty-six thousand parts. Cole, *Ardennes,* 652.

2. The long-barreled, high-velocity gun rightly impressed Triplet. The tank destroyer proved itself in the Battle of the Bulge, especially when equipped with a 90-mm. gun. Meanwhile, the Germans placed an 88-mm. on their destroyers. Effective tank destroyers were self-propelled;

those that were towed suffered heavy losses, as often they were dug in, impossible to get out except with a truck or tractor, lost when tow vehicles were immobilized. Cole, *Ardennes,* 655.

3. The German attack in the Ardennes, the Battle of the Bulge, began December 16, an assault on a front of sixty miles, with five armored divisions and twelve and two-thirds infantry divisions. By January 2, just before the Allied counterattack that drove in the bulge, the Germans had thrown in three more armored and seven infantry divisions. Of the estimated eighteen hundred German tanks in the Ardennes, perhaps 250 were Mark VIs; the remainder divided evenly between Mark IVs and Mark Vs. During the eighteen days of the German offensive the Americans used eight armored divisions, sixteen infantry, and two airborne. All American battle tanks were M4s. Cole, *Ardennes,* 650–52.

4. John H. Collier (1898–1980), West Point 1919, commissioned in the cavalry, commanded CCA in 1944–1945. After the war he was commandant of the Armor School and retired a lieutenant general in 1958.

5. S-3 was operations.

6. As a full colonel Triplet ranked 6, numbers beginning with second lieutenant—first lieutenant, captain, major, lieutenant colonel. Generals rated variations of 6. Big Six was General Harmon. Collier was A-6.

7. This was the division's sobriquet.

8. The other two best men were Lieutenant Tank Destroyers, mentioned in the next chapter, whose reconnaissance and subsequent excellent shooting blew up a Panther, and a redheaded lieutenant who wished to charge a machine-gun nest (chap. 8). The captain whose name Triplet did not learn was George T. Bonney. Cole, *Ardennes,* 436. The entrapment killed thirty of the enemy, in addition to the men taken prisoner.

9. The Panzerfaust was a German bazooka, highly effective, much more so than the lighter American weapon.

Ten. They've Got a Lot of Stuff in There

1. A platoon leader in the Meuse-Argonne on September 26–29, 1918, until gassed and wounded, Triplet never forgot the spirit of his fifty men as he led them into machine-gun fire.

Eleven. Defeat

1. This is a reference to the "bridge too far" at Nijmegen when support troops could not get up fast enough, hemmed on roads surrounded by waterlogged farmland.

2. TOTs were time-on-target artillery shells, timed from various points to fall on a given target simultaneously.

3. Veterans of the war of 1941–1945 will remember the distinction

between the C-ration, mentioned earlier, and the K-ration. The latter was preferable. C-rations were small cans of slimy meat that tasted all right if cooked. K-rations showed imagination, several recipes, and frequently included delicious candy; troops were known to open K-rations solely for the candy.

4. The D-ration, a sizable bar of calorie-reinforced chocolate, hard as a rock, had its moments, and sufficed for a day of other nutrients.

5. A Tennessee sharpshooter, Alvin C. York won the Congressional Medal of Honor in the Meuse-Argonne for killing seventeen Germans with seventeen shots and capturing 132 prisoners and thirty-five machine guns.

Twelve. To the Seventh Armored

1. A special meanness of German defenders was to stretch wire lines across roads, decapitating American drivers with windshields up, for the wire while loose would rise to the top of the windshield and drop down. A cowcatcher with a hooked top for the wire, set at the top of the hood, solved everything.

2. Otto Skorzeny, the rescuer of Mussolini after Italy joined the Allies, was in charge of infiltrators of American lines.

3. John L. Ryan, Jr., class of 1926, after serving with the Sixth Cavalry and attending cavalry school was assigned to the First Armored Car Troop at Fort Bliss, Texas, in 1931. After two years in the Philippines, and duty at Fort Knox, together with the Twelfth Armored, he served as commander of CCR of the Seventh Armored and divisional chief of staff. After the war he was promoted to lieutenant general.

4. Bruce C. Clarke rose to the four stars of a full general. He served in World War I, afterward graduated from the Academy (in 1925; he was not, as Triplet related, a member of Ryan's class, which was 1926). During World War II he at first was with the Fourth Armored Division. He then became commander of CCB of the Seventh. He enjoyed a remarkable postwar career, and during the Korean War commanded I Corps and later X Corps (Group). He trained the First Army (Republic of Korea) and was deputy commander of the Eighth Army (U.S.). After the Korean War he became commanding general of army forces in the Pacific, army commander in Europe, and commander of NATO Central Army Group, until retirement in 1962. Clarke died in 1988.

5. Robert W. Hasbrouck entered West Point in the class of 1914 and served in France with artillery during World War I. "I then came into the [postwar] service with the American Polish Relief Expedition, followed by duty with our forces occupying Germany. I returned to the United States in September, 1920. Between wars, my duties included schools, troop and

teaching assignments. . . . An approaching World War II found me on the army general staff, engaged in planning the mobilization of our army. I next found myself on the cadre for activation of the Fourth Armored Division. After subsequently serving with the First and Eighth Armored Divisions, I was ordered to London, where I became the deputy chief of staff of Bradley's Twelfth Army Group. In September 1944 a vacancy for combat commander occurred in the Seventh Armored Division and I got the assignment. On November 1, 1944, General Bradley ordered me to assume command of the division. Immediately following World War II, I retired and became chairman of the Federal Services Finance Corporation, a position I occupied for ten years, before final retirement." *The Seventh Armored Division: A Historical Overview, 1942–1945,* I, 244. Hasbrouck died in 1985.

6. Combat Command Reserve comprised divisional troops.

7. John P. Wemple graduated from Louisiana State University in 1923 and was commissioned a second lieutenant in the Reserves. Ordered to active duty in 1941, he reported to the Second Armored at Fort Benning, then commanded by Brigadier General Patton, who, Wemple believed, made a "fairly good" soldier out of him and six hundred other Reserve officers. Transferred to the Seventh Armored in 1942, he took command of the third battalion of the Thirty-first Armored Regiment, which upon reorganization became the Seventeenth Tank Battalion. He remained with the Seventeenth until the end of the war and was promoted to full colonel while on terminal leave. He spent most of his subsequent business career with the North Central Oil Corporation, from which he retired as senior vice president.

8. Robert L. Rhea, a native of Chicago, served in the National Guard and was brought into federal service in 1941, thereafter the Eighty-fifth, 103rd, and Sixty-fifth Divisions. He joined the Seventh Armored in 1944 and assumed command of the Twenty-third Armored Infantry Battalion in the Netherlands in 1944, with which he continued until the end of the war. He continued with the Regular Army and served in the Japanese occupation, becoming a full colonel in 1951. After stateside assignments he retired in 1962, to pursue a career as a metallurgist.

9. James W. Milner graduated from the Academy and resigned, receiving a master of science degree from the University of Michigan. Inducted into federal service in 1940, he served in all the Seventh Armored's campaigns.

10. Morris E. Sorenson was a Latter Day Saints missionary in Sweden in 1934–1937, graduated from Brigham Young University in 1939, and received a master's degree from the University of Utah in 1940. Enlisting, he was commissioned a second lieutenant and assigned to the Seventh

Armored at Camp Polk, Louisiana, with service in armored infantry regiments and as S-2 (intelligence) for CCA and finally division G-2. After the war he was assigned to military government in Germany and then the staff and faculty at Benning. A member of the UN truce delegation during the Korean War, he later served again in Germany.

11. Public relations officer.

Thirteen. Hunnange

1. Matthew B. Ridgway, an airborne officer, was to have a notable career after World War II. He took command of the Eighth Army in Korea in December 1950 when the attacking Chinese were forcing a retreat south to the unfordable Han River and expecting to trap the Americans against it. Ridgway's divisions managed to get across, regrouped, and turned on the densely bunched Chinese, cutting them to ribbons with artillery fire and pushing back into North Korea. Ridgway replaced MacArthur as UN commander in Tokyo and served as NATO commander and army chief of staff.

2. Like Tar Baby in the Second Armored, Triplet's command tank in the Seventh, Tiger Bait, was an M5.

3. Twenty-third Airborne Infantry Battalion.

Fourteen. Recapture of St. Vith

1. "Good news—Wemple's surgeon reported no casualties from the strafing and Wemple stated that only a few vehicles had incurred minor damage. Made me wonder about the effectiveness of our flyboys when they operated against the enemy. I asked Wemple to send birdman over to the OP. When he arrived the young man seemed somewhat embarrassed. I reassured him. 'That's all right, lieutenant. Mistakes will happen. I just want to ensure that they don't happen to us again. I like your gung-ho attitude and if you continue to want to win the war you can be the bow gunner in a tank, you can sight in an M-1 and do some sniping, or you can get someone to take you on a patrol. But never again can you talk to the air force on your radio.' He took it well. Wemple reported that the lad did pretty good bow-gunning during our next show."

2. The battle was in November 1917.

Fifteen. High Ground

1. Bill Mauldin's cartoons in *Stars and Stripes* featured a weary, disheveled infantryman known as Sad Sack.

Sixteen. In and Out

1. POWINT was prisoner-of-war intelligence.

2. R-R&R was rest, relaxation, and rehabilitation.

3. Coombs had arrived at CCA as communications officer at the same time as Colonel King, and possessed the same personality—a "can do" sort, inclined to choler. Effective officers, both were reminiscent of Colonel Edwards of the Thirteenth Armored. Triplet was attracted to self-starting assistants. In the case of Coombs, the commander of CCA had been having difficulty keeping radios in working order. General Hasbrouck recommended Coombs to get him out of division headquarters where, he said, the lieutenant had been a disciplinary case, although it was true that he could fix a radio with bailing wire and old beer cans. Upon the lieutenant's arrival Triplet confronted him with his criminal past. As Coombs described it, "They had me running the headquarters movie machine as an additional duty. I got this can of film that was all torn up, twenty-three breaks; those bastards back in Army recreation hadn't bothered to repair it. It teed me off, I just got out my splicing kit, shuffled the pieces, and spliced them together. Some of them came out upside down and backwards. Everybody else thought it was funny but the general wasn't amused."

Seventeen. Remagen–Rolandseck–Bad Godesberg

1. Dr. Bernardi was the CCA surgeon.

Eighteen. The Autobahn War

1. H, HQ meant headquarters and headquarters company.

2. OD is olive drab.

3. Here Colonel Triplet wrote: "It should be remembered that at that time there was only one road in the United States to compare with it, the forty-mile stretch of four-lane highway between Washington and Baltimore." He overlooked the Pennsylvania Turnpike of the mid-1930s and the similar if much shorter Merritt Parkway in Connecticut.

Nineteen. On the Way to Giessen

1. Triplet had instructed his task force commanders that "When your vanguard enters a village, your riflemen dash into a house and capture a civilian who lives there. Ask him how best to get to the next village on your route, let's say it's Misthaufen. . . . You then seat the civilian on the turret of your lead tank and tell him to guide you to Misthaufen. When you arrive you grab another civilian and ask him the name of the place. If he says 'Misthaufen' give your first guide a pack of cigarettes and let him go. If he says any other name shoot the first guide to keep the second one honest and tell him where you want to go."

2. A Cossack post was manned by a half squad.

3. OCS was an officer candidate school.

Twenty. To Hemer

1. Captain Powell, headquarters commandant, mistakenly had sent Triplet's personal possessions to salvage after the colonel was nearly killed, when Triplet had asked for his soiled uniform to go to salvage. The Gruen watch, all his clothes, liquor, and shotguns went to salvage. Powell went to the replacement pool and his substitute was "a very sharp lad, Captain Donaldson."

2. Betty Boop was a machine gun designed by Triplet and his command armorer, with a sight for quick use and two magazines. The original Betty Boop was a comic newspaper figure.

3. Triplet had organized CCA in a balanced task force formation, each force consisting of one rifle company reinforced by heavy weapons units, one medium tank company, one light tank platoon, one tank destroyer platoon, and one engineer platoon. In addition General Hasbrouck attached Chappuis's AIB battalion and the third battalion of the 359th Infantry, the latter from the Ninetieth Division, which he thereafter described as Danube Blue. Because this was an infantry battalion he gave it a platoon of tanks from Dailey's task force and a section of destroyers for tank-sniping. He liked the battalion's commander: "He was mid-sized, square-cut in face and figure, very earnest, and had a workmanlike attitude when I described his probable job."

4. Bismarck did not seek to destroy the nobility; he joined it, accepting the title of prince.

5. FO is forward observer.

Twenty-One. The Baltic Front

1. This may well have been a high figure, but any such deaths were saddening commentary on the purpose of the camp. The estimate of 300 deaths daily was perhaps high—a clipping from an American newspaper related 150 deaths, and the official U.S. Army history says 100 (Charles P. MacDonald, *The Last Offensive*, 368). The prisoners were mostly Russian. Among them were ninety-nine Americans, in fair condition as they had been there only a few days.

2. Triplet should have sent food and medical officers, whatever the needs of his men.

3. The pontoon bridge at Bleckede was eleven hundred feet long. Ridgway's engineers put it down in fifteen hours.

4. Counterintelligence corps, counterintelligence division.

5. Lieutenant Kirschbaum had found the agents in one of his caches and employed them.

Bibliographical Essay

The numbers of books on World War II are legion and surely have over-taken and surpassed books on the next most popular topic in American history, the Civil War. Those on American participation alone, excluding that of Britain, the Soviet Union, and other nations, are now beyond counting, beyond calculation. And rightly so, for if battlefield deaths in World War II were not as high as for the great conflict of the nineteenth century, the issues both for the United States and the world were much larger (slavery would not have lasted, nor the economy of cotton). It is of course true that issues raised by the Civil War lasted into the twentieth century and some are still in evidence. But those produced by World War II pursued the American nation until the end of the last century and give evidence of lasting far into the third millenium.

General books on American participation are too many to mention. For commanders in Europe they again are too many, and one may only point out such volumes as pertain to Colonel Triplet's service, beginning with Russell F. Weigley, *Eisenhower's Lieutenants: The Campaign of France and Germany, 1944–1945* (Bloomington: Indiana University Press, 1981). Two autobiographies by corps commanders are Matthew B. Ridgway, *Soldier* (New York: Harper, 1956) and J. Lawton Collins, *Lightning Joe* (Baton Rouge: Louisiana State University Press, 1979). The U.S. Army published a massive multivolume account of its participation in World War II and volumes for Triplet's European service are Hugh M. Cole, *The Ardennes: Battle of the Bulge* (Washington, D.C.: Government Printing Office, 1965); Charles B. MacDonald, *The Siegfried Line Campaign* (1963); and the same author's *The Last Offensive* (1973). Series accounts often are thick with detail about divisions and lesser units, full of small-unit action, bewilderingly so. The books by Cole and MacDonald are very well done.

When Triplet was assigned to amphibian tanks and carriers he was under General William H. Simpson, for whose command see *Conquer: The Story of Ninth Army, 1944–1945* (Washington, D.C.: Infantry Journal Press, 1947); MacDonald describes the book as in a special class, "a sober and invaluable volume." Alas, he also writes that most of the divisional and other unit histories are heavy on the side of unit pride. Moreover, those books appear to be in two categories, both unfortunate. One constitutes publications that came out shortly after the end of hostilities, that is, in the next years, when veterans were close to their experiences and interested in purchasing accounts of them. The resultant books were laudatory to a fault. The other category of unit histories seems to have been of recent vintage, by authors or editors of indeterminate quality, published by private houses of uncertain repute. These volumes appeal to the memories of old veterans—the men of World War II are now in their seventies and well beyond. A sign of the books' nature, of their studied appeal, is long and detailed accounts of members of units, rundowns that seem to have been invited and put together with little editing or arrangement other than alphabetical order for quick reference. The sketches usually are accompanied by photographs of then and now, 1941–1945 together with decades later, interesting and often saddening juxtapositions. Even more than the first group of unit histories, the recent books seem economic ventures. See *The Thirteenth Armored Division: A History of the Black Cats from Texas to France, Germany and Austria and Back to California* (Baton Rouge: Thirteenth Armored Division, 1945). The very title would have aroused Colonel Triplet, who understandably makes no appearance in the book. The account has very little narrative and offers photographs of officers and men beginning with a portrait of General Wogan. E. A. Trahan, ed., *A History of the Second United States Armored Division: 1940 to 1946* (Atlanta: Love, 1947 [?]) is a similar book, with maps containing black-crayon markings, confusing to anyone. Donald F. Houston, *Hell on Wheels: The 2d Armored Division* (San Rafael, Calif.: Presidio, 1977) has an interesting provenance as it was a dissertation at Oklahoma State University. Perhaps because Triplet was with the Second Armored only for a short time, there is no mention of his presence. See also Philip A. St. John, *Second Armored Division: Hell on Wheels* (Paducah, Ky.: Turner, 1991); the author possessed a Ph.D. and the book had a printing of one thousand copies, doubtless showing the diminishment of the division's rolls. Much of it is an assemblage of Signal Corps photographs, the rest contemporary and later photos of whoever sent in likenesses and accounts. For the Seventh Armored there is *From the Beaches to the Baltic: The Story of the 7th Armored* (Heidelberg: Gutenberg-Druckerei, n.d.), a booklet printed just after the end of the war, nicely written, given out to or perhaps sold to men of the division. It is carefully uncritical and mentions each of the ranking officers, Hasbrouck of course, Clarke, Ryan, Triplet, Haskell, and the lieutenant colonels. Description of actions is general, a *Reise durch*, runthrough. *The Seventh Armored Division: A Historical Overview, 1942–1945* (2 vols., Farmington Hills, Mich.: Seventh Armored Division Association,

1982–1987) contains in its first volume detailed description of actions by date, together with the usual contemporary and later photographs of division members. The second volume gives the impression of publication of leftovers; among other information it relates Hasbrouck's death in 1985.

For anyone interested in what happened beyond the army's official series, and willing to go beyond Weigley's splendid general volume and the two autobiographies by corps commanders, the history of the Ninth Army, and the indifferent to poor divisional histories, the first recourse should be to the manuscript diaries, memoirs, and letters in the army's collections in the Military History Institute at Carlisle. Established through the initiative of Colonel George S. Pappas in the late 1960s, the institute opened in the nick of time and one might even contend almost too late, but it is the best resource for unit histories. Papers are filed by divisions principally, with an earlier arranged file by commanders and other individuals. The system is simple. After a researcher consults with search room archivists, materials come out in Hollinger boxes, emerging from storage areas within minutes. Beyond the resources at Carlisle it is necessary to visit the National Archives in its enormous new building near College Park, Maryland, known as Archives II. There research might appear much more formidable than at Carlisle with its small search room lined with Civil War portraits. Again, the ready cooperation and helpfulness of archivists makes the study of records easy.

Because of the lateness in establishing the army's archives at Carlisle Barracks, and despite the institute's sending out of thousands of questionnaires to veterans in hope not merely of responses but of sending in of ancillary materials, diaries and memoirs and letters, many personal records have been lost, thrown into trash bins by veterans or their uninterested relatives. Some have gone to library collections across the country. Sizable public libraries maintain manuscript collections that include World War II materials, and so do college and university libraries, and state and sometimes local historical societies. It is not always easy to locate such materials, but if the inquirer knows an individual's name it is possible to search the National Union Catalog of Manuscript Collections, a serial compiled and published by the Library of Congress. Not all libraries cooperate with the LC by sending in forms listing collections for "Nucmuc," as the serial is known. At that juncture each researcher is on his or her own and must become a library manuscript collection detective.

Index